AFTER
SECESSION

AFTER SECESSION

*Jefferson Davis
and
the Failure of
Confederate
Nationalism*

PAUL D. ESCOTT

LOUISIANA STATE UNIVERSITY PRESS
BATON ROUGE AND LONDON

Copyright © 1978 by Louisiana State University Press
All rights reserved
Manufactured in the United States of America

Designer: Albert Crochet
Type face: VIP Caledonia
Composition: LSU Press
Printer: Thomson-Shore, Inc.
Binder: John H. Dekker & Sons, Inc.

LIBRARY OF CONGRESS CATALOGING IN PUBLICATION DATA

Escott, Paul D   1947–
  After secession.

  Bibliography: p.
  Includes index.
  1.   Southern States—Politics and government—Civil
War, 1861–1865.   2.   Davis, Jefferson, 1808–1889.
3.   Confederate States of America—Politics and govern-
ment.   4.   Secession.   I.   Title.
E487.E8   973.7'13   78–5726
ISBN 0-8071-0369-1

To my mother and father
Fannie M. Escott
and
William E. Escott

Contents

Preface

In the winter of 1860–1861, the South's dominant planter class, fearing for its property interests in slaves, led eleven states out of the Union. This initial success did not ensure the future of their revolution, however, for many problems remained, above and beyond the military ones which soon became evident. The slaveholding elite had to secure the support of the South's non-slaveholding yeomen, who made up the bulk of the population. An effective government had to be established, and devotion to the new nation had to take root in what had been no more than a region or section before. Secession was only the beginning, the beginning of the trial of Confederate nationalism.

This book focuses on Jefferson Davis' attempt to build a spirit of Confederate nationalism and on the internal problems which he encountered. To Davis fell the responsibility not only of prosecuting the war but also of articulating a unifying ideology, resolving social conflicts, and strengthening morale. If his government was to survive, he had to build unity and determination among the people, for the South needed all its energy and endurance in a contest against the more powerful North. The Confederate president brought dedication, intelligence, and considerable flexibility to his task, but he failed to elicit the kind of support he needed. Southerners grew critical of their government, demoralized about the cause, often disaffected, and in some cases disloyal. Economic suffering, class resentments, and political controversies sapped the strength of the Confederacy and started an internal collapse which preceded and promoted military defeat.

The potential for internal strife and weakness had been present from secession. Even as the lower South left the Union there were signs of ambivalence and opposition. Many advocated secession as a means of promoting a settlement, and nonslaveholders often broke with the planters and supported compromise. In the upper South, substantial majorities refused for months to secede. Thus, as he assumed the presidency, Davis needed to build a tentative sense of national identity into a strong and sustaining faith.

During the first year of the war he seemed to be succeeding. By enunciating a conservative, nondivisive ideology, he avoided potential pitfalls and obtained maximum benefit from the South's avowed posture of nonaggression. Aided by Lincoln's provoking call for troops from all the southern states, Davis created the conditions for a great outpouring of enthusiasm and patriotic dedication based on a feeling of regional identity. The thin flame of Confederate nationalism seemed to be growing into a sturdy blaze.

Quickly, however, morale declined, unity turned into division, and enthusiasm devolved toward despair. From all sectors of society came growing criticism of the Richmond administration. A large segment of the planter class clung to its privileges instead of sacrificing for the cause. Nonslaveholders staggered under crushing burdens and then turned away from a government which neglected their needs. Desertion from the armies caused grave concern, while in parts of every southern state many citizens ceased to cooperate with the authorities, effectively withdrew from the war, and sheltered others who resisted the law. By 1864 Jefferson Davis was fighting to hold his disintegrating nation together.

It is the central argument of this study that the primary cause of waning loyalty was the failure of the Davis administration to respond to the problems of the common people, who were the backbone of the Confederacy. Most of these southerners were small farmers who owned no slaves, lived in rural independence and isolation, and felt little identification with the world of the planters. Yet these farmers constituted the great majority of the white population, and their support was essential to the maintenance of military strength. In part, of course, the steady crumbling of their support for a southern nation was due to military defeat and the discouragement which accompanied it, but these causes only contributed to a separate and independent process. War burdened the common people, who often had a hard life at best, with tremendous additional difficulties. Volunteering and conscription robbed one-man farms of their main source of labor, while shortages, rampant inflation, and profiteering increased the problems of the women and children left behind. Faced with destitution for the first time, many southerners turned in desperation to their government. Traditional concepts of limited government melted away before the fact of suffering and want, and citizens called on the authorities for assistance.

To these needs Jefferson Davis failed to respond, and in fact his government often made conditions worse or stirred resentment by policies which either favored the wealthy or seemed to do so. Ignoring pleas from citizens and the recommendations of a few high officials, Davis took no significant steps to alleviate distress and continued to call for greater sacrifice from those who already had reached the limit of endurance. At the same time, Confederate statutes and administrative regulations allowed slaveowners and the rich special privileges and exemption from service. Such treatment angered and disillusioned many individualistic southern yeomen, who reacted by giving higher priority to the needs of their families than to the requirements of Confederate nationalism. As a result, a growing number of the common people of the South quietly withdrew their support from the government or left the armies.

Davis also lost the united support of the planter class as a result of personality clashes and differences over policies and principles. Accepting the concept of federalism, Davis moved early in the conflict to build a strong central government capable of meeting the requirements of war. His policies stirred opposition from a small core of leaders who held an extreme view of states' rights and from many others who could not surmount parochial perspectives, the desire for patronage, or political pressures to protect their suffering constituents from the demands of the Richmond administration. Whatever the reasons for the opposition of political leaders and the press, their criticism caused further depression and lack of confidence in the government.

Davis was aware of internal weakness, for it affected his definition of the South's ideology, impelled him to make three trips into the deep South, and forced the dispatch of troops to disloyal areas. But he underestimated this crucial challenge to his leadership and failed to produce the conditions in which Confederate nationalism could grow. Internal dissensions seriously weakened the Confederacy, for there is a clear link between the failure of Jefferson Davis to build a spirit of Confederate nationalism at home and the inability of southern generals to establish Confederate independence on the battlefield.

The aims of this book have to do with this aspect of the South's defeat. The work is not intended as a biography of Jefferson Davis, although it focuses on him in considerable detail because he occupied the most important single position in regard to southern nationalism. Events at the bottom level of society, far from Richmond, receive equal attention, since changes in the lives of the common people had major ramifications. The narrative moves from cabinet meetings to rural farms in pursuit of the same goal: to analyze developments within Confederate society which affected national unity and the national spirit. It does not attempt to provide a comprehensive political, military, or diplomatic history of the Confederacy.

Acknowledgments

In the preparation of this work I have contracted many debts which I am happy to acknowledge. My greatest debt is to Robert F. Durden of Duke University, who steered me toward this topic and gave me his friendship, encouragement, and thoughtful criticism throughout. Three other scholars at Duke University made important contributions. Raymond Gavins of the history department helped me with a careful reading and criticism of the dissertation on which this book is based, and Richard L. Watson, Jr., of history and Donald Roy of sociology also made valuable suggestions. Jeffrey Crow, who for three years was my fellow student and who now is historical publications editor for the North Carolina Division of Archives and History, has read almost every word and furnished long, detailed comments on substance and style. Whatever deficiencies remain are entirely my responsibility.

The staffs of many libraries have been friendly and helpful. I want to single out for special mention the extremely able staff of the National Archives in Washington, D.C., and particularly Michael Musick; also Mattie Russell and E. Ford of Perkins Library at Duke University; Barbara Lisenby, Charles Lowry, Virginia Kerr, and Lorraine Penninger of Atkins Library at the University of North Carolina at Charlotte; the staff of the Library of Congress; and members of the staff of the North Carolina Department of Archives and History.

Two historians have shown that professional courtesy is very real and extends to great lengths. John B. Robbins gave me the research materials which he had collected on the Confederacy, including several rolls of microfilm containing documents whose originals are found in libraries throughout the South. Bell I. Wiley very graciously made available to me his large collection of letters of Confederate congressmen. This collection, which he has gathered over a lifetime, draws on the holdings of libraries throughout the United States. To both men I am very grateful.

I also wish to thank four secretaries of the history department at UNCC—Paulette Busey, Diane Cloninger, Ann Cormier, and Ann Oliver—who swiftly and skillfully typed the manuscript.

And last but certainly not least, I want to thank my wife, Randi, who often listens to my mumbling over some puzzling issue after a tiring day of legal work of her own.

I gratefully acknowledge permission to reprint portions of this book which first appeared in these publications: *Civil War History*, XXIII (September, 1977), © Kent State University Press; *Georgia Historical Quarterly*, LXI (Spring, 1977); *Journal of Mississippi History* (May, 1977); *South Atlantic Quarterly*, LXXVII (Spring, 1978).

AFTER SECESSION

1

Preparation for the Presidency: Jefferson Davis 1846–1860

Before the Civil War, Jefferson Davis spent fifteen years in public life. These were years of turmoil for the nation and growth for Davis, and at the end neither was the same. In certain ways, the United States prospered, nearly doubling its territory, expanding its economy, and adding varied immigrant groups to its population. But the nation also faltered under the disintegration of the second party system and the birth of a radically new one. Politicians first compromised the slavery issue, then struggled desperately in a fluid and changing situation, and finally lost the ability to control increasing sectional acrimony.

Jefferson Davis influenced some of these events, but they altered him as well. On the surface, his direction seemed straightforward and his rise rapid. From the isolated life of a Mississippi planter Davis entered the House of Representatives late in 1845, then became a military hero in the Mexican War and a United States senator in 1847. Bitter defeat four years later threatened to end his political career, but after serving as secretary of war under Franklin Pierce, Davis reentered the Senate and became a leading spokesman for the South. There secession and the formation of the Confederacy found him.

Below surface appearances, however, Davis was changing from a hot-blooded Mississippi leader into a southern moderate who could take a wider view of his section and the nation. Although his career unfolded in a time of passion and heated controversy, events offered ample opportunities for political education, and Davis took them. As

1

he studied the dynamics of northern politics, he also became more sensitive to the nature of southern society. In this period the soaring ambitions of a rising young politician died, and a sober realization of the power of sectional enmities took their place. Davis first expected to gain national eminence through regional prominence. Later he hoped only to avert disaster by playing the limited role of sectional leader. Changing from a prophet of defiance to a seeker of compromise, Davis found that while his determination to defend the South remained steady, his desire to preserve the Union became more intense. At the end he took the final step of secession with a reluctance and fondness for the Union which characterized many southerners. In this way the decade and a half before the Civil War was Davis' preparation for the Confederate presidency.

Davis had risen from humble origins through the aid of his older brother. Joseph Emory Davis found financial success in the rich bottomlands near the Mississippi River, and he gave young Jefferson a chance for further success by sending him to the United States Military Academy. West Point offered Davis a means to confirm and advance his social status, and in later years he frequently encountered former classmates who held leading positions in southern society. After a brief military career, Davis returned to Mississippi and began the life of a planter. Through reading and discussions with his older brother, he developed his political philosophy, which coincided with that of southern states' rights Democrats.[1]

In 1845 Davis won election to Congress, and he entered the House of Representatives at a time when territorial issues were dominating politics. He supported compromise over the Oregon territory but as a southern advocate demanded strong measures to gain New Mexico and California. Disagreeing with John C. Calhoun, who viewed the war with Mexico as immoral and unconstitutional, Davis enthusiastically declared that American cannon should be sent as the new am-

---

1. For more complete accounts see: Hudson Strode, *Jefferson Davis* (3 vols.; New York: Harcourt, Brace & Company, 1955–1964), I, Chaps. 1–9; Varina Howell Davis, *Jefferson Davis, Ex-President of the Confederate States of America: A Memoir* (2 vols.; New York: Belford Company, 1890), I, Chaps. 1–18, hereinafter cited as *A Memoir*.

bassador to Mexico City. To suit these bellicose emotions, he resigned his seat in Congress and led a Mississippi regiment into battle. Within a few months a determined stand at the Battle of Buena Vista had transformed Davis into a wounded hero and a United States senator. In the Senate he favored adding generous amounts of Mexican land to the United States, probably with an eye toward more slave territory and a southern railroad route to California. Such sectional ambitions had already rekindled the smoldering slavery issue, as David Wilmot and many northerners proposed banning slavery from all lands acquired from Mexico. In the coming years Davis would devote most of his energy as a leading spokesman for the South to this one issue—slavery in the territories.[2]

Through the many debates which followed, several elements of Davis' thinking remained unchanged. He followed Calhoun in reasoning that the Constitution was a compact between sovereign states, and therefore each state had equal rights under the compact and equal rights in the territories. Southerners were entitled to bring their human property into the territories just as northerners had the right to immigrate with their forms of property. A final and crucial point in this argument was that only states were sovereign; therefore, only when a territory became a state could its residents decide to exclude slavery. From 1848 through secession Davis consistently opposed any idea that the settlers in a territory could take action to bar slavery. The South, he said, must be allowed "an experiment." If slavery proved unprofitable in a territory, few southerners would settle there and the area would naturally become a free state. Where they did settle thickly, southerners should be able to pass "police regulations" against runaways in the territorial legislature. For several years Davis apparently believed that slavery would prove profitable in mining and irrigated agriculture in the Southwest.[3]

2. *Appendix* to *Congressional Globe*, 29th Cong., 1st Sess., 212–17; Dunbar Rowland (ed.), *Jefferson Davis: Constitutionalist; His Letters, Papers, and Speeches* (10 vols.; Jackson, Miss.: Little & Ives Co., 1923), I, 46; *Senate Executive Documents*, 30th Cong., 1st Sess., Vol. VII, No. 52, p. 18; Rowland (ed.), *Jefferson Davis*, II, 89.

3. Rowland (ed.), *Jefferson Davis*, I, 290–91, 297; *Congressional Globe*, 31st Cong., 1st Sess., 1019–20; Rowland (ed.), *Jefferson Davis*, I, 289.

But if he developed these ideas from Calhoun's, Davis based another element of his thinking on a political strategy which opposed
the famous South Carolinian. As early as 1845 Calhoun had called
for the formation of a Southern party. Throughout the sectional conflict, however, Davis fought to preserve the national Democratic
party. He believed that a system of national parties protected the
South while suppressing threats to the Union. Davis urged southerners to keep the northern Democrats as their "natural allies" and
wrote that "the worst of all political divisions" was "one made by geo-
graphical lines merely."[4]

A final persistent element in Davis' thinking concerned the form
of a possible compromise between North and South. In 1847 he proposed "extending the Missouri compromise" line to all new states.
During the debates on the Compromise of 1850, he deplored any
tendency to stop short of this and denied that the Compromise was
an acceptable solution. "I here assert," said Mississippi's young senator, "that never will I take less than the Missouri compromise line
extended to the Pacific Ocean, with the specific recognition of the
right to hold slaves in the territory below that line."[5]

This position was popular with Mississippians in 1850, as the state
legislature commended Davis for his stand and censured Mississippi's other senator for supporting the Compromise. Soon, however, Davis and his allies were on the defensive in state politics. The
legislature called for a convention to meet in November, 1851, and
consider how to oppose Congress' action. Before this date it had become apparent that the South as a whole would not contest the Compromise. Left in an untenable position, Davis' party prevailed on
him to resign his Senate seat and wage an uphill battle for governor.
In a short campaign he reduced a large deficit to only 999 votes, but
the defeat was bitter. Davis regarded it as a humiliation and vowed
"never to return to public life until called by the people of Mississippi."[6]

4. Rowland (ed.), *Jefferson Davis*, I, 95.
5. *Ibid.; Congressional Globe*, 31st Cong., 1st Sess., 249.
6. Cleo Hearon, *Mississippi and the Compromise of 1850* (Chicago: n.p., 1913), 205–215.

One year later, however, Jefferson Davis reentered politics as secretary of war in Franklin Pierce's administration. Pierce, a personal friend, had won a smashing victory which hastened the Whig party into oblivion and seemed to reunite the Democrats. Moreover, Pierce was a strict constructionist who believed that the Constitution recognized and protected slavery, and he favored vigorous territorial and commercial expansion. For a moment it seemed that the slavery issue had been left behind and that a new president might reshape national politics in ways which pleased the South. Initially, at least, there was wide support for Pierce's expansive nationalism.[7]

Davis played a large role in the new administration and introduced its first major proposal: the construction of a railroad to the Pacific. As secretary of war he continued to promote this project and sent survey teams across the West to map the best route. When the results finally judged a southern route to be best, Davis probably was delighted, for he felt that a southern road would encourage slaveholders to settle in the territories and help the South regain its equality in the Senate. He also shared the cabinet's interest in acquiring Cuba through purchase or possibly war and supported the president's battles against internal improvements and for tariff reduction.[8]

All of Pierce's major projects, however, came crashing down in the general wreck of the administration. The Pacific railroad encountered opposition and was abandoned; Cuba remained in the possession of Spain; the tariff and internal improvements never became dominant issues as Pierce had hoped. The utter failure of the administration was due partly to Pierce's blunders and to his failure to understand that he had been a compromise nominee rather than the leader of his party. But the chief cause of the disaster was the Kansas-

7. Roy F. Nichols, *Franklin Pierce: Young Hickory of the Granite Hills* (Philadelphia: University of Pennsylvania Press, 1931), 222–23, 237–38.

8. *Ibid.*, 280–81; Rowland (ed.), *Jefferson Davis*, II, 242–45, 250–51, 256–61; James D. Richardson (ed.), *Messages and Papers of the Presidents* (10 vols.; Washington: Government Printing Office, 1897), V, 221–22; Robert R. Russel, *Improvement of Communication with the Pacific Coast as an Issue in American Politics, 1783–1864* (Cedar Rapids, Iowa: Torch Press, 1948), 168, 178–80; Percy Lee Rainwater, *Mississippi, Storm Center of Secession, 1856–1861* (Baton Rouge: Otto Claitor, 1938), 26–27; William E. Dodd, *Jefferson Davis* (Philadelphia: George W. Jacobs & Company, 1907), 154.

Nebraska bill, which originated in Congress and was not an administration proposal. This act revived the sectional controversy with greater bitterness than ever before, and occasioned the greatest possible failure of the government in domestic policy.[9] Free-soilers and abolitionists felt that Congress had thrown free territory open to slavery and decried another step in the aggressive march of the "Slave Power." The bloody struggles between proslavery and antislavery forces in Kansas exacerbated feelings in all parts of the nation and led antislavery and reform forces in the North to coalesce. From this nucleus arose the Republican party, which showed astonishing strength in the 1856 elections. For the first time the United States had a powerful sectional party based on opposition to the extension of slavery.

These developments deeply disturbed Jefferson Davis. He feared that the momentum of the Republicans and antislavery forces would take them beyond the prohibition of slavery in the territories. In a letter to a friend he wrote that the abolitionists would gain little by excluding slavery from the territories if they were not planning "to disturb that institution in the States." In 1857 he told Mississippians that the desire to exclude slavery from Kansas was part of a design to throw a cordon around slave regions and thus cut off slavery's expansion and begin its destruction. Kansas would be the entering wedge for abolitionism, which then could spread to Missouri, Arkansas, New Mexico, and Texas.[10]

In 1856 these views may have seemed a bit extreme in Mississippi, for Davis won reelection to the Senate by a narrow margin.[11] In the next few years, however, this situation was reversed. Sentiment in Mississippi quickly grew more radical, but Davis moved in the opposite direction and worked to restrain the extremists in the state. From 1858 to secession in early 1861 he actually followed a course of moderation. Davis remained committed to defending the South's rights, but, becoming convinced that there was hope of avoiding dis-

9. Nichols, *Franklin Pierce*, 287–89, 308, 333, 343, 396.

10. Rainwater, *Mississippi*, 26; *Mississippian and State Gazette* (Jackson, Miss.), October 21, 1857, p. 1.

11. John Ezell, "Jefferson Davis Seeks Political Vindication, 1851–1857," *Journal of Mississippi History*, XXVI (1964), 321.

union, he determined to try. Jefferson Davis at the end of the 1850s was a man struggling to protect the South within the Union. He worked to find the common ground between the sections, maintain the unity of the Democratic party, and preserve the Union.

As Davis reentered the Senate, events from an unexpected quarter influenced his entire approach to the sectional crisis. A summer trip to New England revealed to him a new strategy for protecting the South and preserving the Union. Illness set these events in motion. High-strung, tense, and dyspeptic, Davis suffered from poor health throughout his political career. Early in 1858 a bad cold reawakened a chronic neuralgia of his left eye. After great pain and long illness, he barely saved his sight. On the advice of his doctors, the Davises took a sea voyage that summer, and chose to visit Maine. Sun and sea air had the desired effect on his health, but the trip had far more important effects on his political outlook.

Amazed at the friendly reception which he and his family met everywhere in New England, Davis began to see new possibilities of understanding between South and North.[12] When he served in the cabinet under Pierce, Davis had found some evidence of northern sympathy for the South's view of her constitutional rights. The president's opinions had usually coincided with Davis', and in addition Attorney General Caleb Cushing of Massachusetts had been as strict in his constitutional constructions as any southerner could desire. Now Davis discovered additional evidence of fraternity and congenial political attitudes in the North. The summer in New England gave him faith that there were supporters of states' rights in the North on whom his section could rely.

Laying aside the catechism of states' rights, Davis became a fervid advocate of patriotism and national unity. His nationalism was not a hypocritical gesture. Throughout the antebellum South men of both parties had felt an almost mystical sort of reverence for the idea of the Union. Although they believed in states' rights, they saw the United States as the greatest example of representative government

12. Varina Howell Davis, *A Memoir*, I, 575; Rowland (ed.), *Jefferson Davis*, III, 214, 228–31, 215, 279, 306.

in the history of the world, a government hallowed by the labors and sacrifices of earlier patriots. Adopting a vocabulary of patriotism and inspiration, Davis spoke often in New England, trying to strike chords which would resonate in the hearts of northerners and southerners alike.[13]

On the fourth of July he predicted that "this great country will continue united" and stressed the fraternity and unselfishness which established the Union as a "temple of liberty" intended for "perpetuity." A few days later he asked: "Has patriotism ceased to be a virtue, and is narrow sectionalism no longer to be counted a crime? . . . We cannot sink to the petty strife which would sap the foundations, and destroy the political fabric our fathers erected, and bequeathed as an inheritance to our posterity forever." In September he told listeners at the Maine State Fair, "The whole confederacy is my country, and to the innermost fibers of my heart I love it all, and every part." Davis also spoke of the nation's destiny and endorsed the expansive nationalism used so effectively by other politicians including Stephen A. Douglas. To warm applause he declared that American theory and practice "fits our government for immeasurable domain."[14]

Speaking in Boston's Faneuil Hall to the Massachusetts Democracy in October, Davis summed up his new attitudes: "I have learned since I have been in New England the vast mass of true States Rights Democrats to be found within its limits. . . . And if it comes to the worst . . . I believe that even in Massachusetts . . . the State Rights Democracy . . . can and will whip the Black Republicans."[15] Davis had found a new strategy. He decided to join with the true Democrats of the North to defend the Constitution and beat back the fires of abolitionism. In a frank and open letter to his friend Franklin Pierce, Davis said, "That tour convinced me that the field of useful labor is now among the people." By honestly exchanging their views with

---

13. Paul C. Nagle, *One Nation Indivisible: The Union in American Thought, 1776–1861* (New York: Oxford University Press, 1964), Chaps. 3, 5, 6.

14. Rowland (ed.), *Jefferson Davis*, III, 273, 277; 309, 312–13, 321.

15. *Ibid.*, 326–27, 331.

each other, men of both sections could master the forces which threatened to drive them apart. "The difference is less than I had supposed," Davis concluded.[16]

To cement this new partnership, initiatives from the South were vital. Southerners needed to assure northern Democrats of their good will and scotch the myth of a monolithic "Slave Power" plotting to spread slavery over the entire nation. To aid this rapprochement Davis made one of the most remarkable speeches of his career in 1858. With courage which was rare for a southern politician, Davis tried to defuse the explosive issue of slavery in the territories, which he realized had diminishing practical significance even as its symbolic role increased.[17]

Stephen A. Douglas had just enuniciated his famous Freeport Doctrine a few weeks previously in debate with Abraham Lincoln. To counter the Supreme Court's decision in the Dred Scott case, which held that slavery could not be barred from the territories, Douglas argued that the decision technically did not extend to a situation involving a territorial legislature. Furthermore, the Illinois Democrat declared that it made no difference what the Court might decide, because the people of a territory could bar slavery either by passing laws against it or simply by refusing to enact the police regulations which slavery needed. As a southern leader, Davis endorsed part of the Freeport Doctrine and stressed that slaveholders wanted only their fair chance to settle the territories: "If the inhabitants of any territory should refuse to enact . . . police regulations [to give security to] slave property, the insecurity would be so great that . . . the owner would be practically debarred by the circumstances of the case, from taking slave property into a territory where the sense of the inhabitants was opposed to its introduction. So much for the oft repeated fallacy of forcing slavery upon any community."[18]

16. Jefferson Davis to Franklin Pierce, January 17, 1859, in Rowland (ed.), *Jefferson Davis*, III, 498–99.

17. Davis' awareness that slavery in the territories had diminishing practical significance can be traced in Rowland (ed.), *Jefferson Davis*, III, 172, 303–304, 364, and IV, 322–23, 327–28.

18. *Ibid.*, III, 299.

Davis' bold new departure toward the northern Democrats caused an angry reaction in Mississippi. Friendly newspapers strained their ingenuity to defend him, and when Davis addressed the state legislature in December, 1858, he clearly was on the defensive. Throughout the speech his tone was conciliatory, but though he explained himself, Davis retracted nothing. After making a few prosouthern assertions on collateral issues, Davis preached his new message to the legislature. The northern Democracy was reliable, for his trip had shown him that there were many "who maintain our constitutional rights as explicitly and as broadly as we assert them." He declared that due to the principled stands taken by northern Democrats who risked their political futures, "a great reaction had begun" against the abolitionists.[19]

Davis gained this faith in the northern Democrats at a crucial time for the Democratic party in Mississippi. Some of the state's political leaders had always realized that there was a link between the future of the Democratic party and the future of the Union. In the Jacksonian era southerners learned that national parties tended to override sectional differences, and one of Mississippi's newspapers ran a succinct but eloquent motto under its masthead—"The Union of the Democracy for the Salvation of the Country." Another paper rejoiced that when ties between North and South were breaking, "the Democratic party looms gradually up, its nationality intact, and waves the olive branch over the troubled waters of politics." Jefferson Davis believed "that the downfall of [the] Democracy would be its [the Union's] destruction."[20] By 1858, however, many Mississippians were becoming convinced that the differences between North and South were radical and irreconcilable and that it was futile to try to compromise and preserve what remained of a national framework. One person who held these opinions was Albert Gallatin Brown, Davis' rival in the Senate. In 1858 Brown "was willing to let the 'na-

19. Rainwater, *Mississippi*, 56; *Mississippian and State Gazette*, September 3, 1858, p. 2 and 3; Rowland (ed.), *Jefferson Davis*, III, 356, 359, 348, 340, 351.

20. Woodville (Miss.) *Republican*, August 25, 1858; *Mississippian and State Gazette*, September 1, 1858, p. 1; Rowland (ed.), *Jefferson Davis*, IV, 262.

tional Democratic party go.'" Davis' strong defense of northern Democrats and his national prestige prevailed, however, and Mississippi's Democrats continued to work within the party.[21]

The radicalization of opinion in Mississippi was a grave threat to Davis' national strategy. The triumph of extremists in his own state would destroy his credibility as he tried to strengthen the alliance with the Democrats in the North. Davis had to restrain the more outspoken fire-eaters, but at the same time he had to protect his own position. As a southern leader he could not appear to be weak on southern rights. Davis found a politician's ingenious solution to this problem. He used fiery rhetoric whenever a topic had no practical application, but he was much more circumspect when he discussed actual policies to be adopted.

In 1859 and 1860 Davis employed this method to deflect the growing agitation in certain southern quarters to reopen the African slave trade. The southern Commercial Convention voted in favor of reopening the slave trade in 1859, and Mississippi was one of the states which gave strongest support to this issue.[22] Realizing that this question could become prominent in the approaching election, Davis joined one of his allies, O. R. Singleton, and four other candidates in taking a deceptively strong position on the issue. Together these men opposed two statutes which seemed to stigmatize slavery, but they favored other laws on the books which abolished the slave trade.[23] Davis also used his influence behind the scenes at the Mississippi Democratic Convention in July, 1859, to block a demand for reopening the trade.[24] Simultaneously he took steps to reassure his northern allies. To correct any misapprehension, Davis wrote to Franklin

21. Hearon, *Mississippi and the Compromise of 1850*, p. 33; Rainwater, *Mississippi*, 55, 62.

22. Harvey Wish, "Revival of the African Slave Trade in the United States, 1856–1860," *Mississippi Valley Historical Review*, XXVII (1941), 569–88; W. J. Carnathan, "The Proposal to Reopen the African Slave Trade in the South, 1854–1860," *South Atlantic Quarterly*, XXV (October, 1926), 410–29.

23. Jefferson Davis to C. C. Clay, May 17, 1859, in Clement C. Clay Papers, Duke University; Rowland (ed.), *Jefferson Davis*, IV, 55–6, 66–70; O. R. Singleton to Jefferson Davis, June 27, 1859, in Jefferson Davis Papers, Library of Congress.

24. Rainwater, *Mississippi*, 95–99.

Pierce that the idea that the South wanted to reopen the trade was a "fiction." He also denied that the South wanted Congress to enact a slave code for the territories.[25]

After coping with radical tendencies in Mississippi, Jefferson Davis attempted to relieve mounting southern fears on the national level. As the 1860 election approached, the Democratic party faced the problem of choosing its presidential nominee. This would be a crucial decision for the party, which was badly divided over the slavery issue. Davis played an important role in this decision, for many southern congressmen looked to him to define the minimum position acceptable to the South. Throughout all the complicated political manueverings Davis tried to protect the South and also avoid splitting the party.

Davis led a movement to block the nomination of Stephen Douglas. These two men had often quarreled with each other in the Senate, but personalities were not the primary reason for Davis' decision to oppose Douglas. Davis believed that the dynamics of northern politics presented a grave threat to the South. The Republicans were not simply another political party, although they had a diverse membership. As the antislavery movement wrought changes in northern opinion, the Republican party fed upon and accelerated those changes. The direction of this trend was clear, and it was pushing conservative politicians, like Abraham Lincoln and other former Whigs, into antislavery positions. Because it was intimately connected with the reforming, antislavery ferment of the North, the Republican party constituted a revolutionary threat. In October, 1860, Davis wrote that "the vital element" of the Republican party was hostility to slavery. Early in 1861 he looked back over the course of events and concluded, "The progress has been steady towards a transfer of the government into the hands of the abolitionists."[26]

Davis had decided that the best way to counter the Republican

    25. Jefferson Davis to Franklin Pierce, September 2, 1859, in Rowland (ed.), *Jefferson Davis*, IV, 94.
    26. *Ibid.*, IV, 540, and V, 39.

threat was to unite northern and southern Democrats and make a clear stand on the South's constitutional rights. Remembering the New England Democrats who had stood with him in 1858, Davis hoped and believed that the "gallant minority" which defended southern rights in the North was "daily becoming more numerous." Some of Davis' allies, such as Pierce, believed that northerners were growing exasperated with antislavery fanatics and might even resist the abolitionists forcibly. Davis wanted the Democratic party to follow his strategy and take a firm stand against the Republicans.[27]

Stephen A. Douglas, however, was the epitome of the northern Democrat who steadily adjusted his position to the antislavery movement, and as early as November, 1858, Davis had declared that Douglas would be unacceptable as the party's nominee. To preserve his position with free-soil elements in the North, Douglas had always maintained that territorial legislatures could pass laws prohibiting slavery. Furthermore, in 1859 in an article in *Harper's Magazine* Douglas echoed the Republican charge that protection of slavery in the territories would lead to imposition of slavery in all the states.[28]

By the end of 1859 southern congressmen were thoroughly alarmed by the waxing power of the Republican party and by John Brown's recent raid on Harper's Ferry. They decided that at the Democratic convention in Charleston their party should take a stand on the South's rights in the territories. Jefferson Davis' resolutions on the "relations of states" emerged from Congress as the statement of southern territorial demands. Avoiding any call for immediate action by the legislative branch, Davis restricted himself to enunciating a general principle of federal protection. The key parts of his resolutions declared that neither Congress nor a territorial legislature had the power to abridge southerners' constitutional right to take their slaves into the territories and keep them there during the territorial stage. If the judiciary and the executive proved unable to ensure adequate

27. *Ibid.*, IV, 119, 335.
28. *Ibid.*, III, 348; reprinted as Stephen Douglas, *Popular Sovereignty in the Territories* (New York: Harper & Brothers, 1859), 28–29.

protection, Davis continued, or if the territorial government refused to provide needed remedies, Congress had a duty "to supply such deficiency."[29]

These resolutions brought down upon Davis' head the charge that he, and the South in general, wanted to impose a slave code on the territories. The vagueness of the wording left him open to such an accusation, although Davis' goal was not a congressionally imposed slave code. Thoughtful southerners realized that Republican amendments could transform any slave-code bill and make it far worse than nothing at all.[30] Davis' position remained the same as it had been in 1850 and 1858. Through his resolutions he meant to strike at Douglas' belief that a territorial legislature could pass laws to prohibit slavery. If such a case should arise, Davis believed that Congress had an obligation to strike down the law. On the other hand, Davis held that territorial governments did not have to legislate in favor of slaveholders. In fact, they naturally would not do so if slavery were unsuitable in a particular region. Davis explicitly denied, to the Senate and in private, that he sought a slave code, as he had denied the same charge before the Mississippi Democratic Convention.[31]

Sometimes these beliefs placed Davis in a difficult position in relations with his fellow southerners. In the charged atmosphere on the eve of the convention, he could not admit, as he had in Maine, that all a territory needed to do to exclude slavery was to pass no laws on the subject at all. Once one of Senator Douglas' supporters pointed out that Davis had encouraged the exclusion of slavery by nonaction as much as had Douglas. When he asked Davis directly whether a territorial legislature could thus bar slavery, Davis became completely evasive and refused to answer the query.[32]

Although Davis was trying to block Douglas' nomination with these resolutions (which passed the Senate), he still struggled to avoid a

29. Rowland (ed.), *Jefferson Davis*, IV, 204.
30. Chauncey S. Boucher, "*In Re* That Aggressive Slavocracy," *Mississippi Valley Historical Review*, VIII (1921), 72–73.
31. Rowland (ed.), *Jefferson Davis*, IV, 122, III, 586, IV, 274, 94, 77–78.
32. *Ibid.*, IV, 125.

split of the Democratic party. To hold the party together, and possibly through it the Union, Davis, as one of many concerned Democrats, cast about for a solution. In January, 1860, three months before the convention met, Davis had settled on a plan. Reporting his strategy to Franklin Pierce, Davis wrote: "Govr. Dana of Me. is still here and much concerned lest our party should be divided at Charleston. I have not been able to show him how the question could be adjusted by "resolution" but have told him of the only way I have seen, and which is that of nominating the man who will be accepted by both sections without a platform."[33]

At Charleston Douglas' forces used parliamentary maneuvers to marshal a majority behind their version of the platform. As enraged southern delegates considered whether to walk out of the convention, they pondered various messages of advice from Washington. Jefferson Davis sent L. Q. C. Lamar, a Mississippi congressman who later became a prominent figure in the New South, as his emissary to argue against a withdrawal on the platform. Lamar told the delegates that Davis considered it far more important for the Gulf states to stay in the convention and defeat Douglas. But after Douglas' platform was adopted, the delegations from Alabama, Mississippi, Louisiana, South Carolina, Florida, and Texas left the convention. Parts of the Georgia and Arkansas delegations followed the next day.[34]

After years of stress, the Democracy had split apart. However, since the Douglas forces were unable to nominate their candidate even after the southern walkout, they recessed the convention for six weeks. In the interim Davis continued speaking out against Douglas and for a candidate who was acceptable to the South. But Davis also

33. *Ibid.*, 185.
34. James B. Murphy, *L. Q. C. Lamar: Pragmatic Patriot* (Baton Rouge: Louisiana State University Press, 1973), 51; Roy F. Nichols, *The Disruption of American Democracy* (New York: Macmillan, 1948), 305–306.

urged the rebellious southern delegations to attend the second meeting of the convention. He hoped that the party would find a compromise candidate. If the nominee were a man whom the South could trust, the platform, Davis thought, would be unimportant.[35] Five days before the convention reconvened in Baltimore, Davis wrote to his trusted friend, Franklin Pierce: "I have urged my friends to make an honest effort to save our party from disintegration as the last hope of averting ruin from the country. They would gladly unite upon you, or [former vice-president George M.] Dallas and would readily be brought to any one of the like character and record."[36]

But the results of the Baltimore convention were as dismal as those of Charleston. Douglas' supporters walked out to form their own convention. The remaining Democrats finally nominated Douglas; southern Democrats nominated John Breckinridge of Kentucky. The Constitutional Union party had already nominated John Bell. The vote against Lincoln was likely to be divided among these three candidates.[37]

Jefferson Davis later wrote that he made one more effort to unite the Democrats. During the campaign he suggested to Douglas, Breckinridge, and Bell that all three withdraw in favor of some conservative candidate. Breckinridge and Bell agreed, but Davis carried the idea to Stephen Douglas in vain. The Illinois senator refused to cooperate on the grounds that he alone had a chance of winning in the North.[38] Returning to Mississippi for the remainder of the campaign, Davis endorsed Breckinridge and defended the South's rights but refused to commit himself to secession.[39]

By the end of the first week of November, the South knew that

35. Rowland (ed.), *Jefferson Davis*, IV, 299–300, 335.
36. Jefferson Davis to Franklin Pierce, June 13, 1860, *ibid.*, 496.
37. Nichols, *The Disruption of American Democracy*, 317–18.
38. Jefferson Davis, *The Rise and Fall of the Confederate Government* (2 vols.; London: Longmans, Green and Co., 1881), I, 52. The existence of such a plan and Davis' role in it is questioned in Damon Wells, *Stephen Douglas: The Last Years, 1857–1861* (Austin: University of Texas Press, 1971), 246. Hard evidence of Davis' role is lacking, but such a plan certainly did exist. See Franklin Pierce to James Campbell, October 17, 1860, and Campbell to Pierce, October 22, 1860, in Franklin Pierce Papers, Library of Congress.
39. Rainwater, *Mississippi*, 152–56.

the Republicans had elected a president. Abraham Lincoln carried the election by winning sufficient electoral votes in the North alone. Southern leaders quickly divided into two groups. The fire-eaters favored immediate secession by individual states, a plan which would guarantee that results came before talk and would build pressure for secession. The "cooperationists" favored a conference of southern states and a coordinated demand that the federal government take steps to meet the South's grievances. This method of resistance offered the maximum number of opportunities for compromise and negotiation and it multiplied the chances of delay and settlement.

Throughout the crisis, Jefferson Davis was firmly in the cooperationist camp. On November 10, 1860, he told Robert Barnwell Rhett, Jr., South Carolina's fieriest advocate of secession, not to expect early secession by Mississippi, and he recommended that South Carolina wait also. Two weeks later Governor John J. Pettus summoned Mississippi's entire congressional delegation to meet with him and advise on the course their state should take. Davis was one of a minority of three who opposed separate state action. He still favored the slower and less certain method of cooperation.[40]

Even after the secession of Mississippi became certain, Davis played an important role in Congress. On January 10, 1861, he warned the Senate that war, if it came, would be terribly destructive. Although disunion appeared inevitable, he still urged separation in a way which would allow the possibility of later reconstruction. Most importantly, Davis agreed to serve on the Committee of Thirteen, established by the Senate to examine the possibilities of compromise. Kentucky's John J. Crittenden and others had suggested a variety of proposals including the extension of the Missouri Compromise line to the eastern border of California. When the committee took up Crittenden's proposals, Jefferson Davis and Robert Toombs of Georgia were ready to support them, but the Republicans on the committee refused to agree. Davis' longtime antagonist, Stephen A. Douglas, himself a member of the committee, reported

40. Rowland (ed.), *Jefferson Davis*, IV, 541–43; Murphy, *L. Q. C. Lamar*, 55.

the failure of this last chance to the Senate and noted that "Senator Davis himself, when on the committee of thirteen, was ready, at all times, to compromise on the Crittenden proposition."[41]

In fifteen years as a prominent southern leader Jefferson Davis had not changed the details of his positions on slavery in the territories or the nature of an acceptable compromise. But emotionally and in the context of his surroundings, he had moved from a proponent of defiant resistance who was too extreme for the South to follow in 1850 to a reluctant secessionist who hoped until the end for compromise and lagged behind opinion in his state. By the close of the 1850s, Mississippians were beginning to suspect him of too much affection for the Union. But if Davis risked losing the confidence of radical politicians in Mississippi, he gained an identification with the great majority of people in the South. The reluctance, regret, and agony with which Davis approached secession made him a more representative southerner than any fire-eater. Davis' transformation from an eager prophet of defiance to one who tried to protect both the South and the Union was vital preparation for his term as president of the Confederacy.

41. Rowland (ed.), *Jefferson Davis*, V, 21, 32, 23; quoted in James Ford Rhodes, *History of the United States from the Compromise of 1850* (9 vols.; New York: Harper and Brothers, 1913–1922), III, 151–55.

2

The Problem of Unity: Regional Identity or Confederate Nationalism?

In 1860 the deepening sectional quarrel between North and South led the South to consider anew its position in the nation. Events forced southerners to decide whether bonds of interest and affection still held them to the Union or whether the time had come to form a new nation. In a sense, the clash between two entire regions reached its culmination in the minds and hearts of southerners, as they prepared to make a choice between American nationalism and southern nationalism.

The South had long had a sense of regional identity springing from facts of climate, geography, and social organization. But in addition, at some time in the preceding half-century, the spirit of southern nationalism had come into being. To men who felt this spirit, the South belonged not to the nation but to itself and was a different, even superior, entity.[1] For many years these views were the extravagant notions of a few, but as the slavery controversy drove a wedge into national unity, the idea of southern nationalism gained wider currency. Concerned men in both sections wondered how far this tendency had developed.

In 1860–1861, the secession crisis posed a clear test of the extent of southern nationalism. If southerners truly felt this new force, they would strengthen the sense of belonging to their own world as they severed their connections with American society. On the other hand, if they actually saw themselves as Americans, a new southern government based only on regional identity or on a premature national-

1. For a suggestive discussion of the South's self-image in literature, see William R. Taylor, *Cavalier and Yankee* (New York: G. Braziller, 1961).

ism would face significant problems. Uncertainty or lingering union-ism might grow, and divisions that had been hidden within society might surface with disruptive effect.

For Jefferson Davis the secession crisis represented a special op-portunity. Although he did not know it in 1860, it would soon become his responsibility to foster all the sources of southern nationality. By watching developments during the winter of 1860–1861, he could identify the South's unifying forces while he located weaknesses in southern will and traced the lines of fracture within the society. Events could indicate to the future Confederate president whether southern nationalism would sweep all before it or whether its nur-ture would be a difficult and uncertain task.

Davis did not seek the responsibility which he was given. In fact, he had taken what he believed were "adequate precautions . . . to prevent" such a selection and preferred to be a general in the army.[2] His wife feared that he was unsuited for the office and would be un-able to use his talents in such a position. "I thought his genius was military," she wrote, "but that, as a party manager, he would not succeed. He did not know the arts of the politician, and would not practice them if understood."[3]

Varina Howell Davis had grasped an important truth. In many ways Jefferson Davis was unsuited for the office of president, but he also had many talents to bring to this new position. Intelligence, dil-igence, and iron determination were all part of his character. His years as a senator had trained him to express constitutional principles in lofty, dignified terms. In addition, Davis' growing moderation be-spoke an innate sympathy with the temper of the whole South in the secession crisis. These attributes contributed significantly to his suc-cess as a revolutionary leader. In 1861 they helped him reach his

2. Jefferson Davis, *The Rise and Fall of the Confederate Government* (2 vols.; London: Longmans, Green and Co., 1881), I, 230, 237; Dunbar Rowland (ed.), *Jefferson Davis: Con-stitutionalist; His Letters, Papers, and Speeches* (10 vols.; Jackson, Miss.: Little & Ives Co., 1923), V, 47–49.
3. Varina Howell Davis, *Jefferson Davis, Ex-President of the Confederate States of America: A Memoir* (2 vols.; New York: Belford Company, 1890), II, 12, hereinafter cited as Davis, *A Memoir*.

greatest effectiveness as Confederate president and enabled him to guide the new southern nation to early unity. Under his leadership a great outpouring of regional loyalty occurred, though the state of Confederate nationalism remained uncertain.

Several times in the 1840s and 1850s John C. Calhoun and others had tried without success to unite the South in defense of its interests, but as the presidential election of 1860 approached, a new group of southern leaders had high hopes of at last obtaining support for southern independence. These men, led by such figures as William L. Yancy and Robert Barnwell Rhett, Jr., did not share the unionism of leaders such as Calhoun and Jefferson Davis. They were emphatically not interested in defending the South within the Union. They would be satisfied with nothing less than the destruction of the Union and the formation of a purely southern confederacy. More importantly, these men had a strategy. To achieve their aim, they had decided to abandon all measures of gradualism and compromise. They were determined to force action, take a daring position, and rely on the pressure of events to push the rest of the South after them. They stood ready to use their strategy as the four-cornered presidential race of 1860 began.

With such a wide range of candidates and platforms in the field, it seemed that the South had a clear choice on the slavery issue and on the future of the Union, and during the campaign there were some charges and counter-charges concerning the issue of union or disunion. But in general the campaign blurred the choice of alternatives. Seeking the greatest number of voters, each party tried to adjust its principles to the attitudes of the majority. As a result, each presented its purposes as compatible with the maintenance of the Union. The course of the campaign demonstrated that no candidate had been willing to run on a program of secession and that most of the South had not wanted to choose between disunion and union.

From the opening of the contest, unionist newspapers assailed the fire-eaters and their alleged conspiracy to destroy the Union. Repeatedly these journals printed William L. Yancey's "scarlet letter" to James S. Slaughter in 1858, a letter which appeared to propose a secessionist conspiracy. After condemning the fire-eaters, many newspapers tried to link the radicals' purposes with the candidate whom they supported, John Breckinridge of the southern rights party. The New Orleans *Bee* charged that every disunionist in the land was enthusiastic for Breckinridge, and a Texas paper delivered an earthy verdict on Breckinridge's close associations with the contemptible fire-eaters: "Mr. Breckinridge claims that he isn't a disunionist. An animal not willing to pass for a pig shouldn't stay in the stye."[4]

Breckinridge considered the charge of disunionism so damaging that he reversed his decision to remain silent during the campaign. He delivered a single speech in which he flatly denied that he was a disunionist or belonged to any organization whose aim was secession. Quickly his supporters spread this denial, and one of them ridiculed the idea of secession in case of a Republican victory as "political suicide." In North Carolina, Virginia, and Kentucky, Breckinridge speakers "went out of their way to stress their loyalty." Soon the Breckinridge press was strongly professing its devotion to the Union.[5]

These pro-Union testimonials helped the Kentuckian, yet it is likely that many southerners voted for Breckinridge simply because he was the candidate of their party, the southern Democracy. Areas which had normally voted Democratic continued to express that preference in the 1860 election. Sometimes the question of secession was almost totally absent. In Arkansas, for example, there had been little excitement about the burning sectional issues of the 1850s. Citizens in that growing state had given most of their attention to economic development, and the state as a whole was strongly unionist. The salient issues in the 1860 campaign were local, as an inde-

4. Donald E. Reynolds, *Editors Make War: Southern Newspapers in the Secession Crisis* (Nashville: Vanderbilt University Press, 1970), 84–86.

5. Avery O. Craven, *The Growth of Southern Nationalism, 1848–1861* (Baton Rouge: Louisiana State University Press, 1953), Vol. VI of 10 vols., in Wendell Holmes Stephenson and E. Merton Coulter (eds.), *A History of the South*, 341; Reynolds, *Editors Make War*, 88.

pendent Democrat ran against the "machine control" of the bosses who controlled the Democratic party. Breckinridge's Arkansas supporters presented their party's stand on southern rights not as the prelude to independence but as the best way to save the Union. Similarly, in North Carolina few felt that a vote for Breckinridge had any relation to a vote for secession.[6]

The results of the election revealed a sectional vote. Lincoln and Douglas attracted few supporters outside the North, and Breckinridge and Bell drew poorly beyond the South.[7] But the vote was sectional within the South as well. Breckinridge carried nine southern states with his strength concentrated in the lower South. The taint of disunionism had weakened him outside the cotton states. Only Texas, Mississippi, Alabama, Florida, and South Carolina gave Breckinridge strong majorities. In two other states, Arkansas and North Carolina, he gained a majority, but here Bell and Douglas together won 48.6 percent of the total vote, despite the moderate stands of the southern rights party. In Louisiana and Georgia the supporters of Breckinridge were not even a majority; 52.4 percent of the voters in these two states preferred the moderate, unionist programs of Bell or Douglas.[8] Thus, when one considers that many who cast their ballots for Breckinridge did not favor secession, it is clear that the voters did not desire secession in at least four of the nine states that he carried.

In the upper South, the unionist forces were clearly in control. John Bell and the Constitutional Unionists won pluralities in Virginia, Tennessee, and Kentucky. Missouri supported Douglas. Two other slave states, Maryland and Delaware, which never had governments loyal to the Confederacy, also gave the preponderance of their

6. Seymour Martin Lipset, *Political Man: The Social Bases of Politics* (Anchor Books ed.; Garden City, N.Y.: Doubleday and Company, 1963), 374–76; Jack B. Scroggs, "Arkansas in the Secession Crisis," in John L. Ferguson (ed.), *Arkansas in the Civil War* (Little Rock: Arkansas History Commission, n.d.), 12–13; Joseph C. Sitterson, *The Secession Movement in North Carolina* (Chapel Hill: University of North Carolina Press, 1939), 174–75.

7. W. Dean Burnham, *Presidential Ballots, 1836–1892* (Baltimore: Johns Hopkins Press, 1955), 76, 78.

8. *Ibid.*, calculations based on data given on 250–54.

votes to Breckinridge's opponents. In Virginia and Tennessee, Bell and Douglas won 55.5 percent of the total vote, even though the Breckinridge forces in those states had denied any connection with attempts to disrupt the Union. Kentucky and Missouri, states which the Confederacy would claim but never effectively control, gave an impressive 70.7 percent of their vote to the opponents of Breckinridge.[9] The upper South desired compromise and the preservation of the Union, not a radical assertion of southern rights which would lead to secession.

By taking the combined vote of six of the eleven states that would eventually form the Confederacy, one can see the strength of antiextremist sentiment in the South in the fall of 1860. Arkansas, North Carolina, Louisiana, Georgia, Virginia, and Tennessee, taken together, gave only 46.9 percent of their votes to Breckinridge, and many of these ballots had not been endorsements of secession. A solid majority in these states, 53.1 percent, favored candidates whose position definitely supported the Union.[10] Thus radical southern nationalism had not dominated the South during the presidential campaign, and probably a great majority of southerners hoped that some compromise could be reached.

But frail hopes had to contend with stern realities, and as a practical fact the radicals' strategy proved effective. Separate state secession worked as they had hoped that it would, transforming talk into action and pushing events in the direction of disunion. When South Carolina seceded on December 20, 1860, her action placed pressure on other southern states to follow, not only to support the South Carolinians but also to accent grievances felt elsewhere in the South. By seceding, South Carolina had deflated the mystique of an indissoluble Union and made the ultimate step a less momentous one. After December, many radicals could argue that secession was already a reality, and that southerners who wanted to compromise could make a better bargain with the United States out of the Union than in it. According to this argument secession was no longer an irrevocable

9. *Ibid.*
10. *Ibid.*

step, but simply a way of proving the South's seriousness about its demands.

Moreover, the logic of events tended in the direction of secession. After Lincoln's election and the secession of South Carolina, there were many efforts at compromise. Both houses of Congress established special committees to search for means of adjustment. A multitude of proposals poured into Washington from both sections. Potential compromisers like Senator John J. Crittenden of Kentucky emerged, hoping to play the role so often acted before by Henry Clay. Virginia took the lead in organizing a peace convention which met in Washington. But all these efforts failed.[11] The Republicans refused to cooperate in any compromise, largely because they were convinced that no compromise would be necessary and that unionists in the South would reassert control there. At times southern leaders in Congress declined to seek measures of compromise, largely because they had decided that only a resolute stance could convince the Republicans of the gravity of the South's concern. Committees met without result, weeks passed, and nothing was accomplished. The progression of events destroyed hopes of compromise and pushed southerners toward a step which most did not want to take.

Still, the voting on secession illustrated the reluctance and ambiguity with which southerners left the Union. The turnout of voters everywhere was significantly lower than it had been just a few months previously in the presidential election. In a few cases this low turnout stemmed from the fact that voters in an area were so united in feeling that candidates for union or secession ran unopposed. In most states, however, the small vote indicated that southerners were confused and unhappy with the alternatives from which they had to choose. Not knowing what to do, and feeling dissatisfied with both possible courses of action, many people simply stayed home in frustration.

Georgia was a pivotal state in the voting. Its location and the economic importance it would have to any southern confederacy caused

11. Craven, *Growth of Southern Nationalism*, 377–80, 385–86.

many southerners to watch its action closely. Perhaps a refusal by Georgia to bend with the tide would determine the whole South's course as it had in 1850, when the great majority of Georgians had supported compromise and union. Most historians have accepted newspaper reports that in 1861 the voters gave the secessionists a majority by a margin of 50,243 to 37,123. A painstaking recent study, however, concluded that "the most generous estimate of the popular sentiment for secession is just over 51 per cent of those voting" and that "an estimate that is probably more accurate placed the majority for cooperation at just over 50 per cent of the voters." Sentiment in north Georgia was very strong against secession, and delegates from that area needed "tutoring" by secessionists when they arrived at the convention. Alexander Stephens made a strong appeal for the Union, but an ordinance of secession carried, 164 votes to 133.[12] Stephens felt that the most powerful argument in the campaign had been T. R. R. Cobb's: "We can make better terms out of the Union than in it."

In Alabama three-fourths of those who had voted in November went to the polls and elected fifty-four secessionists and forty-six co-operationists. The latter group ranged in opinion from those who wanted to secede with other states to those who opposed secession in all circumstances. The vote had been close, and the *Southern Advocate* claimed that cooperationists would have been the majority except for bad management in two counties. Here as elsewhere South Carolina's action and a feeling that secession would be peaceful aided the radicals. On a strict party division the secessionists won, to the disgust of a delegate from north Alabama who wrote: "Here I sit & from my window see the nasty little thing flaunting in the breeze which has taken the place of that glorious banner which has been the pride of millions of Americans and the boast of freemen the wide world over."[13]

12. Michael P. Johnson, "A New Look at the Popular Vote for Delegates to the Georgia Secession Convention," *Georgia Historical Quarterly*, LVI (1972), 259–75; Horace Montgomery, *Howell Cobb's Confederate Career* (Tuscaloosa, Ala.: Confederate Publishing Company, Inc., 1959), 21–22; Craven, *Growth of Southern Nationalism*, 372; Horace Montgomery, *Cracker Parties* (Baton Rouge: Louisiana State University Press, 1950), 245–46.
13. Craven, *Growth of Southern Nationalism*, 366–68.

In Texas, the slavery issue was thoroughly tangled up with resentment over the federal government's inadequate protection from Indian raids, and this feeling aided secession.[14] Florida and Louisiana had organized opposition to secession, and in Louisiana a large portion of the opposition wanted to remain in the Union as it was, even without a compromise. In each state, however, the secessionists triumphed, although the official vote was suppressed in Louisiana. Both conventions refused to submit their work to the ratification of the people.[15]

Even in Mississippi, where the ardor of the fire-eaters had earned that state a reputation of eagerness to leave the Union second only to that of South Carolina, there was considerable opposition to secession. The radicals were prepared with answers to all arguments, however, and asserted that civil war would not occur and that only courageous resistance by the South could command the attention of the Republicans. Only 60 percent of those who had voted in the presidential election went to the polls. After passing an ordinance of secession, the state convention refused to submit the act to the people for ratification and adjourned.[16]

Even at this point, with seven states out of the Union, secession was far from irresistible. A strong majority of the people of North Carolina, Arkansas, Virginia, and Tennessee steadfastly refused to leave the Union, although a new Confederacy had been organized in Montgomery. Elections in February went heavily against the secessionists in Virginia and North Carolina. In the Old North State "the overwhelming majority of the people obviously did not regard Lincoln's election as a sufficient cause for secession."[17] In Arkansas the voters agreed to hold a convention, but they cast 23,626 votes for Union delegates and only 17,927 votes for secessionists. The secessionist press admitted that there was an even stronger majority for the Union among those not voting, and some sections of the state, such as northwest Arkansas, "remained singularly devoid" of hysteria. Tennessee also clung to the Union as long as it was possible to

14. *Ibid.*, 375–77.
15. *Ibid.*, 368–69, 374–75.
16. *Ibid.*, 363–65.
17. Sitterson, *Secession Movement in North Carolina*, 223, 180; Henry T. Shanks, *The Secession Movement in Virginia, 1847–1861* (Richmond: Garrett and Massie, 1934), 153.

do so in peace, with the eastern part of the state harboring especially strong feelings of loyalty to the Union.[18]

The balloting on secession raised another vital question: What was the attitude of the nonslaveholders? Southern leaders had always regarded the loyalty of the yeoman class as somewhat problematic, although outright revolt was rare. For many years politicians had tailored part of the proslavery argument for the enlightenment of the nonslaveholding portion of the population. According to one line of argument, slavery provided a direct economic advantage to the non-slaveholder because it elevated the wages of all white laborers. Such a wage floor did not exist in the North, proslavery advocates warned, and if the abolitionists succeeded in destroying slavery, all white workers in the South would be forced to live on wages paid to slaves. Another line of argument presented the slaveholder as an example of the gospel of success. Proponents of this view hoped to enlist the nonslaveholders' ambitions and hopes in pursuit of the rewards offered by a slaveholding society. Another common argument relied on racial fears. Among the horrible consequences of emancipation would be domination by black men, sexual abuse of white men's wives and daughters by black males, and widespread miscegenation.[19]

One of the favorite arguments directed to nonslaveholders relied not on the dire consequences of some possible future event, but on present, compelling advantages which slavery provided. The poor man would not oppose slavery because it elevated his status. Jefferson Davis told a gathering at Aberdeen, Mississippi, in 1851: "Distinctions between classes have always existed, everywhere, and in every country, where civilization has been established among men. . . . Wherever a distinction in color has not existed to draw a line, and mark the boundary, the line has been drawn, by property, between the rich and the poor." Then he stressed that the South was the sole exception to this melancholy rule. In its slave society, the

18. Scroggs, "Arkansas in the Secession Crisis," 28, 39–40; Ralph A. Wooster, *The Secession Conventions of the South* (Princeton: Princeton University Press, 1962), 181, 187.

19. Ralph E. Morrow, "The Proslavery Argument Revisited," *Mississippi Valley Historical Review*, XLVIII (1961), 81–94.

nonslaveholding southerner could "*stand upon the broad level of equality with the rich man.*" Pointedly Davis reminded the poor that "their all is suspended upon their *superiority* to the *blacks*."[20] Any social revolution such as that desired by the abolitionists would lower the status of nonslaveholders immediately.

During the secession crisis this concern over the reliability of the nonslaveholder surfaced once more. On the eve of the 1860 presidential election the Montgomery *Mail* charged that the aim of the Republicans was "to free the negroes and force amalgamation between them and the children of the poor men of the South. The rich will be able to keep out of the way of the contamination." In the hill country of South Carolina a letter to the Edgefield *Advertiser* revealed a similar fear that the nonslaveholders needed to be controlled. The writer, Robert S. Hudson, warned of the "evil" of too few slaveowners and urged planters to sell one tenth of their bondsmen to the yeomen. "By that means," Hudson reasoned, "you might make interest supply the deficiency of patriotism." About the same time *De Bow's Review* suggested that slaves be confined to agricultural work so that white mechanics would cease to be foes of slavery.[21] This nagging anxiety over the loyalty of the nonslaveholder was widespread and did not abate, for the planters' fears proved to be justified.

The pattern of voting on secession showed that a crucial problem for the Confederacy might be the reluctance of nonslaveholders to sacrifice for the cause. There were signs that small farmers who owned few or no slaves might be unwilling to march into war for the interests of slaveholders. Even in Mississippi, one small fact should have given the thoughtful fire-eater pause. Of five Mississippi counties with a slave population of less than 25 percent, only one sent a secessionist delegate to the state convention.[22]

This tendency emerged far more clearly in Georgia, where the

20. Rowland (ed.), *Jefferson Davis*, II, 74.

21. Reynolds, *Editors Make War*, 125; Edgefield (S.C.) *Advertiser*, November 28, 1860, p. 1; *De Bow's Review*, quoted in Edgefield (S.C.) *Advertiser*, February 27, 1861, p. 1.

22. Wooster, *Secession Conventions*, 45.

northern section, a hilly, red-clay area, and the southeast (except along the coast), were predominantly white. Thirteen counties in these regions were more than 90 percent white, and eight of them opposed secession, while two sent split delegations to the state convention. Of counties in north Georgia that were 75 to 90 percent white, nine opposed secession, three were split, and only three supported leaving the Union. Of a total of twenty counties in north Georgia that opposed secession, all twenty were more than 60 percent white and seventeen were more than 75 percent white. A similar situation existed in southeastern Georgia, where seven of the eight counties that opposed secession were more than 60 percent white. Georgia's black belt counties, on the other hand, generally supported secession.[23]

Many of Georgia's nonslaveholders had supported Breckinridge but voted against secession. This reversal of allegiance was even more pronounced in Alabama. The northern half of Alabama was an area of few slaves, and political battles between the different areas of the state had been quite common during the 1850s. In 1860 northern Alabama gave Breckinridge a strong majority, with almost exactly the same percentage of the vote as Breckinridge won in the rest of the state. The vote for the secession convention revealed a different situation.

Political leaders from the northern half of the state worried that the predominantly nonslaveholding voters there might oppose disunion. Leroy Pope Walker, who would soon become Confederate secretary of war, long had been prominent in north Alabama's politics and had stumped the region during the presidential canvass in order to combat its unionist proclivities. As the vote on delegates to the secession convention approached, Walker once again spoke out against unionism. Using strongly worded predictions of racial upheaval if the state did not secede, he warned that Alabama must avoid the Republican "tide of fanaticism." On one occasion he declared that the issue was: "Shall negroes govern white men, or white men

23. These data were compiled from maps in U. B. Phillips, *Georgia and State Rights* (Washington: Government Printing Office, 1902), 204–209.

govern negroes: Remember now, that universal emancipation and universal suffrage, go together. When this point is reached, and the ballot is free alike to black and white—my God! the infamy of such a possibility!"[24] Even these powerful racial appeals, however, failed to deter the voters of northern Alabama. Walker's own county and neighboring counties elected opponents of secession. In fact, in the vote for delegates to the convention, the state split sharply into two opposed areas. By an overwhelming margin, the southern half of the state selected secessionist delegates for the convention. Almost 75 percent of the vote in the southern part of Alabama was secessionist. In northern Alabama, on the other hand, the people chose coopera-tionist candidates by a margin of 57.3 percent to 42.7 percent.[25] Ala-bama's nonslaveholders and small farmers were markedly less eager to risk the dangers of secession than were the planters of the state's black belt. This split among Alabamians indicated a possible fault in the structure of southern nationalism.

In Louisiana also there was a cleavage between "hillfarmer and planter, especially in North Louisiana." The hillfarmers tended to be moderate on the issue of secession. However, under the state constitution of 1852, Louisiana's sugar planters enjoyed an over-representation that helped them to carry the state out of the Union. Only 32 percent of the delegates to the state convention were co-operationists, although they had been elected by 48.5 percent of the state's white voters. The predominantly slave counties in Louisiana shifted toward secession between the presidential election and the selection of a convention. By contrast, of the counties with relatively few slaves, the number supporting secession dropped off by one third.[26]

Seymour Martin Lipset, a leading sociologist, has analyzed these

24. William C. Harris, *Leroy Pope Walker: Confederate Secretary of War* (Tuscaloosa, Ala.: Confederate Publishing Company, Inc., 1961), 15.

25. These calculations were made from tables of election returns presented in Lewy Dorman, *Party Politics in Alabama from 1850 Through 1860* (Wetumpka, Ala.: Alabama State Department of Archives and History, 1935), 176–77, 194–95.

26. Perry H. Howard, *Political Tendencies in Louisiana* (Rev. ed.; Baton Rouge: Loui-siana State University Press, 1971), 97–99, 101–102.

tendencies for seven states in the South—Virginia, Alabama, Georgia, Mississippi, North Carolina, Tennessee, and Louisiana. He classified the counties in these states according to the number of slaves held within them. In the presidential election, only 52 percent of the counties with a high proportion of slaves supported Breckinridge, whereas 64 percent of the counties with a low proportion of slaves voted for the southern rights candidate. This difference reflected the fact that traditionally the Whig party in the South had been strongest among the large planters, whereas the Democrats were the party of small farmers. Party loyalty had guided voters as they selected a presidential candidate. In the vote on secession, however, the situation was reversed. Of the counties with many slaves, 72 percent supported secession. The counties with few slaves which had supported Breckinridge very strongly, now shifted toward a moderate position, 63 percent of them sending cooperationist or unionist delegates to the secession conventions. Fully one-half of the lowslave counties that had voted for Breckinridge shifted to unionist candidates, and 86 percent of the low-slave counties that had voted for Bell or Douglas continued to support moderate candidates in the convention elections.[27]

Thus during the secession crisis both reluctance to leave the Union and another more disturbing tendency appeared. Southerners began to divide along class lines in their devotion to the South, or more specifically in their willingness to incur risks and possibly make sacrifices over the issue of slavery. Slaveholders embraced a cause which was theirs, but southerners who owned few or no slaves seemed reluctant to support a southern nation. It was clear that Confederate leaders would face a formidable task in building loyalty among the population and cementing the social fractures which lay beneath the facade of a rebellious South. Southern nationalism at the beginning of 1861 was still a fragile and weak organism.

Its skillful nurture was not the task for the radicals and fire-eaters, for they were the group most unsuited to unify upper South and

27. Lipset, *Political Man*, 376–79.

lower South, slaveholder and nonslaveholder. Their aggressive ideology only threatened to make the fissures in southern society deeper, and the antidemocratic theories which they sometimes stressed, with their emphasis on aristocracy and rule by the well born, were unacceptable in the democratic South.[28] Delegates to the Montgomery Convention soon learned that fire-eaters like Yancey or Rhett and extreme proslavery views were unattractive to Virginia and the upper South, and therefore they began to present a more moderate image of the Confederacy.[29] For these reasons a shift in power occurred, signaled by Jefferson Davis' election as president.

Davis had been one of the leading contenders for the presidency throughout the Montgomery Convention, and many delegates shared T. R. R. Cobb's feeling that the Mississippi senator would be the eventual choice. In later years Alexander Stephens disseminated a story that Robert Toombs would have been president but for confusion about the preference of the Georgia delegation. Stephen's account contradicts that of T. R. R. Cobb, a trained legal reporter, and conflicts with an abundance of other evidence about sentiment at the convention. It is far more likely that Davis' election was the natural product of a widespread desire for unanimity, respectability, and above all, moderation. The Mississippian represented the right man for the time. He was probably the most widely known of the South's leaders and was acceptable to all parts of the divided South. His moderation inspired enthusiasm in the upper South, and he could project an image of unimpeachable dignity for the new nation.[30]

The desire for moderation and respectability which helped elect

28. Arguments against placing government in the hands of the common people frequently appeared in the Charleston *Mercury*. See also Robert H. Smith to W. C. Rives, January 1, 1864, in W. C. Rives Collection, Library of Congress.

29. Charles Robert Lee, Jr., *The Confederate Constitutions* (Chapel Hill: University of North Carolina Press, 1963), 73; William W. Boyce to R. M. T. Hunter, February 5, 1861, in R. M. T. Hunter Papers, University of Virginia.

30. Lee, *Confederate Constitutions*, 72–73; Alexander H. Stephens, *A Constitutional View of the Late War Between the States: Its Cause, Character, Conduct and Results* (2 vols.; Philadelphia: n.p., 1870), II, 328–33; Albert N. Fitts, "The Confederate Convention: The Provisional Constitution," *Alabama Review*, II (April, 1949), 91–95; Ralph Richardson, "The Choice of Jefferson Davis as Confederate President," *Journal of Mississippi History*, XVII (July, 1955), 161–76.

Davis was also evident in the drafting of a Confederate constitution. Both the provisional constitution, under which he took office, and the permanent constitution, which was completed on March 16, 1861, took as their model the Constitution of the United States. The fundamental law of the Confederacy closely followed that revered earlier document with a few changes designed to emphasize the South's philosophy of states' rights. To restrain the expansion of authority of the central government, the drafters of the Confederate constitutions dropped the "general welfare" clause and prohibited Confederate-sponsored internal improvements and a protective tariff. The Confederate Convention also added a few measures of reform, such as limiting the president to one six-year term, permitting cabinet members to sit in Congress to discuss proposed legislation, and making the amending process easier to initiate. But the constitutions' provisions on slavery revealed that, in the southern context, the documents were essentially moderate. Although they mentioned slavery by name and provided for its protection, both Confederate constitutions contained an absolute ban on the African slave trade.[31]

As the Confederate framers finished their documents, Jefferson Davis' work had just begun. He faced several immediate challenges when he took office, chief among them being the South's lack of means to defend itself in what he feared would be a "long and bloody" war.[32] Moreover the entire upper South—including Virginia, North Carolina, Tennessee, Arkansas, and the other slaveholding states of Maryland, Delaware, Kentucky, and Missouri—was still in the Union. To be successful, Davis first had to be a nation builder and find some way to add many of these states to the Confederacy. The machinery of govenment had to be organized, and Davis needed to establish the Confederacy's independence in a practical sense. The new government had to function as a nation and win the recognition of other sovereign countries. In regard to foreign recognition, the South's defense of slavery might pose a problem, as it did to unity within the Confederacy.

31. Lee, *Confederate Constitutions*, 145–50, Appendices B and C.
32. Rowland (ed.), *Jefferson Davis*, V, 21, 32; Davis, *Rise and Fall*, I, 230.

With a sure hand, Davis accepted these challenges and began to prove that he was the man whom the Confederacy needed in 1861. One would like to know what Davis thought as he approached his tasks, but it is difficult to reconstruct his views precisely. He was an exceedingly private individual, and though his course of action was clear, he kept his own counsel and rarely committed his inner thoughts to paper. One can define Davis' attitudes with some assurance, however, by examining his past behavior, the factors relevant to his decisions, and the pattern of his actions. One of the most important decisions that he reached in 1861 involved the issue of slavery.

Davis decided to deemphasize slavery's role in the Confederacy's ideology, and throughout 1861 he consistently adhered to a strategy of relegating the slavery issue to a subordinate position. He scrupulously avoided mentioning it whenever possible, despite the fact that fear for slavery's future under the Lincoln government had been the cause of secession. Davis himself had come to favor secession because he believed that slavery was not safe within the states.[33] But as the leader of the Confederacy, he realized that the issue of slavery entailed dangers both foreign and domestic.

Southerners long had known that most of the world was hostile to their peculiar institution. During the four decades before the Civil War, opponents of slavery in Britain had succeeded in abolishing the institution from that empire's Atlantic possessions and had waged war on the international slave trade. The antislavery movement in Europe, particularly in Britain, had many ties with its counterpart in the northern United States. When Confederate commissioners arrived in England, they encountered considerable criticism of their new nation's racial arrangements. Their first report to the Davis administration dealt with the strength of the antislavery sentiment in England: "We are satisfied that the public mind here is entirely opposed to the Government of the Confederate States of America on the question of slavery, and that the sincerity and universality of this

---

33. *Mississippian and State Gazette* (Jackson, Miss.), October 21, 1857, p. 1; Percy Rainwater, *Mississippi: Storm Center of Secession, 1856–1861* (Baton Rouge: Otto Claitor, 1938), 26; Rowland (ed.), *Jefferson Davis*, IV, 540, V, 39.

feeling embarrass the Government in dealing with the question of our recognition." Although the commissioners later concluded that other considerations were more important with foreign governments, the European aversion to American slavery remained a stumbling block for the Confederate government.[34] Thus considerations of foreign policy provided one reason for Davis to avoid making slavery the symbol of the Confederacy.

Other reasons for deemphasizing slavery pertained to the internal morale of the South. As a slaveholder and an experienced southern politician, Jefferson Davis knew that slavery was potentially a divisive force in the Confederate body politic. He had worried about the loyalty of nonslaveholders earlier in his political career, and now he tried to ensure that they would not defect from the Confederate cause.[35] Because it was unwise to make slavery the explicit and paramount foundation for a government which nonslaveholders would have to defend, he refused to define the new southern nation by its support for slavery. Instead he took pains not to mention the institution and reached for themes which would inspire and unify the South as a whole.

In stark contrast to Davis, the Confederacy's vice president, diminutive and volatile Alexander Stephens, spoke out loudly about slavery. In a speech in Savannah, Georgia, on March 21, 1861, Stephens said: "The new constitution has put to rest forever all agitating questions relating to our institutions. . . . *Our new government is founded . . . its foundations are laid, its cornerstone rests, upon the great truth that the negro is not equal to the white man*; that slavery, subordination to the superior race, is his natural and normal condition."[36] Stephens also was concerned about the doubtful loyalty of the nonslaveholder, for later in this speech he exhorted southerners to avoid

34. W. L. Yancey and A. Dudley Mann to Robert Toombs, May 21, 1861, in James D. Richardson (comp.), *A Compilation of the Messages and Papers of the Confederacy, Including the Diplomatic Correspondence, 1861–1865* (2 vols.; Nashville: United States Publishing Company, 1906), II, 37, and W. L. Yancey and A. Dudley Mann to Robert Toombs, August 1, 1861, p. 53.
35. Rowland (ed.), *Jefferson Davis*, II, 73–75.
36. Augusta *Constitutionalist*, March 30, 1861.

internal divisions. Perhaps in an impulsive manner he was trying to confront the Confederacy's embarrassing connection with slavery and dispose of its dangers immediately by an argument of racial unity. Davis probably knew that such an approach would not work, for he remained devoted to his own strategy. Perhaps he hoped that Stephen's speech would be the forgotten exception to what a distinguished historian has termed "the moderate posture struck by every other Confederate." [37]

Lincoln's silence on the slavery issue helped Davis immeasurably. For reasons of his own Lincoln shunned this issue throughout 1861 and much of 1862. In fact, the North and the South fought the first fifteen months of the war which freed the slaves with scarcely an official mention of slavery. Aside from the need to conciliate northern Democrats as well as moderate Republicans, Lincoln was counting on a resurgence of unionism in the South and struggling to hold some of the border states. For these reasons he did not want to broach an issue which would alarm many in both the North and the South. In addition, the U.S. president knew that large segments of northern opinion would not tolerate emancipation unless it was an unavoidable necessity. [38] As long as Lincoln held his silence the issue could not be drawn, and this fact furthered Jefferson Davis' purpose.

In all of 1861 Davis made only two public references to slavery. The first of these afforded him an opportunity to separate the Confederacy from extreme proslavery views. Article I, section 7 of the Provisional Constitution required the Confederate Congress to pass laws which would "effectually prevent . . . the importation of African negroes from any foreign country other than the slave-holding States of the United States." Congress passed a bill on this subject and sent it to Davis. But on February 18, 1861, Davis vetoed the bill because it did not satisfy the "emphatic" requirements of the constitution. One provision would allow the sale at public auction of il-

37. Frank E. Vandiver, *Their Tattered Flags* (New York: Harper's Magazine Press and Harper & Row, 1970), 24.
38. David M. Potter, *Lincoln and His Party in the Secession Crisis* (New Haven: Yale University Press, 1942), Chap. 1, 141–42, 316–18; C. Vann Woodward, "Our Racist History," *New York Review of Books*, XII (February 27, 1969), 5–11.

legally imported Negroes who could not be returned to Africa by foreign states or societies. Such sales, Davis insisted, might lead to disguised renewal of the African slave trade, and would violate the constitution.[39]

The Confederacy's chief executive also referred to slavery on April 29, 1861, when he delivered his war message to the congress. In the first part of this message Davis reviewed the causes of the conflict, and he scarcely could avoid mentioning slavery. But he characteristically placed a clash of constitutional theories first among the causes of the war and attacked the greed of manufacturing and shipping classes in the North. Only then did he mention slavery in a way which praised the morality and humanity of slaveholders. The planters' "increasing care and attention for the well-being and comfort of the laboring class," had multiplied the number of slaves and converted "brutal savages into docile, intelligent, and civilized agricultural laborers" blessed with "careful religious instruction."[40] After making this justification for the South's institutions, Davis avoided any public mention of the subject during the rest of 1861. This low-key approach to slavery tended to remove a possible cause of strain in society and freed Davis to build Confederate nationalism on themes of common interest.

The first step in developing Confederate nationalism was to establish independence as the South's primary goal. Some delegates in Montgomery were concerned that Davis was a reconstructionist, but the new president had put his earlier hopes of compromise behind him.[41] On his arrival in Montgomery, Davis slammed the door on possibilities of compromise. "The time for compromise," he said, had "passed, and our only hope [is] in a determined maintenance of our position, and to make all who oppose us smell Southern powder and feel Southern steel. . . . Our separation from the old Union is complete. NO COMPROMISE: NO RECONSTRUCTION CAN

---

39. Richardson (comp.), *Messages and Papers of the Confederacy*, I, 5–6, 59.
40. *Ibid.*, 64–68.
41. T. R. R. Cobb to his wife, February 15, 1861, in T. R. R. Cobb Letters, University of Georgia, Athens, Georgia; Lawrence M. Keitt to James H. Hammond, February 13, 1861, in MS Hammond Papers, Library of Congress.

NOW BE ENTERTAINED."[42] In his inaugural address, Davis made a similar declaration and indicated to northerners and southerners alike that the Confederacy would not return to the Union under any circumstances. He anticipated that more states would join the Confederacy, "but beyond this," he said, "a reunion with the States from which we have separated is neither practicable nor desirable." Davis told his audience that the long history of conflict with the North had demonstrated that a nation needed homogeneity for unity. Without an essential similarity among the states, antagonisms would develop which "must and should result in separation."[43] These statements marked the beginning of a determination to win southern independence which would remain unshakable even in the last days of the war.

As he wrote such passages, Davis may also have felt the need to discourage hopes for reconciliation in the South, for some Confederates were disturbingly ready to compromise. Many men had supported secession in the hope of winning better terms from the Republicans, and unionists were delaying secession in the upper South. Georgia's Howell Cobb was quite disturbed about unionism in the northern part of his state, and his brother, T. R. R. Cobb, wrote from Montgomery that some of Alabama's representatives were "not only reconstructionists but absolutely union men." One secessionist reported in March, 1861, that there were enough unionists in Alabama to vote that state back into the United States. In the same month newspapers in Nashville carried stories of citizens' meetings in Frankfort and Athens, Alabama, for the purpose of reconstruction.[44] Davis tried to make clear at the outset that he was seeking loyalty to the Confederate States of America, not compromise with the United States.

The new president made his main ideological appeal to the people of the South in his inaugural. Although he demanded allegiance to

42. Rowland (ed.), *Jefferson Davis*, V, 48.
43. Richardson (comp.), *Messages and Papers of the Confederacy*, I, 35, 34.
44. T. R. R. Cobb to his wife, February 4, 1861, in T. R. R. Cobb Letters; Montgomery, *Howell Cobb's Confederate Career*, 26, 29, 33–34; Nashville *Daily Democrat*, March 30, 1861, p. 2; Nashville *Republican Banner*, March 22, 1861.

the Confederacy, Davis took care to define his new nation in terms
which would appeal to all who still had some love for the Union. The
burden of his message was that the Confederacy was the true embodiment of American principles of government. Rather than destroying the American system, the formation of the Confederacy
preserved and vindicated it. The Confederacy had become the guar-
dian of the founders' legacy. Those who loved the Union did not have
to surrender their feelings of affection but merely transfer them to
their true object, the new government in Montgomery. The Confederate Constitution differed from the founders' only "in so far as
it is explanatory of their well-known intent. . . . The Constitution
framed by our fathers is that of these Confederate States." Davis
concluded his address by calling on God to help the new nation "to
perpetuate the principles which [the founding fathers] were able to
vindicate, establish, and transmit to their posterity."[45]

Thus Davis identified the South's new government with the fundamental principles of the original United States. This decision gave
him an ideology which would have the broadest possible appeal to
southerners. For those who already supported the new nation, Davis
offered an inspiring and dignified justification of its existence. For
the doubtful he offered reassuring continuity with the American heritage and with the Union which they loved. This definition of the
Confederacy's ideology was not original with Davis. Many others
turned to the same theme, for it answered a deeply felt need among
Confederates. Not only did the identification of the Confederacy
with American principles provide a ready justification for secession,
it also eased the transfer of strong loyalties to a new and untried government.

This definition of the Confederacy's purpose also satisfied the need
for a social myth. The slaveholding class, aided by forces of racial and
regional unity and the absence of desirable alternatives, had led the
South out of the Union in order to protect slavery. But having done

45. Richardson (comp.), *Messages and Papers of the Confederacy*, I, 32–36. Davis
wanted to retain the United States' flag as the banner of the southern nation. See Varina
Howell Davis, *A Memoir*, III, 36.

so, the dominant class had to justify its action and secure the loyalty of all the citizens. The assertion that the Confederacy was the true embodiment of American principles of government answered these purposes admirably. Southerners could explain to themselves and to the world that with peaceful intent they had formed a new nation in order to preserve constitutional government.

Davis had barely begun to establish his government—by forming a cabinet and arranging to purchase arms in the North and Europe —when war broke out.[46] An extensive body of literature has grown up concerning the events leading to the first shot, but no detailed examination of this question is necessary here, except to note Davis' basic attitudes.[47] The Confederate president wanted to avoid war but was never optimistic about the chances of doing so. He publicly displayed this lack of optimism in his inaugural and later told South Carolina's governor Pickens, "I have not been [one] of those who felt sanguine hope that the enemy would retire peaceably from your harbor." Davis' main goal throughout the crisis over the forts off the southern coast was to establish the Confederacy as a separate, independent government. His prime responsibility was to alter the status quo, which was intolerable to any sovereign nation, whereas Lincoln could accept the status quo in the short run. Functioning as the head of a government that did not exercise one of the essential attributes of sovereignty—control of its own territory—Davis regarded possession of the forts as absolutely essential, whereas avoidance of war was merely desirable. Thus, when Lincoln sent a supply ship to the besieged garrison in Charleston harbor, Confederate forces opened fire and captured the fort.[48]

The shooting had begun, but the act which precipitated the next

46. Harris, *Leroy Pope Walker*, 79–84.
47. Charles W. Ramsdell, "Lincoln and Fort Sumter," *Journal of Southern History*, III (1937), 259–88; Richard N. Current, "The Confederates and the First Shot," *Civil War History*, VII (December, 1961), 357–69; Grady McWhiney, "The Confederacy's First Shot," *Civil War History*, XIV (March, 1968), 5–14; Ludwell H. Johnson, "Fort Sumter and Confederate Diplomacy," *Journal of Southern History*, XXVI (1960), 441–77.
48. Richardson (comp.), *Messages and Papers of the Confederacy*, I, 32–34; Rowland (ed.), *Jefferson Davis*, V, 61.

series of events came from Abraham Lincoln. Since a Federal garrison had been fired upon by forces in South Carolina, Lincoln adopted measures to defend the authority of the United States. On April 15, 1861, he called on all the states for 75,000 volunteers to put down "combinations too powerful to be suppressed by the ordinary course of judicial proceedings, or by the powers vested in the Marshals by law."[49] This action ended the upper South's hope of avoiding a choice between the two American governments, and the rest of the southern states now had to decide where their loyalties belonged. Lincoln's call for troops and Davis' subsequent acts resulted in the secession of four more states in the upper South.

Virginians, including all moderates and many unionists, had been opposed to Federal coercion since the meeting of their convention in February. They argued that whether a right of secession existed or not, coercion would alter the nature of the Union. Certainly it would force them into a choice which they did not want to make. Opponents of secession in Virginia had been able to retain the support of the moderates on the strength of Seward's promise that Sumter would not be reenforced. As rumors of a Federal operation to resupply the garrison at Sumter multiplied, a shift in opinion developed. The news that a relief ship was on its way to Charleston harbor and that firing had begun accelerated the momentum toward secession. A last-minute proposal for a conference of the border states failed, and on April 17, 1861, Virginia seceded from the United States. Seven days later the state entered into an alliance with the Confederacy.[50]

Noting the pattern of events in Virginia, Davis determined to do nothing which would arrest the process generated in the upper South by Lincoln's call for troops. In his address to the Confederate Congress on April 19, which explained the outbreak of war, Davis kept the sentiments of foreign nations and the upper South in mind. He

49. Quoted by Davis in Richardson (comp.), *Messages and Papers of the Confederacy*, I, 74.
50. Shanks, *Secession Movement in Virginia*, 191, 199, 197, 204; Richardson (comp.), *Messages and Papers of the Confederacy*, I, 102.

began by mentioning the happy expectation that other states would soon join the Confederacy, thus strengthening its ability to defend "constitutional liberty." Then he reviewed the history of the United States and stressed that the South had always upheld the Constitution. Reluctantly, when there was no other way to defend its rights, the South had left the Union in peace. Now Lincoln's government had created a war: "But for the interference of the Government of the United States in this legitimate exercise of the right of a people to self-government, peace, happiness, and prosperity would now smile on our land."[51]

The Confederacy, Davis asserted, "ardently desired" peace. He traced his government's attempts to find a solution short of war and gave considerable attention to the exchanges which took place between Confederate commissioners who had been sent to Washington and Secretary of State Seward. Seeking a peaceful settlement, the commissioners "waived all questions of form" and "went so far even as to hold during that long period unofficial intercourse through an intermediary." Repeatedly they received assurances that Fort Sumter would be evacuated and that no change prejudicial to the Confederacy would occur at Fort Pickens. The progress of events, however, revealed what Davis charged was a pattern of deceit on the part of the Lincoln administration. The United States "had profited by the delay created by their own assurances in order to prepare secretly the means for effective hostile operations." Davis castigated the acts of the Federal government in strong terms: "The crooked paths of diplomacy can scarcely furnish an example so wanting in courtesy, in candor, and directness as was the course of the United States Government toward our commissioners in Washington."[52] To emphasize the Confederacy's good faith and peaceable intentions, Davis made public the commissioners' correspondence with the United States.

These protestations of Confederate innocence and good faith helped hasten the upper South's movement into the new southern

51. Richardson (comp.), *Messages and Papers of the Confederacy*, I, 70.
52. *Ibid.*, 71, 72.

nation. In North Carolina, as in Virginia, Lincoln's call for troops had jolted the secession movement off dead center. All factions supported the Tarheel governor's refusal to supply Lincoln with any troops. North Carolina's legislature arranged for a convention to meet and in the intervening period prepared for war. On May 20, 1861, the convention met and seceded from the Union that same day.[53] Arkansas still displayed some resistance to secession and a desire for neutrality. But Lincoln's actions and Davis' response had shifted the burden of proof onto the opponents of secession. On May 6, 1861, the Arkansas convention reconvened and seceded by a vote of 65 to 5. On the same day Tennessee, where there also remained some reluctance to secede, entered into a military alliance with the Confederacy. In June a referendum approved the legislature's action and made secession official. In Missouri, Kentucky, and Maryland, sentiment was too divided for conclusive measures, and the Lincoln administration exerted strong efforts to check any attempts at secession in those states.[54]

These events broke the long season of tension and uncertainty in the South. A wave of excitement and enthusiasm replaced the hesitation which had gone before as men welcomed the prospect of action. During the secession crisis, many southern leaders had boasted that any war with the North would be brief and victorious. Encouraged by these predictions, southerners now organized for war. In every state preparations went forward, and eager young men banded into companies. Jefferson Davis tried to exploit this enthusiasm and to strengthen it during the succeeding months. It was a propitious time for him to hammer away at his main themes in order to build the people's spirit. Davis used the months after the capture of Fort Sumter to complete his definition of Confederate ideology and stimulate the citizens' will to fight. He sought to make Confederates certain of their goals and steadfast in their determination.

Davis continued to identify the Confederate cause with the true

53. Sitterson, *Secession Movement in North Carolina*, 240, 241, 243–44, 247.
54. Scroggs, "Arkansas in the Secession Crisis," 40; Wooster, *Secession Conventions*, 188; Craven, *Growth of Southern Nationalism*, 390.

heritage of the United States, and frequently drew an analogy between the American Revolution and the South's war for independence. The founding fathers had fought against tyranny to establish liberty on the American continent. The South's high duty now, Davis declared, was to preserve that legacy. When he arrived at Richmond, the Confederacy's new capital, on May 30, 1861, Davis told the throng waiting at the new fair grounds, "I look upon you as the last best hope of liberty." Later in the summer he insisted that southerners would defend "their right to self-government," and in November he described the Confederacy's war as a battle against tyranny. According to Davis, the Confederates were "fighting for the sacred right of self-government and the privileges of a freeman." [55]

To strengthen the Confederacy's identification with American values, Davis charged that the United States had abandoned its original principles. Only in the Confederacy were man's inalienable rights safe from despotism. Launching a propaganda campaign against Lincoln's actions in the North, Davis argued that executive usurpations there had utterly destroyed the basic freedoms which Americans were supposed to enjoy. He told the congress when it reassembled in Richmond that Lincoln had claimed that the executive had the power to suspend the writ of *habeas corpus*. The northern president then had proceeded to delegate that power to military commanders. Davis also ridiculed Lincoln's argument that he was justified in violating "to a very limited extent" a law whose "extreme tenderness of the citizen's liberty" favored guilty parties more than the innocent. "We may well rejoice," Davis concluded, "that we have forever severed our connection with a government that thus tramples on all the principles of constitutional liberty, and with a people in whose presence such avowals could be hazarded." [56]

Four months later Davis pointed in mock horror to "the scenes which are now being enacted in the United States": a president was making war without the assent of Congress; the executive branch

55. Rowland (ed.), *Jefferson Davis*, V, 104; Richardson (comp.), *Messages and Papers of the Confederacy*, I, 123–24, 137.
56. Richardson (comp.), *Messages and Papers of the Confederacy*, I, 122.

was threatening judges "because they maintain the writ of *habeas corpus* so sacred to freemen"; the United States had trampled justice and law "under the armed heel of military authority"; and innocent men and women found themselves "dragged to distant dungeons upon the mere edict of a despot." Most alarming to southerners, Davis argued, was the fact that people who had been free only a short time before were willing to tolerate such acts. Since the North had abandoned completely the traditional American concepts of freedom, southerners would "shrink with aversion from the bare idea of renewing such a connection."[57]

Another part of Davis' strategy to stimulate southern resistance consisted of accusations that the United States was waging an uncivilized war. Davis hoped to enrage southerners with these charges and use indignation to strengthen their will to fight. Particularly in the early days of the conflict, he had a basis on which to rest his charges. Confused by the constitutional problems involved in fighting a war against a government which it did not admit to exist, the United States initially was unwilling to treat captured Confederates as prisoners of war. In July, 1861, the United States Navy captured the schooner *Savannah*, which was sailing under Confederate authority. Rather than treating the crewmen as prisoners of war, the United States began to charge them with piracy and treason. In a letter of protest to Lincoln, Davis wrote that his own government wanted to conduct the war in a manner which would "mitigate its horrors as far as may be possible." But if the United States continued its prosecution of the *Savannah*'s crew, Davis threatened to retaliate with identical punishment for prisoners held by the Confederacy.[58]

Extending his indictment of the North, Davis alleged two weeks later that the Federal government was attacking civilians "with a savage ferocity unknown to modern civilization," stating that "in this war, rapine is the rule." Davis told the congress that the United States

---

57. *Ibid.*, 140.
58. J. G. Randall and David Donald, *The Civil War and Reconstruction* (2nd ed.; Boston: D. C. Heath and Company, 1961), 334; Richardson (comp.), *Messages and Papers of the Confederacy*, I, 115–16.

troops were destroying homes, crops, and every useful implement. Reaching for rhetorical heights, he said, "Mankind will shudder to hear the tales of outrages committed on defenseless females by soldiers of the United States . . . prompted by inflamed passions and the madness of intoxication." Alluding to the blockade, Davis also condemned the United States' effort, as he saw it, to deny necessary medicines to the sick. The humanity of southerners, he insisted, prevented them from "waging a like war upon the sick, the women, and the children of the enemy." Davis continued this catalog of Federal atrocities in November by expressing outrage at the arson and rapine which he said took place during forays along the border. In addition he charged that the United States had fitted out a large naval expedition "with the confessed purpose . . . to incite a servile insurrection in our midst."[59]

By listing such outrages, Davis was trying to reach southerners' pride, self-respect, and sense of decency, and thereby steel their determination to fight. Southerners were individualists who usually did not take an insult lying down. According to Davis' version of events, they had been attacked by fanatics who waged a cruel, inhuman type of warfare and wanted to destroy every Confederate's rights. "I know," he asserted in a speech in May, 1861, "that there beats in the breast of Southern sons, a determination never to surrender—a determination never to go home but to tell a tale of honor. (Cries of 'Never!' and applause.)" Later he boasted that the idea of subjugation was "incomprehensible" to southerners, for "to resist attacks on their rights or their liberties is with them an instinct." The men of the Confederacy would fight for one, three, or five years, or however long the enemy persisted. In his speeches Davis challenged southerners to prove that "numbers cease to avail" against people fighting for such a sacred cause as that of the Confederacy.[60]

Davis' attempts in 1861 to define the South's ideology and give southerners a set of reasons to fight proved successful. He struck

59. Richardson (comp.), *Messages and Papers of the Confederacy*, I, 119–20, 141.
60. Rowland (ed.), *Jefferson Davis*, V, 104; Richardson (comp.), *Messages and Papers of the Confederacy*, I, 124, 137.

themes which had a wide appeal in the South and established in effect a lowest common denominator of Confederate values. The success of his ideological leadership derived not from its originality but from its sensitivity to the basic attitudes of southerners. Many of Davis' themes had been common in southern newspapers before he made them part of the official justification for the nation. His speeches reinforced these themes and gave them central importance as the Confederate ideology both for the world in general and for its own citizens.

The Charleston *Mercury*, destined to become one of Davis' severest critics, gave considerable support to his ideological appeals in the early days of the war. R. B. Rhett, Jr., the *Mercury*'s editor, held many views that were more extreme than those of Davis and therefore less serviceable as appeals to the South as a whole. Slavery, in particular, held a more prominent place in the Confederate scheme of things for the *Mercury* than it did for Davis. But the *Mercury* also supported many of Davis' arguments, and during the winter and spring of 1861 no southern paper was more vigilant in denouncing alleged executive usurpations by Abraham Lincoln. The *Mercury* saw a despotism in the North even before Jefferson Davis brought it to the attention of the southern public.[61]

The influence of Davis' inaugural address was visible in an editorial of the North Carolina *Whig* in April, 1861, before the Old North State had seceded from the Union. Davis had argued that the lower South had created a new government by peaceful and democratic means, and the *Whig* echoed his stress on "the American idea that governments rest on the consent of the governed," a principle perverted by the North. The attack which Davis made on the character of the northerners also had wide support in the South. Some papers went so far as to pronounce the North guilty of "total and universal moral depravity" and declare that Lincoln was determined to institute "a grand military despotism" in Washington. Even in northwest Georgia an editor saw in Lincoln's popularity the "unmistakable proof

61. Such denunciations of Lincoln occur in almost every issue of the *Mercury* during the first five months of 1861.

of the unabated existence of the same blind and abominable fanaticism which defies the Constitution." By the end of the year this paper, the Rome *Weekly Courier*, believed that the Constitution and the Bible were "obsolete institutions" in the North, a land of "Folly and Corruption." The famous South Carolina diarist Mary Boykin Chesnut wrote that Abraham Lincoln's vigorous use of executive powers had made the United States completely "consolidated . . . with no states but with the army organized by the central power." The governors of two states echoed Davis' theme that liberty had been destroyed in the North.[62]

Understandably, the treatment of Confederate prisoners was a source of concern throughout the South, and Davis' condemnation of Federal policy toward southern soldiers evoked a strong response. The Richmond *Dispatch* demanded in August, 1861, that the administration retaliate against Union prisoners for the treatment that some Confederates were receiving from the enemy. Many other southern newspapers took up the same cry and eventually criticized Davis for being too slow to anger. On December 6, 1861, the North Carolina convention passed a series of resolutions which virtually repeated Davis' address to Congress of the month before. The convention expanded on the "cruel and barbarous manner" in which the enemy was waging war and charged that the United States had imprisoned old men and helpless women without warrant. Also noting alleged cases of robbery, arson, and incitement of servile insurrection, the North Carolina convention declared that it was convinced of the South's "radical incompatibility" with the North, an incompatibility which required that separation be final.[63]

The outbreak of war and Davis' appeals to southern determination

---

62. Charlotte (N.C.) *Whig*, April 23, 1861, May 28, 1861; Rome (Ga.) *Weekly Courier*, March 1, 1861, December 20, 1861; Mary Boykin Chesnut, *A Diary from Dixie*, ed. Ben Ames Williams (Sentry ed.; Boston: Houghton Mifflin Company, 1949), 121; *The War of the Rebellion: A Compilation of the Official Records of the Union and Confederate Armies* (130 vols.; Washington: Government Printing Office, 1880–1901), Ser. IV, Vol. I, 709, 725, hereinafter cited as *Official Records*.

63. Richmond *Dispatch*, quoted in Charlotte (N.C.) *Whig*, August 20, 1861, p. 2; *Official Records*, Ser. IV, Vol. I, 776–77.

created a great wave of martial spirit. Southern men and boys turned out in great numbers to defend their homes and their cause, in the broad terms in which Jefferson Davis defined it. The response to Confederate requests for troops was so great that the administration could not employ all the soldiers who wanted to fight. On July 24, 1861, secretary of war Leroy P. Walker reported that if arms could be found "no less than 200,000 additional volunteers for the war would be found in our ranks in less than two months." Walker was not merely guessing at the total number of volunteers. He based his statement on the number of applications which were on file in the War Department. One month later he wrote Henry Hotze, a Confederate propaganda agent in Europe, that the Confederacy "could bring into the field and maintain there with ease 500,000 men were arms and munitions sufficiently abundant." As a result of the surplus of manpower over firepower, the administration adopted a policy of accepting only volunteers for three years or the duration of the war. Since more men came forward for this type of service than could be armed, it made no sense to accept volunteers for shorter terms of service.[64]

The dimensions of this groundswell of support for the Confederacy were truly impressive. An army of 500,000 men would have represented a formidable organization for a nation which had only about eight million white inhabitants. During the entire war, in fact, the Confederate armies never reached the level of strength which could have been marshaled in 1861 but for the lack of guns and ammunition.[65] Under Davis' leadership it was clear that the South had achieved a high degree of early unity. Both slaveholders and non-slaveholders, both the upper South and the lower South, were pulling together with a common purpose.

The solidification of regional loyalty was the primary cause of this

64. *Official Records*, Ser. IV, Vol. I, 496–98, 596, 380.
65. The Confederate armies approached this level of strength most closely in April, 1863, when official returns showed 304,236 officers and men present for duty, 360,097 men in all present, and 498,169 men present and absent. The official returns of the Confederate armies are given in *Official Records*, Ser. IV, Vol. I, 822, 962–64, 1176, and Vol. II, 380, 530, 615, 1073, and Vol. III, 520, 1182.

early unity. There were many men like Robert E. Lee, who did not want to have to choose sides in a war but who was determined to follow the decision of his state.[66] When the shooting began, Virginians and other citizens of the upper South discovered what many had suspected all along: that their basic loyalties were with the agricultural, slaveholding South rather than with the industrializing, free-labor North. Southerners had a sense of regional identity which asserted itself strongly in the final crisis of war.

The natural reaction of self-defense also played a role. Virginians and North Carolinians, among the last to secede, knew that their states would face invasion as surely as would South Carolina. Men in the lower South often feared that the Federal army would save its greatest wrath for them.[67] Throughout the Confederacy southerners shared a natural desire to defend their homes from invasion, whether they had taken an active interest in politics or not.

But Jefferson Davis also should receive considerable credit for effective leadership during 1861. He aided the development of unity by enunciating a nondivisive ideology. Avoiding potential dangers and finding positive sources of enthusiasm, Davis gave southerners a cause which few of them found easy to criticize. He grounded the Confederacy's appeal on the heritage of the United States, which all professed to honor. He muted the latent strains of conflict between slaveholders and nonslaveholders, who would rediscover during the war that their interests sometimes diverged—and sharply so. By claiming the United States Constitution as a sacred text for the Confederacy, Davis helped to found the government in a manner which lessened the sense of a break with the past. At the same time he sharpened resentment against the North through carefully chosen words of criticism. Davis attacked the United States for acts which almost all southerners would disapprove, and in this way he tried to

66. Douglas Southall Freeman, *R. E. Lee* (4 vols.; New York: Charles Scribner's Sons, 1934–1935), I, 418.

67. The Charleston *Mercury* and many South Carolinians feared that Charleston would be the target of major Federal attacks. For private correspondence revealing the same attitude, see Robert M. Myers (ed.), *The Children of Pride* (New Haven: Yale University Press, 1972).

enlist the pride of an individualistic people in the battle against a formidable adversary.

In the first months of the war Davis seemed to have made dramatic progress toward building a nation. The capstone of his achievement came on July 21, 1861, at a small stream near Washington called Bull Run. Outnumbered Confederate troops directed by Generals Joseph E. Johnston and P. G. T. Beauregard routed a much larger Federal force and sent the Union army reeling back to Washington. This defeat disturbed the picnics of many who had come out from Washington expecting to watch a Federal victory, and it caused great rejoicing in the South. Jefferson Davis left Richmond and reached the scene of the battle in time to see part of the engagement and the retreat of one body of Union troops. It must have gratified him to watch the first victory of his government's forces and observe "that the watchword of 'On to Richmond' had been changed to 'Off to Washington.'" The Confederate capital took on a carnival atmosphere, and the entire Confederacy experienced a great increase in confidence and élan.[68]

Before January, 1862, there would appear more than one portent of the darker days which lay ahead. Soon after the victory some southerners began to question whether the Confederate forces should not have rushed on and taken the Federal capital. This issue developed into a full-scale controversy, and Davis felt obliged to collect statements from the generals who were in the field in order to defend himself against hostile criticism. Newspapers particularly noticed what they felt was a conflict of strategies between General Beauregard and President Davis, and many credited Beauregard with the desire to advance into Maryland and blamed Davis for keeping the armies below the Potomac. Demands for a forward movement grew in volume before the end of the year. A nasty quarrel also arose between Davis and General Joseph E. Johnston, who felt that Davis had discriminated against him by not giving him the highest place among Confederate generals. Johnston had held the highest rank in

68. Varina Howell Davis, *A Memoir*, II, 98; Vandiver, *Their Tattered Flags*, 84.

the United States army, but Davis had not considered Johnston's last promotion because it was a staff, not a line position.[69]

These controversies cast a few clouds on the horizon at the end of 1861. But they were only small shadows in a brilliantly hopeful atmosphere. The year 1861 marked the bright days of the new southern nation. Morale in the armies and among the civilian population seemed high. The Confederacy seemed united both geographically and socially. In the fall elections Davis won a full six-year term as president without opposition.[70] People appeared to be ready to follow his lead in adopting measures which were necessary for success. As 1862 began, Davis had already begun to fashion these measures.

69. Rowland (ed.), *Jefferson Davis*, V, 157–61; Charleston *Mercury*, October 22, 1861, February 28, 1862. For the letters between Johnston and Davis, see Varina Howell Davis, *A Memoir*, II, 144–54.

70. *Daily Richmond Enquirer*, September 16, 1861, p. 2; *Daily Richmond Examiner*, September 16, 1861, p. 2, September 18, 1861, p. 2.

3

The Debate

over

Centralization

Like most new governments, the Confederacy initially represented an aspiration more than a reality. Its government lacked clearly defined powers, a corps of civil servants, or even a permanent capital, and the first days of the new administration constituted a formative period in which precedents would be established for the future. Davis did not hesitate to provide them. With clear and purposeful leadership, he set out to build a strong central government capable of meeting the tremendous challenges of war with the United States. Demonstrating that he was not afraid to exercise power, he sought to use all the authority which the Confederate Constitution gave him.

In the process the Confederacy's president raised fundamental questions about the nature and purpose of the southern nation. Davis believed that states' rights did not negate federalism or preclude a strong central government that was active in its sphere, but others discovered that their definition of states' rights was more strict. Stung into angry opposition, these southerners cried that the central government was subverting the purposes for which the nation had been established. Thus as Confederates fought their external foe, they also engaged in a fierce internal debate about their political values and goals. At issue was the concept of the southern nation. Jefferson Davis unhesitatingly expounded his vision of the Confederacy and fought with determination and the powers of his office to make that vision a reality.

On the whole, he won; for a powerful and extensive central government came into being, and many Confederates realized that it was needed. The victory was not without cost, however, for the acrimonious debate which developed had injurious effects on morale. Criticism by states' rights advocates eroded Davis' support among the planter class and contributed to a broader decline. As part of the planters turned away from the Confederate government, they laid down a blistering attack which became a stimulus and focal point for subsequent discontent. Political enemies of the president found a weapon they could use to undermine his legitimacy and influence.

From the Confederacy's inception, Davis strove to turn abstract power into tangible realities and make his government an effective instrument of southern independence. Finding when he reached Montgomery that the forts, navy yards, guns, and ammunition needed to wage war were all in the hands of the states, he promptly told the congress that "efficiency requires the exclusive control" by the central government. Some states responded quickly, but Davis declined to accept any half measures. Virginia, for example, gave the Confederacy many soldiers and supplies, but valuable arms-making machinery which troops had found at Harpers Ferry remained in the state's possession. Gently but persistently Davis pressed Governor John Letcher for these machines and impatiently waited for other states to transfer their weapons to Confederate authority.[1]

As a West Point graduate, Davis knew that the Confederacy also needed a unified national army under central direction. Professional soldiers had favored a national army for many years, and the limited resources of the South augmented the need to avoid waste and duplication of effort. Still, the United States had never possessed such a fighting force. In all of America's previous wars, independent state units had cooperated with the small nucleus of professional officers and regulars who tried to infuse some coherence into what was essentially a patchwork army. During the Civil War Presidents Davis

1. James D. Richardson (comp.), *A Compilation of the Messages and Papers of the Confederacy, Including the Diplomatic Correspondence, 1861–1865* (2 vols.; Nashville: United States Publishing Company, 1906), I, 34, 56–57; Dunbar Rowland (ed.), *Jefferson Davis: Constitutionalist; His Letters, Papers and Speeches* (10 vols.; Jackson, Miss.: Little & Ives Company, 1923), V, 101–102, 108–109.

and Lincoln ended this tradition and imposed stronger central control. The first army act of the Confederate Congress relied on the states for troops, but, as Davis noted well, it established the principle that all units became integral parts of the Confederate army when they entered national service. By the spring of 1861 the congress had authorized Davis to accept volunteers directly in order to speed recruitment, and he began to assemble and train an army without going through state authorities. In fact, the governors of Virginia, Missouri, and Texas soon learned that he would not allow state recruiting to interfere with Confederate efforts or accept less than full control of troops.[2]

Davis intended to employ Confederate forces on a national scale and shift units from one locality to another as the need arose. In most cases, the instincts and desires of state governors directly opposed this plan. Responsible only for their states and dependent on their constituents' votes, governors often thought first about the home front and later about the nation. Davis rejected this approach so completely that his opinion became known throughout the Confederate bureaucracy. A clerk in the War Department, J. B. Jones, showed his awareness of Davis' view when he wrote in his diary on November 29, 1862. The president had asked his new secretary of war, James Seddon, for advice on North Carolina's plan to organize an army of 10,000 men for its own defense. With wry humor Jones noted that this request put Seddon in "a delicate and embarrassing predicament. . . . He must know that the President frowns on all military organizations not under his own control. . . . Beware Mr. Seddon! The President is a little particular concerning his prerogatives. . . . Forget your old State-Rights doctrine, or off goes your head."[3]

The situation in North Carolina was typical. After the fall of Roa-

2. James M. Matthews (ed.), *The Statutes at Large of the Provisional Government of the Confederate States of America* (Richmond: R. M. Smith, 1864), 43, 106; Rowland (ed.), *Jefferson Davis*, V, 105, 183–85; Richardson (comp.), *Messages and Papers of the Confederacy*, I, 160.

3. J. B. Jones, *A Rebel War Clerk's Diary*, ed. Howard Swiggett (2 vols.; New York: Old Hickory Bookshop, 1935), I, 198–99.

noke Island, Tarheel citizens grew alarmed about the defense of their state and urged that some North Carolina troops recently sent elsewhere be returned. Davis replied with soothing words but refused to order the troops back and explained that he had to use soldiers from all the states "for the common defense as its necessities require." Turning aside similar requests from Virginia in September, 1861, and the two Carolinas in the winter of 1862–1863, he repeatedly resisted the governors' attempts to disperse troops for garrison duty in each state. Perhaps the clearest statement of his policy came in March, 1863, in a letter to the Arkansas congressional delegation, which was convinced that the government had neglected their protection. Davis insisted that "the idea of retaining in each State its own troops for its own defense" was a "fatal error": "Our safety—our very existence—depends on the complete blending of the military strength of all the States into one united body, to be used anywhere and everywhere as the exigencies of the contest may require for the good of the *whole*." To the governor of Arkansas Davis explained that Confederate operations around Vicksburg were strategically equivalent to posting men in Arkansas.[4]

The Confederate commander-in-chief proceeded to shuttle his troops from point to point as the need arose. One of the most daring movements of southern troops came in the fall of 1862, when Davis and his generals constructed a pipeline of soldiers traveling by train from Tupelo, Mississippi, through Atlanta to Chattanooga, Tennessee. In effect the circuitous railroad route allowed each successive unit to defend the points through which it passed as it moved toward its final destination. Nor did Davis' imagination stop at transfers of Confederate forces. To achieve a concentration of troops at vital times, he called on the governors to lend their state forces. When A. S. Johnston and Beauregard were fighting the enemy at Shiloh

4. Rowland (ed.), *Jefferson Davis*, V, 193, 131, 354–55, 432, 462, 465–67. Generally speaking, Davis' strategy was to defend all of the South, and for this policy he has been criticized. For an able discussion of this issue, see Archer Jones, *Confederate Strategy from Shiloh to Vicksburg* (Baton Rouge: Louisiana State University Press, 1961), Chap. 2, and Thomas L. Connelly and Archer Jones, *The Politics of Command: Factions and Ideas in Confederate Strategy* (Baton Rouge: Louisiana State University Press, 1973).

and Corinth, for example, Davis wired the executives of five nearby states and requested short-term reinforcements.[5]

These efforts by a determined president created a national army under central direction, but they were only a hint of his approach to the war. A narrow military commander might have done as much solely in the interest of military efficiency, but Davis realized that he would have to go much further. The unprecedented scale of the Civil War required the marshaling of society's energies from every source. To have a chance of success, the Confederate government would have to intervene deeply in the southern economy. Davis understood this fact better than many of his contemporaries and often fought for his programs against great opposition. After the congress gave him control over telegraph companies, he turned his attention to the railroads. Asking the congress for special powers, Davis argued that it was essential militarily to build new lines connecting key points. Unless the central government built these lines and furnished the capital necessary for certain other activities, such as manufacturing locomotives and rerolling old rails for use in new locations, the South could not hope to win its independence. Outlining a broad interpretation of the constitution's powers to wage war, the president told Congress that "certain appropriations which otherwise could not be constitutionally made by the Confederate Government come within the range of its power, when absolutely necessary for the prosecution of the war. . . . When this military necessity ceases, the right to make such appropriations no longer exists."[6]

Thus Davis demonstrated that he was not afraid to confront the shibboleths of limited government which southerners had created in prewar days. Despite an explicit constitutional ban on Confederate-sponsored internal improvements, he recommended measures which admittedly would have been unconstitutional in peacetime. His arguments and the wartime emergency proved convincing, and eventually the government completed two new railroad lines. One con-

5. Connelly and Jones, *Politics of Command*, 106; Rowland (ed.), *Jefferson Davis*, V, 231.

6. Richardson (comp.), *Messages and Papers of the Confederacy*, I, 152–53, 139–40.

nected Danville, Virginia, and Greensboro, North Carolina, and the other linked Meridian, Mississippi, and Selma, Alabama. In addition the central government started construction on two other railroads, but the fortunes of war prevented their completion.[7]

The Confederacy soon became even more involved in railways and other business enterprises. In the middle of 1862 Davis informed the congress that the government needed more power in order to control military transportation. Going beyond the idea of government aid, he sought legislation which embraced the possibility of superseding private ownership. When the lawmakers failed to respond, he renewed his request in January, 1863, and explained that "the control of the roads under some general supervision and resort to the power of impressment" was necessary. This time the congress gave him what he had asked.[8] To free the Confederacy from dependence on foreign supplies, Davis proposed that the government encourage and engage in the mining and manufacturing of essential materials. Hoping to stimulate these vital industries, the congress passed a law which offered loans and inducements to potential manufacturers of saltpeter, small arms, coal, and iron. The Confederacy also undertook the production of salt in Louisiana, and the Ordnance Department, under the capable direction of Josiah Gorgas, developed from nothing an immense capacity to produce guns and ammunition.[9]

To Davis the development of industry was more than a wartime exigency. Both his previous career and his early statements as president indicated his desire to strengthen the economy of the South by introducing useful industries. Although cotton was king, there was a gap in the structure of the southern economy. Without a healthy in-

7. Charles W. Ramsdell, "The Confederate Government and the Railroads," *American Historical Review*, XXII (1917), 801–803.

8. Richardson (comp.), *Messages and Papers of the Confederacy*, I, 236, 295.

9. Rowland (ed.), *Jefferson Davis*, V, 357; *The War of the Rebellion: A Compilation of the Official Records of the Union and Confederate Armies* (130 vols.; Washington: Government Printing Office, 1880–1901), Ser. IV, Vol. I, 1070–1071, 1074, hereinafter cited as *Official Records*; Rowland (ed.), *Jefferson Davis*, V, 344, 360–61, VI, 121; Frank Vandiver, *Ploughshares into Swords* (Austin: University of Texas Press, 1952).

dustrial capacity, the South would always be subservient to outside commercial interests. As early as 1851, when he was running for governor of Mississippi, Davis had called for the development of natural resources and the encouragement of manufacturing.[10] This had been an integral part of his program of southern resistance.

This interest in industrialization was not unique to Davis. Periodically from the end of the eighteenth century to the Civil War, southerners had debated the value of industry. Usually they assumed that southern industry would be slave-based and under the control of the planter class. Many leading planters favored industrial slavery as a means to profit, commercial independence, and the maintenance of a slave society. In the long run, as the major student of industrial slavery has noted, "extensive industrialization would have been difficult, if not impossible, under a rigid slave system."[11] But in the 1850s and 1860s southern leaders did not see an incompatibility between their economic dreams and their society's racial arrangements. Industry, they felt, would be a valuable addition to the southern social system.

Making this one of his basic goals, Davis claimed in November, 1861, that the Confederacy could fight indefinitely, because as the war reduced external supplies, southerners learned to develop their own resources. He stressed that southerners were "becoming more and more independent of the rest of the world" and noted that in this context even the blockade was a good thing.[12]

Southern leaders from many quarters echoed this determination to achieve industrial self-sufficiency. Alabama's Governor John Gill Shorter emphasized to the legislature when he took office in December, 1861, that the Confederacy was fighting to gain not only independence but also "a deliverance, full and unrestricted, from all commercial dependence" upon the United States. To Robert Barnwell Rhett and his son, who edited the Charleston *Mercury*, the

10. Rowland (ed.), *Jefferson Davis*, II, 105.
11. Robert Starobin, *Industrial Slavery in the Old South* (New York: Oxford University Press, 1970), 189–190, Chaps. 5 and 6.
12. Richardson (comp.), *Messages and Papers of the Confederacy*, I, 143; Rowland (ed.), *Jefferson Davis*, V, 201, 394.

"grand object of the struggle" was "to rid ourselves of Yankee domination, politically, commercially, and socially." The *Mercury* warned in 1861 that one of the North's goals was to make the southern states into commercial colonies. After the war, the *Mercury* insisted, there must be no commercial reconstruction: "If we are kept *commercially* dependent upon them, the same game of impertinent intervention in our domestic institutions, and of unscrupulous plunder and domination, will be renewed towards our posterity; and the great struggle in which we are engaged will have settled nothing."[13]

Although it supported Davis' commercial program, the Charleston *Mercury* probably did not realize how deeply the central government would have to intervene in the economy. As R. B. Rhett, Jr., wrote these editorials, Davis' administration was planning measures which would alarm the fiery South Carolinian. Soon the *Mercury* would denounce the Confederacy's president for harboring tyrannical designs. Jefferson Davis was no despot, but he did advocate measures which reached deep into southern society and brought individual citizens into direct contact with the Richmond government.

Reflection on the bold steps which he would have to take may have caused Davis some moments of doubt. His clear understanding of the need for extensive measures only heightened his appreciation of the controversy which they aroused. At times Davis may have wondered whether the southern people would be willing to make all the sacrifices demanded of them. Military reverses on the seacoast and in the west early in 1862 contributed to an atmosphere of gloom, and at his inauguration as president of the permanent government on February 22, 1862, wretched weather dampened Davis' attempt to inspire the people with brave words about progress and future success. In the face of these events, his optimism flagged and gave way to depression about the future.

Already his leadership, which was crucial to public morale, had become a target of criticism. Mary Boykin Chesnut, the famous diarist who moved in the highest levels of Confederate political society,

13. *Official Records*, Ser. IV, Vol. I, 771–74; Charleston *Mercury*, September 11, 1861, p. 1.

reacted with surprise and some dismay to the rapid development of feeling against Davis among other politicians. Less than two weeks after he took office in 1861, she wrote in her diary, "Men are willing to risk an injury to our cause, if they may in so doing hurt Jeff Davis." Within days after the brilliant southern victory at Bull Run, she learned that "many leaders here [in Richmond] hate Jeff Davis." By August, 1861, a coalition against the president had formed and supposedly included such prominent figures as Howell Cobb, James H. Hammond, and Lawrence Keitt. Six months later Vice President Stephens was trying to organize an opposition party, and attempts by some of the leaders of secession to change the government reportedly were under way.[14]

Davis encountered this opposition to his leadership in the congress and in the press, and in his daily work the failure of state leaders to cooperate with the central government caused him much vexation. No less than four governors—the executives of South Carolina, Georgia, Florida, and North Carolina—were clamoring for the return of state-owned arms in January, 1862, when the Confederacy was short of powder and armaments. In irritation and disgust, Davis declared, according to Attorney General Thomas Bragg, that "if such was to be the course of the States . . . we had better make terms as soon as we could." Faced with future troubles and present opposition, Davis may well have wondered whether he would be able to unify southerners and lead them to independence. For a brief period, he reportedly considered resigning.[15] Soon, however, he put those thoughts behind him and set to work on plans to bolster the Confederacy's strength.

In the spring of 1862 Davis recommended to the congress a num-

14. Mary Boykin Chesnut, *A Diary from Dixie*, ed. Ben Ames Williams (Sentry ed.; Boston: Houghton Mifflin Company, 1949), 9, 96, 107; T. R. R. Cobb to his wife, January 12, 1862, in T. R. R. Cobb Letters, University of Georgia, Athens, Ga.; A. R. Wright to Francis C. Shropshire, February 26, 1862, in G. M. Battey, *History of Rome and Floyd County* (2 vols.; Atlanta: n.p., 1921), I, 144–45.

15. Thomas Bragg Diary (Southern Historical Collection, University of North Carolina), p. 115; Edward Younger (ed.), *Inside the Confederate Government: The Diary of Robert Garlick Hill Kean* (New York: Oxford University Press, 1957), 88–89, hereinafter cited as *Diary of R. G. H. Kean*.

ber of extensive new war measures. If adopted, these proposals would extend government power even farther into the southern economy and social system. The central government would acquire the power to affect citizens' lives on every farm and in every village. Davis was giving substance to his vision of a central government equipped to cope with the great problems of war.

At the end of February, 1862, the congress, prodded by complaints of illegal arrests by civil and military officers, had voted the suspension of the writ of *habeas corpus*. The necessity which moved the congress to pass this law stimulated Davis into quick enforcement of its provisions. By the end of March he had imposed martial law on port cities in Virginia and several parishes in Louisiana. The congress renewed the executive's power to suspend the writ of *habeas corpus* in October, 1862, but this law expired in February, 1863. During the summer of 1863, with elections approaching and considerable criticism of the administration in the air, Congress failed to restore Davis' power to use martial law. Before many months had passed, he asked for reenactment of the law.[16]

Soon after the first suspension of the writ of *habeas corpus*, the executive branch sought a power new in American history—conscription. Never before had an American government raised a national army by legal coercion, but Davis saw that conscription would be necessary and acted before northern leaders reached the same conclusion. The initial impetus for the adoption of conscription came from a critical shortage of Confederate manpower, for many soldiers were one-year volunteers whose terms of service were due to expire early in 1862, just as the spring campaign began. For a long time, Secretary of War Judah P. Benjamin hoped that voluntary reenlistments would fill the gap. He offered a liberal bounty and furlough to all who would reenlist for the war, but the results were disappointing. Next he called on the governors to raise volunteers, but they, too, had little success, and three states—Georgia, Texas, and South Carolina—threatened or instituted a draft. At this point Davis sent

16. John B. Robbins, "The Confederacy and the Writ of *Habeas Corpus*," *Georgia Historical Quarterly*, LV (1971), 83–101.

the congress a message advocating the conscription of men between eighteen and thirty-five.[17] To him it was not merely a way to fill the armies and distribute the burden of military service, but also a way to organize society's human resources for the completion of those tasks most vital in wartime.

The congress accepted this principle and drafted an exemption bill which became law on April 21, 1862. This act excused selected categories of men from military duty, such as railroad workers, river pilots, telegraph operators, iron miners, foundrymen, superintendents and operatives in wool and cotton factories, some apothecaries, and officers of state and Confederate governments. Initially overseers were not included, and the administration refused to exempt them despite howls of protest.[18] In practice this law proved to be only a crude first step toward management of the Confederacy's entire supply of manpower, and subsequent laws made further refinements in a steadily expanding scheme of government supervision. A total of 2,443 agents went out under the aegis of the Bureau of Conscription to execute the law and forward men to duty. Eventually Davis pressed for authority to replace exemptions with details of only those men whose skills were needed, but he had to be satisfied with the power to make details or exemptions which increased agricultural production or satisfied a "public necessity."[19]

The concern for agricultural productivity grew out of a shortage of food for the armies which arose in the fall of 1862. Hoping to relieve the shortage without dependence on outside sources, Davis made crop production one of his high priorities in 1863.[20] He praised Geor-

17. *Official Records*, Ser. IV, Vol. I, 760–64, 825–27, 902–903, 913, 918–21, 980–82, 973–75; Richardson (comp.), *Messages and Papers of the Confederacy*, I, 205–206.

18. Allen D. Candler (ed.), *The Confederate Records of the State of Georgia* (6 vols.; Atlanta: Chas. P. Byrd, 1910), III, 201–202; Rowland (ed.), *Jefferson Davis*, V, 238, 262–63.

19. Paul P. Van Riper and Harry N. Scheiber, "The Confederate Civil Service," *Journal of Southern History*, XXV (1959), 457; Jefferson Davis to Congress, December 7, 1863, in Rowland (ed.), *Jefferson Davis*, VI, 117–18; James M. Matthews (ed.), *Statutes at Large of the Confederate States of America, Fourth Session, First Congress* (Richmond: R. M. Smith, 1864), 214.

20. Davis resisted but eventually approved Confederate trade with the enemy in order to obtain food for the army. *Official Records*, Ser. IV, Vol. II, 151, 157–160; Jones, *A Rebel War Clerk's Diary*, I, 180, 186; Younger (ed.), *Diary of R. G. H. Kean*, 32, 45.

gia for legislating to reduce cotton production in favor of food and urged other states to do the same. When Mississippi militiamen petitioned for a furlough to go home and attend their crops, Davis gave his assent and recommended to Governor Pettus that they be furloughed in order to avoid "our worst fear—the want of food." To stress the importance of food production, Davis made a special address to the people of the Confederacy on April 10, 1863. The expectation that 1863 would be the last year of the war, he said, had induced many farmers to plant increased amounts of cotton and tobacco. Warning that this hope might prove illusory, Davis urged farmers to raise more provisions. The administration also cooperated with state authorities to enlarge food supplies. At the request of one governor, a Confederate general seized corn to stop the distilling of liquor and even threatened to impress the cooper from the stills. Secretary of War James Seddon adopted a suggestion from Governor Zebulon Vance and sent detailed men in various branches of the War Department home to North Carolina for two to three weeks in order to help with the harvest.[21]

The granting or revoking of details also proved to be a useful tool in supervising manufacturing. From the beginning of the war the central government operated its own clothing and shoe factories to supply the army. As the war continued, Davis' administration extended its supervision to private factories making necessary supplies. The exemption act of October 11, 1862, assured exemptions to textile workers as long as their employers did not exceed a profit of 75 percent on government contracts. Under a new law in 1864 which replaced exemptions with details, Confederate officials tightened their control over factories. The quartermaster general reduced profits and demanded most of the clothing produced. Textile mills complied rather than lose their supply of manpower.[22]

A large part of the manpower of the South was black. Some south-

21. Candler (ed.), *Confederate Records of Georgia*, III, 324–25; Rowland (ed.), *Jefferson Davis*, V, 439–41, 468; Richardson (comp.), *Messages and Papers of the Confederacy*, I, 331–35; *Official Records*, Ser. IV, Vol. II, 510–11, 513, 595–96.

22. Charles W. Ramsdell, "The Control of Manufacturing by the Confederate Government," *Mississippi Valley Historical Review*, VIII (1921), 231–49.

erners boasted that the war would prove the value of slavery, as slaves stayed home and grew crops while white men fought on the battle-field, but Davis' administration saw that the Confederacy had to make more thorough use of black labor. From the beginning of the war some Confederate generals impressed slaves over owners' protests and used them to build fortifications. On November 26, 1862, Davis sent a circular letter to the governors and asked that the states pro-vide for impressment of slaves through the governors. As the war continued, Confederate reliance on slave labor increased. James H. Brewer's recent study of this important topic has shown that slave labor was vital to the Confederate war effort in both skilled and un-skilled roles and that despite delays the Confederate government obtained slave labor from the states on a large scale.[23]

In addition to slaves, the Confederacy also impressed its citizens' nonhuman property. The practice of impressing supplies from farm-ers began in 1861. As a general rule army officers felt justified in taking needed items from nearby farms when the army's own supply system failed. Citizens received certificates of credit, or, more rarely, payment for the items involved. Even when the army paid for im-pressed goods, however, many inequities remained in the system. Soldiers impressed supplies only in the area of their operations and did not spread the burden equally over adjoining counties. Fre-quently, Confederate troops returned again to regions which had in-voluntarily supported the army at an earlier date. Thus some farm-ers suffered while others in the same state enjoyed relative plenty. The Confederate government always admitted that impressment was, in Davis' words, "so unequal in its operation, vexatious to the producer, injurious to the industrial interests, and productive of such discontent among the people as only to be justified by the exis-tence of an absolute necessity."[24]

23. Candler (ed.), *Confederate Records of Georgia*, III, 305–306; Armstead L. Robin-son, "Day of Jubilo: Civil War and the Demise of Slavery in the Mississippi Valley, 1861–1865" (Ph. D. dissertation, University of Rochester, 1976), 175; James Brewer, *The Confed-erate Negro: Virginia's Craftsmen and Military Laborers, 1861–1865* (Durham: Duke Uni-versity Press, 1969), 142–44, 147, 151, 157.

24. E. Merton Coulter, *The Confederate States of America, 1861–1865* (Baton Rouge: Louisiana State University Press, 1950), Vol. VII of 10 vols., in Wendell Holmes Stephen-son and E. Merton Coulter (eds.), *A History of the South*, 251; Rowland (ed.), *Jefferson Davis*, VI, 120.

The necessity, however, was continual, and Davis' government did not hesitate to seize needed supplies. In an official report to the president, the fourth secretary of war, James Seddon, stated that the Confederate army had relied almost totally on impressment from the fall of 1862. One year later the army depended solely on impressment because no one would voluntarily sell provisions to the government. Rampant inflation encouraged producers to withhold their goods from the market. They knew that no matter how high a price the government offered, it was certain to go higher at a later date. Therefore, to obtain a steady and reliable supply for the army, the government had to impress food.[25] Throughout the war the Confederate army continued to rely heavily on impressment.

The congress acknowledged that impressment would be a more or less regular practice when it passed a law to regulate the system early in 1862. This act authorized impressment when necessary but attempted to place safeguards on its operation by establishing procedures for ascertaining a fair price. To bring uniformity into the assessments, two commissioners in each state, one appointed by the governor and one by the president, would publish periodically a list of prices for standard items. The law also prohibited the army from taking goods necessary for consumption or the normal continuation of business. Davis promptly appointed his share of the commissioners, and the law went into operation.[26] But despite these safeguards, impressment was an onerous burden which graphically illustrated the power of the government.

Less drastic but controversial nonetheless were the demands that the Confederacy made on its citizens through taxes. At the beginning of the war, both the central government and the states proved reluctant to impose taxes and relied on bonds which fed a devastating inflation. Some of Jefferson Davis' initial statements about the na-

25. James Seddon to Jefferson Davis, November 26, 1863, in Letters Sent by the Confederate Secretary of War to the President, in Record Group 109, National Archives, Microcopy M 523, Roll 1, pp. 120–35.
26. General Orders of the Confederate Adjutant and Inspector General's Office, No. 37, April 6, 1863, in Record Group 109, National Archives, Microcopy T 782, pp. 46–51; Rowland (ed.), *Jefferson Davis*, V, 474.

tion's finances were foolishly optimistic, but by the end of 1863, he admitted that the problem was grave and told the congress in no uncertain terms that it would have to enact a direct tax on land and slaves. In making this recommendation, Davis raised a thorny issue. The constitution banned direct taxes at flat rates and required the congress to take a census and thereafter apportion direct taxes among the states according to their populations, including three-fifths of the slaves. Boldly Davis argued that the government had a duty to disregard that provision of the constitution. War had made a census impossible, and with part of some states under enemy control, it would be unjust to apportion the tax on the basis of each state's number of representatives. The only solution, he insisted, was a flat rate of taxation on all property. After Davis took this stand, opposition from the cotton states diminished and on February 17, 1864, the congress levied a 5 percent tax on "property, real, personal, and mixed, of every kind and description."[27]

Shocking as these measures were to some slaveholders, the Confederacy acted even more boldly toward the common people. Before the Civil War, almost all the taxes in the South had been indirect. Ordinary farmers often lived in blissful ignorance of the fact that they were paying some taxes and rarely saw a tax collector.[28] One can imagine, therefore, the shock of many yeomen farmers when the Confederacy reached into their homes and barns to collect a wartime tax. First the government had conscripted their sons; then it conscripted their crops as well. On April 24, 1863, the congress passed a comprehensive tax which became known as the tax-in-kind. Under this law the government levied fees on certain occupations and collected one-tenth of most kinds of farm produce. The law enumerated the crops subject to the tax, such as "wheat, corn, oats, rye, 'buck-

27. Richardson (comp.), *Messages and Papers of the Confederacy*, I, 235; Rowland (ed.), *Jefferson Davis*, VI, 111–14; Article I, Section 2, paragraph 3, and Article I, Section 9, paragraph 5, in Richardson (comp.), *Messages and Papers of the Confederacy*, I, 37–38, 43, also 364–67; Younger (ed.), *Diary of R. G. H. Kean*, 44–45; Coulter, *Confederate States of America*, 181.

28. Georgia Lee Tatum, *Disloyalty in the Confederacy* (Chapel Hill: University of North Carolina Press, 1934), 20.

wheat or rice,' sweet and Irish potatoes, hay and fodder, sugar, molasses, cotton, wool, tobacco, peas, beans, and ground peas."[29] In order not to make farmers destitute, specified amounts were exempt from the tax. The law also created assessors to rule in cases of dispute about the size of a crop. This, surely, was a measure which no weak central government would adopt.

Davis' administration gathered the tax-in-kind with energy and enthusiasm. Secretary of War Seddon soon found that the law was a very valuable addition to the central government's powers. In fact, he recommended that it should be continued and even increased on certain items, such as meat, wheat, rice, and products of sugarcane. To collect the tax-in-kind, the Confederate bureaucracy grew in size. The Treasury Department appointed 1,440 appraisers, and its agents collected those parts of the tax-in-kind which could be paid in money. The War Department collected the crops themselves and dispatched 2,965 men throughout the South to accomplish this task.[30]

Thus, in every area of governmental activity, from the creation and direction of an army to management of the supporting economy, Jefferson Davis built a strong central government. With a sober awareness of the magnitude of his task, he recognized that fighting a war against the United States would require many innovations in the decentralized, individualistic southern style of life. Determined to achieve independence, Davis interpreted his powers broadly and asked southerners to do many things which they considered neither normal nor desirable. Exerting progressively greater control over the nation, the Davis administration by 1863 affected millions of southerners directly every day. To carry out its ambitious programs, the Confederate government grew in size and ultimately employed at least 70,257 civilians. These civil servants formed a vast administrative machine, dwarfing private enterprises in the Confederacy.

29. For the text of the law, see James M. Matthews (ed.), *Statutes at Large of the Confederate States of America Third Session, First Congress, 1863* (Richmond: R. M. Smith, 1863), 115–126.

30. James Seddon to Jefferson Davis, April 25, 1864, in Letters sent by the Confederate Secretary of War to the President, RG 109, NA, Microcopy M 523, Roll 1, pp. 148–57; Van Ripper and Scheiber, "Confederate Civil Service," 454–57.

Compared to the United States' bureaucracy, the Confederate government was considerably larger in proportion to population.[31]

As he built this southern-style leviathan, however, Davis exercised caution and restraint. Though he resolved to create a vigorous central government, he did not seek to destroy the states. Knowing that his proposals were very demanding, Davis tried to soften their impact. The Confederate president did what he thought was necessary but never was heedless of southern traditions or habits of mind. In many ways Davis tried to minimize inequities, correct abuses, and ameliorate the effect of his government's policies.

The suspension of the writ of *habeas corpus* provides a good example of Davis' restraint and sensitivity. In sharp contrast to Lincoln, Davis never imposed martial law without the authority of the congress. During all of 1863, a troubled year for the Confederacy, he waited while Congress postponed a renewal of the suspension of the writ. Although the need was great, Davis did not act until Congress once again gave him the authority in February, 1864. Moreover, when he did use his powers under the suspension of the writ of *habeas corpus*, he took pains to ensure that their exercise would be careful and specific. Frequently he worked with the governors, limiting the areas of suspension and appointing their nominees as provost marshals, for he knew that southerners would accept martial law better if it were administered by local men. He revoked improper orders and instructed his commanders to "limit the application of martial law to cases of absolute necessity."[32]

Davis also knew that conscription had aroused resentment among some of the Confederacy's individualistic citizens. From Halifax County, Virginia, for example, a man named J. M. McCran reported to the War Department that two local residents had refused to go with their company. "They said," wrote McCran, "that no body had the wright to draft men & there for would not [go] untill sent for es-

31. Van Riper and Scheiber, "Confederate Civil Service," 450.
32. Robbins, "Confederacy and *Habeas Corpus*, " *passim*; Richardson (ed.), *Messages and Papers of the Confederacy*, I, 259–60; Rowland (ed.) *Jefferson Davis*, V, 226, 234–35, 237, 245, 310–12, 326, 219–20.

pecially."[33] Davis would not yield the principle of conscription, but he made many efforts to remove all extraneous causes of complaint. His administration tried to punish and eliminate harsh treatment of conscripts. The Bureau of Conscription required its officers to give draftees their full rights to hearings and examinations and to avoid "summary proceedings, in the spirit and style of the press gang." When Governor Vance of North Carolina objected that the head of conscription in his state was not a native Tarheel, Secretary of War Seddon promised a transfer even though no other state had made such a complaint. In 1863 a harsher system of conscription appeared when General Gideon Pillow used untender but very effective methods to gather up men for General Bragg's army. Until the end of the war, however, Davis refused to abolish the less efficient Bureau of Conscription in favor of military conscription.[34]

Complaints about the impressment of slaves also received a sympathetic hearing from Davis. In February, 1863, he ordered the investigation of an individual slaveowner's claim that impressment officers had unjustly discriminated against him. Davis wrote to the general in command and gave these directions: "Inquire into the case that he may not be unequally burdened and that your agent may be required to act equitably and courteously towards the citizens who are called on to contribute for the public defense." Since Virginia was a major theater of battle throughout the Civil War, impressments were particularly heavy there, and Davis displayed concern that no county would have to furnish more than its share of slave labor to the army. Responding to requests from Virginia's politicians, ordinary citizens, and the army's Engineer Bureau, the president or

33. J. M. McCran to the Secretary of War, received on May 8, 1862, Letters Received, Confederate Secretary of War, Record Group 109, National Archives, Microcopy M 437, Roll 60, pp. 493–94.

34. General Orders of the Confederate Adjutant and Inspector General's offices, No. 1, January 3, 1863, RG 109, NA, Microcopy T 782, pp. 1–2; *Official Records*, Ser. IV, Vol, II, 463, 375, 409, 430–45. See also Albert Burton Moore, *Conscription and Conflict in the Confederacy* (New York: Macmillan Company, 1924), 320–34.

his aide frequently asked Governor Letcher to reduce the calls on various counties.[35]

Davis' administration also attempted to protect the rights of non-slaveholders who suffered from impressment. On November 6, 1863, the Adjutant and Inspector General's Office reissued a general order that spelled out the rights of citizens who had their goods impressed. This order reminded all government officers that under no circumstances could they take goods on the way to market or commodities "which a party has for his own consumption or that of his family, employees, or slaves." The War Department was ready to act against officers who violated these regulations, but the complaints from citizens and state officials usually were very imprecise. Repeatedly the administration urged its correspondents to give exact information so that the governor could locate and punish the offending soldier. The War Department also warned against unneccessary impressments, and the quartermaster general required his agents to keep written records, give certificates for all impressed goods to the owners, and distribute the burden of impressment as equally as possible.[36] Although these regulations and instructions were often ignored by troops in the field, they showed a concern on the part of the central government for limiting the severity of its measures.

Perhaps Davis' caution and awareness of the heavy impact of his policies kept him from acting more vigorously in regard to the Confederacy's railroads. Despite legislation which gave him power to control the railroad companies and run them himself, he continually held back. The railroads remained in the hands of their private owners and managers, whose narrow viewpoint and failure to cooperate caused much delay and inefficiency. The leading student of the Confederacy's railroads has judged Davis' failure to take control as "little less than astonishing."[37] His normal determination to take whatever

35. Rowland (ed.), *Jefferson Davis*, V, 437.
36. General Orders of the Confederate Adjutant and Inspector General's Office, No. 114, November 6, 1863, RG 109, NA, Microcopy T 782, p. 259 for 1863; *Official Records* Ser. IV, Vol. II, 875–77, Vol. I, 767.
37. Robert C. Black III, *The Railroads of the Confederacy* (Chapel Hill: University of North Carolina Press, 1952), 164.

steps were required would have produced great benefits if he had applied it to the case of the railroads. As the backbone of the South's system of transportation and distribution, the railroads were vital to the southern war effort. Undoubtedly Davis' failure to use the full extent of his legal powers damaged the Confederacy's chances of success.

The reasons that Davis refused to use the full extent of his powers are not entirely clear, but political pressures certainly played some role. On March 25, 1863, he wrote Governor Letcher of Virginia and acknowledged receipt of a report on the transportation of private freight by rail. Assuring Letcher that the government was considering the matter, Davis said that "efforts have been made to prevent any unnecessary interference with the control of the roads by their respective companies." A month later Davis rejected proposals by his secretary of war, commissary general, and chief military adviser that the government take effective contol of the railroads. Enunciating instead a policy of "co-operation," he hinted at another reason for restraint, his suspicion that management of all the railroads was beyond the government's ability: "I am not encouraged by the past to expect that all difficulties would be removed by transferring the management of these extensive organizations to the agents of the War Department."[38] Whatever the reasons for Davis' timidity, it was ironic that he failed to act boldly on this issue, for the benefits might have been enormous.

Part of the opposition to Davis' strong leadership grew from a sense of state pride, and he recognized that fact. Davis rightly deserves the appellation of southern nationalist, for he sought to build a nation and frequently reminded Confederates of their common values and goals; but he did not try to crush state pride. Like other nineteenth-century men, he felt a stronger identification with his state than most Americans do today. Local loyalties had a place in Davis' vision of the Confederacy. Rather than seeking to destroy them, he sought to use them and make them contribute to the nation's war effort. For

38. Rowland (ed.), *Jefferson Davis*, V, 454, *Official Records*, Ser. I, Vol. LI, Pt. II, 850–52.

example, soldiers often desired to fight in units drawn from their home state. The Confederate Congress wrote this principle into its laws on the organization of the army, and Davis supported it strongly. But from his generals, who always seemed busy with other matters, he encountered substantial opposition. Many times Davis prodded his commanders and went so far as to issue stern rebukes to Beauregard and Joe Johnston. Nor was he above flattering those whose state commanded all their devotion. His messages and correspondence contained occasional bursts of praise for the gallantry and patriotism of some "noble State."[39]

Despite these gestures of deference to state pride, Jefferson Davis' leadership sparked a heated and bitter debate over states' rights. To many southerners the powerful central government which he built was the antithesis of what the Confederacy was supposed to be. They accused Davis of trampling on the constitution and subverting the nation's purpose. From 1862 through the end of the war this controversy raged amid many angry words about strict construction, states' rights, and state sovereignty.

In large part, this debate stemmed from a fundamental confusion among southerners over the nature of their government. The Montgomery Convention had met early in 1861 in an atmosphere of determined unity, and the delegates had possessed neither the time nor the inclination to sift the fine points of their political philosophy. Under pressure to put the government in operation, they borrowed freely from the United States Constitution and steered away from troubled waters. They did not stress their differences or attempt to discover their conflicting assumptions. To be sure, Robert Barnwell Rhett sounded some discordant notes when he tried to bar future nonslaveholding states and keep open the possibility of reviving the African slave trade. But the delegates approved only those of Rhett's proposals which seemed to amplify Jeffersonian tradition, such as a limitation on internal improvements and a ban on the protective tariff. William Boyce of South Carolina raised a fundamental issue

39. Rowland (ed.) *Jefferson Davis*, V, 140–41, 163–64, 242–43; Jones, *A Rebel War Clerk's Diary*, I, 89; Richardson (comp.), *Messages and Papers of the Confederacy*, I, 73; *Official Records*, Ser. IV, Vol. II, 804–805.

when he proposed to write into the constitution an explicit recognition of the right of secession, but after brief discussion the convention tabled his motion. Such a precise allotment of power between
the states and the central government made the delegates uncomfortable, and they preferred to leave that area unclear.[40]

Thus some questions remained unasked. Had the South, for example, merely objected to alleged and prospective violations of the
United States Constitution, or did it reject the entire federal system? Did southerners want to defend slavery from unconstitutional
assaults by the Federal government, or did they actually object to
the concept of a central government supreme in its sphere? Finding
it easy to agree that the states deserved more respect, southerners
failed to notice their latent disagreement about the central government. Some envisioned for the Confederacy a government like the
Articles of Confederation, while others desired the familiar system
of the United States, safely run by southerners. The Montgomery
Convention neither illuminated nor resolved these differences.

Jefferson Davis was one of those who thought that the Confederacy, removed from northern influences, would profit from the federal pattern. Among southerners he saw a reassuring degree of social
homogeneity and a community of interests. The underlying agree-
ment on political traditions would assure a satisfactory government
and protect the rights of the states. In this context Davis felt that an
effective central government would be perfectly appropriate. Taking
the Confederate Constitution literally, he believed that the central
government was entitled to pass laws "necessary and proper" for the
execution of its assigned duties. Moreover, he noted that the constitution made the laws of the Confederate government the supreme
law of the land. Judges in every state had to obey the central government's enactments under the constitution, "anything in the constitution or laws of any State to the contrary notwithstanding."[41] Clearly

40. Charles Robert Lee, Jr., *The Confederate Constitutions* (Chapel Hill: University of
North Carolina Press, 1963), 84, 92, 115, 65–66, 147, 101–102.
41. Rowland (ed.), *Jefferson Davis*, V, 48; Article I, Section 8, and Article VI, Section 3,
in Richardson (comp.), *Messages and Papers of the Confederacy*, I, 43, 52.

the founders of the Confederate States had provided for a national government that had substantial and important powers.

Within this context, however, Davis regarded himself a strict constructionist. From his first days in office he kept sharp watch for provisions in newly passed bills which failed to conform to the constitution. Using his veto power frequently, he rejected many laws on technical grounds that only a strict constructionist would have appreciated. In a number of cases he vetoed bills which would have been popular with the people, such as an act to distribute the pay of deceased soldiers to their families, or one to send newspapers free to servicemen.[42] No departure from the letter of the constitution was unimportant to the president, as the congress found in May, 1861, when it decided to move the government from Montgomery to Richmond and passed a resolution to adjourn to the latter city. Since the Provisional Constitution explicitly stated that Montgomery was to be the "seat of government" until the congress provided otherwise, Davis felt that he could not move the executive departments without authorization. Vetoing the resolution, he forced the congress to reword the measure and designate Richmond as the seat of government.[43]

For other southerners, however, strict construction had a different meaning, and years of opposition to the Federal government had become a habit. The constant repetition of states' rights dogma had led them to feel that the states were all and the central government almost nothing. Having cultivated an exaggerated regard for the states, such men thought that the only way to treat the central government was to oppose it. Magnifying the dangers in every issue, they saw assaults on the sovereignty of the states with great regularity. Belligerent particularism was for them the only safeguard of liberty.

Drawing inspiration from the preamble to the Confederate Con-

42. Richardson (comp.), *Messages and Papers of the Confederacy*, I, 217, 556–58. The veto of this bill was the only one of Davis' presidency which the congress managed to override.
43. *Ibid.*, 100–101.

stitution, the extreme states' rightists sought to make the states the primary forces in the Confederacy. According to the Confederacy's fundamental law, each state had acted "in its sovereign and independent character" to establish the new government.[44] Emphasizing this passage, states' rightists thought more in terms of a system like the Articles of Confederation than of the United States government. Always they stressed what the central government could not do. An amusing example of this mentality came to Mary Boykin Chesnut's attention, and she preserved it in her famous diary. Judge Thomas J. Withers, a member of South Carolina's secession convention, felt that tyranny had begun on February 25, 1861, the eighth day after Davis' inauguration: "They have trampled the Constitution underfoot! They have provided President Davis with a house!"[45] At the time such extreme views proved merely amusing, but before long they caused serious trouble.

The Charleston *Mercury* was a major source of extreme states' rights theory. Early in the war it clarified its approach to the major questions facing the Confederacy and steadily advocated states' rights thereafter. Hammering away at its points without ceasing, the *Mercury* focused and propagated the views of many southerners who saw the states as paramount. Often critical of Jefferson Davis, this paper fostered discontent with Confederate leadership and policies. Of all the weapons in the states' rightists arsenal, certainly the *Mercury* was one of the most formidable.

Shortly after the southerners' capture of Fort Sumter, the *Mercury* tried to define states' rights as the heart of the Confederacy's purpose. South Carolina, the Charleston paper argued, had fought with the Federal government for more than thirty years in order to halt the progress of consolidation. Continually the United States government had "usurped powers not granted—progressively trenched upon State Rights." Unfortunately years of living under Federal usurpation had accustomed southerners to the national government's role. Rhett decried his countrymen's "mistaken proneness to turn to the Central

44. For text, see Lee, *Confederate Constitutions*, 171.
45. Chesnut, *Diary*, 6.

Government for a remedy for all inconveniences or necessities."
Such attitudes threatened the basic foundation of the Confederacy,
Rhett felt, and he saw the need for an educational campaign that
would implant new habits of mind. Through his paper he stressed
that "the new Government . . . leaves the States untouched in their
Sovereignty, and commits to the Confederate Government only a
few simple objects, and a few simple powers to enforce them."[46] In
effect this editorial served notice on the central government to confine itself to its "few simple powers."

Even within the Confederate government the *Mercury* saw griev-
ous dangers. The executive branch often served as the engine of consolidation, Rhett asserted, and in time of war any legislative body
had to be particularly watchful of its rights. After warning against an
increase of executive power at the expense of the congress, the *Mercury* reported a plan to check usurpation. The editor of the Richmond *Whig*, Alexander Moseley, had conceived the idea of "an acci-
dental President—the oldest Senator to exercise the functions of
President for two years." Truly this was a remarkable plan, probably
one of the first to combine the benefits of weakness and possible se-
nility in office. The *Mercury* and the *Whig* were even concerned
that the presidential electors would defer to the choice of the electorate, as they had in the United States, and that this would lead to ag-
grandizement of the executive. The only solution was to "strengthen
the Legislative Departments."[47]

Curiously, one of Jefferson Davis' most rigorous applications of
strict construction provoked bitter criticism from these two papers.
In August, 1861, the congress adjourned before Davis could approve
a measure continuing nominated military officers at their jobs until
the next session. Since the constitution dictated that such a bill "shall
not be a law," Davis called the congress back into session in order to
re-pass this measure. In the Provisional Congress each state had one
vote, and only one member of any delegation needed to be present

46. Charleston *Mercury*, April 19, 1861, p. 1, October 10, 1861, p. 1.
47. *Ibid.*, October 30, 1861, p. 1, October 7, 1861, p.1, February 13, 1861, October 22,
1861, November 29, 1861, and September 19, 1861.

to cast his state's vote. Thus it happened that relatively few congressmen returned to approve Davis' rather unimportant bill. Both the *Mercury* and the Richmond *Whig* raised cries of alarm. The president, they warned, had discovered an easy path to despotism. By calling together six friendly congressmen from different states Davis could claim that the congress had met and given its sanction to his designs.[48] In this case there had been no doubt that Congress favored the bill and that Davis was trying to observe the letter of the constitution. Yet the newspapers accused him of despotism and showed beyond a shadow of doubt that some of the states' rights forces were inordinately suspicious of the executive's power.

The Charleston *Mercury*'s opposition, though formidable in itself, was only the most visible part of a set of attitudes which many state authorities shared. In the short interval between secession and admission to the Confederacy, some governors had considered their states to be independent republics. Georgia's Governor Brown, taking this moment of unfettered sovereignty very seriously, even sent a diplomatic representative abroad with instructions to seek recognition for Georgia from Queen Victoria, Napoleon III, and the king of Belgium.[49] When Davis began to organize the Confederate government, this heady feeling of state sovereignty placed many obstacles in his path. At least four states attached conditions to the transfer of forts and navy yards to the central government. Georgia's convention, for example, merely authorized the Confederacy "to occupy, use, and hold possession of" the former United States facilities "until the ordinance should be repealed by a convention" of the state. Moreover, Brown jealously kept all of his state's guns under his control, and some states attempted to raise entire armies.[50] Secretary of War Benjamin complained to Davis that several states had their own troops, officers, and commissary and quartermaster departments. Competing with the Confederacy for men and scarce supplies, these

48. Richardson (comp.), *Messages and Papers of the Confederacy*, I, 133, 134–35, 41; Charleston *Mercury*, September 7, 1861, p. 1, September 19, 1861, p. 1.
49. Candler (ed.), *Confederate Records of Georgia*, II, 19–24.
50. Rowland (ed.), *Jefferson Davis*, V, 105–180; Candler (ed.), *Confederate Records of Georgia*, III, 170–80.

state armies had seriously affected Confederate recruiting efforts
and caused much waste of energy and money. According to the estimate of Frank L. Owsley, more than 100,000 soldiers remained in
militarily worthless state units until April, 1862.[51]

The leading defender of state prerogatives was Georgia's Joseph E.
Brown. From the first days of the Confederacy, this combative and
shrewd politician emerged as Davis' chief opponent. Skillfully using
states' rights rhetoric to further his fame, Brown threw one obstacle
after another into the path of the harassed Richmond administration.
He threatened to disarm Georgia volunteers who left the borders of
the state and schemed to reserve for himself the greatest possible
powers of appointment.[52] Confederate law allowed the governors to
appoint officers up through the level of colonel in all regiments raised
by the states for national service. Promptly seeing a means to exploit
this provision, Brown offered the Confederacy numerous "skeleton"
regiments which had a full complement of officers but few privates.
Unabashedly he argued that future recruits could fill the vacancies
and thus ignored the army's need for functional combat units.[53] To
win favor with Georgia's voters, he searched for a means to permit
all of the state's men to elect their lower-level officers. Repeatedly
during the war he discovered that units of the army actually were militia and therefore entitled under law to elect their officers. Through
skillful political management Brown got his legislature to support
him in 1863, when Georgia's lawmakers asked the congress to alter
laws which made other provisions for a variety of complex circumstances.[54]

All of Brown's complaints and obstructions, however, paled in comparison to his assault on conscription. Saving his greatest wrath for ·

51. Judah Benjamin to Jefferson Davis, December 14, (?), 1861, in *Official Records*,
Ser. IV, Vol. I, 795; Frank L. Owsley, *State Rights in the Confederacy* (Chicago: University
of Chicago Press, 1925), 25–31.

52. *Official Records*, Ser. IV, Vol. I, 348–50, 355; Candler (ed.), *Confederate Records
of Georgia*, III, 188–89.

53. Joseph E. Brown to Secretary of War George Randolph, May 5, 1862, in Candler
(ed.), *Confederate Records of Georgia*, III, 206–209; Owsley, *State Rights*, 87–90.

54. *Official Records*, Ser. IV, Vol. II, 620–23, 737–39, 878.

this essential measure, he ignored his own inconsistency, for Brown had drafted men from Georgia and even done so without legal authority. The unscrupulous governor did not let this fact bother him. Instead he launched an attack on Davis' administration which reverberated throughout the Confederacy and aroused other states' rightists to opposition. Brown's voice was the loudest in a cacophony of criticism which depressed recruiting and morale. Even Jefferson Davis publicly admitted that "unexpected criticism" had "impaired" the efficiency of the conscription law.[55]

When the congress passed conscription in April, 1862, Brown objected almost immediately. Writing directly to the president, Georgia's governor asserted that there was no need for such a law since his state had always met or exceeded all requisitions for troops. Brown demanded that the government exempt a long list of officials, including state legislators, judges, government employees, state militia officers, students at the state university, overseers, mechanics and manufacturers. Ominously Brown speculated that the conscription act empowered the president to disband the legislature or take over the militia. Protesting that this was a power to "destroy the civil government of each State," the governor ordered his state's enrollment officers to refuse to cooperate with Confederate officials.[56]

Despite the breadth of this first attack, Brown was only warming up. On May 8, 1862, he penned a long philippic against conscription, sent it to Jefferson Davis, and thus opened a fascinating exchange between the two leaders on the nature of the Confederate government. Conscription, Brown declared, was "subversive of [Georgia's] sovereignty, and at war with all the principles for the support of which Georgia entered into this revolution." Rejecting all arguments that war required extraordinary measures and some limitations of states' rights, he suggested that southerners should intensify their defense of their liberties during the crisis. Next Brown plunged into turgid

55. Louise Biles Hill, *Joseph E. Brown and the Confederacy* (Chapel Hill: University of North Carolina Press, 1939), 80; Richardson (comp.), *Messages and Papers of the Confederacy*, I, 234–35.
56. Joseph E. Brown to Jefferson Davis, April 22, 1862, in Candler (ed.) *Confederate Records of Georgia*, III, 192–98.

constitutional arguments and concluded that the Confederacy had
no right under the constitution to draft "the whole militia of all the
States." By defining the militia as "the whole arms-bearing population of the State who are not enlisted in the regular armies of the
Confederacy," Brown denied that most of the men in the South were
subject to conscription.[57]

Davis' first reply to Brown was brief and calm. The Confederacy's
chief executive simply sent the contentious Georgian a copy of the
exemption act and reassured him that the congress had followed the
wishes of the states in regard to organization of troops and election of
officers by the conscripts. In addition Davis observed, "The constitutionality of the act you refer to as the 'conscription bill' is clearly
not derivable from the power to call out the militia, but from that to
raise armies."[58]

After Brown's second letter, Davis composed a substantial and
carefully considered document in rebuttal. Beginning at the level of
general principles, he demonstrated that the historic reason for con-
federations was to improve the management of foreign affairs. Thus
the Confederate government naturally had the primary responsibility
for national defense. Turning to the constitution, Davis listed the
government's war powers and pointed out that these constituted a
broad and nearly unqualified grant of authority. As for Brown's specific assertions, Davis argued cogently that the power to call out the
militia was an additional power which did not impair the power to
raise an army. Though both the army and the state militia relied upon
the same pool of men, conscription did not amount to a wholesale
disbanding of the militia. The Confederate army had the right to induct all men liable to service, but the state organizations could enroll the remainder of the military population and use these men in
an emergency. Ridiculing Brown's definition of the militia, Davis
wrote that unless some law inducted all of the state's men into the
militia, they were "no more militia than they [were] seamen."[59]

57. Joseph E. Brown to Jefferson Davis, May 8, 1862, and Brown to James Seddon, July
10, 1863, in Candler (ed.), *Confederate Records of Georgia*, III, 213–14, 362.
58. Candler (ed.), *Confederate Records of Georgia*, III, 200.
59. Jefferson Davis to Joseph E. Brown, May 29, 1862, in Rowland (ed.), *Jefferson
Davis*, V, 255, 257–61.

Then Davis developed a striking point. Governor Brown had denied that conscription was necessary. After mentioning that he could refute that claim with specific facts, Davis declined to do so. Instead he justified conscription on the basis of a general principle: "I hold that when a specific power is granted by the Constitution . . . Congress is the judge whether the law passed for the purpose of executing that power is 'necessary and proper.'" Rejecting a restrictive definition of these crucial words, he argued, "It is not enough to say that armies might be raised in other ways, and that therefore this particular way is not 'necessary.'" Such an argument could be used against every method of raising armies. No particular method could be necessary as long as there was some alternative. Concluding his bold analysis, Davis wrote: "The true and only test is to inquire whether the law is intended and calculated to carry out the object, whether it devises and creates an instrumentality for executing the specific power granted; and if the answer be in the affirmative, the law is constitutional."[60]

Here was a situation pregnant with irony and drama. Davis had deliberately taken the stage playing a Confederate Hamilton to Brown's Jefferson. The Confederacy was reenacting the famous clash within Washington's administration over the constitutionality of a national bank, and Jefferson Davis purposely chose Alexander Hamilton's role. Despite his description of the Confederacy's authority to make war as a "specific power," Davis clearly was arguing that a broad grant of power carried the implied power to adopt effective means of execution. Just as he argued against a restrictive definition of the word "necessary," so Alexander Hamilton had argued in 1791 that "*necessary* often means no more than *needful, requisite, incidental, useful, or conducive to*." The framers, Hamilton continued, had never meant to give the word *necessary* "the same force as if the word absolutely or indispensably had been prefixed to it." Just as Davis argued that the congress' true test was whether a law "devises and creates an instrumentality for executing the specific power granted," so Hamilton

60. *Ibid.*, 256. This represents a development and extension of Davis' prewar position. See Varina Howell Davis, *Jefferson Davis, Ex-President of the Confederate States of America: A Memoir* (2 vols.; New York: Belford Company, 1890), I, 236–38.

had argued that the criterion of constitutionality must be "the *rela-tion* between the *measure* and the *end*." Davis restated Hamilton's view of implied powers and arrived essentially at Hamilton's conclusion, which was this: "If the *end* be clearly comprehended within any of the specified powers, and if the measure have an obvious relation to that *end*, and is not forbidden by any particular provision of the Constitution, it may safely be deemed to come within the compass of the national authority."[61]

These striking parallels between Davis' position and Hamilton's were not lost on Joe Brown. Quickly identifying the origin of his opponent's argument, Brown deftly wrote that the president's doctrine had been "first proclaimed I believe almost as strongly by Mr. Hamilton." Next to Davis' statements of Hamiltonian doctrine, Brown juxtaposed his authorities—John C. Calhoun and the Jefferson and Madison of the Kentucky and Virginia resolutions. Both these famous resolutions had attempted to set limits on the power of the central government. By underlining parts of the Virginia Resolutions, Brown expressed his conviction that the Confederate government had only the specific powers enumerated in the constitution and no others. The Virginia Resolutions deplored any "design to expound *certain general phrases* . . . so as to destroy the meaning and effect of the particular enumeration which *necessarily explains and limits the general phrases.*"[62]

Charging "a bold and dangerous usurpation by Congress of the reserved rights of the States, and a rapid stride towards military despotism," Brown stood by all his former claims. In addition he developed several new ones. Statements by the founders of the United States proved, he felt, that the states should appoint all militia officers even when the militia was in national service. Denying hard realities, the governor declared that the Confederacy should rely solely on voluntary enlistments, which would be adequate when-

61. Quoted in Richard Hofstadter (ed.), *Great Issues in American History* (2 vols., Vintage Books ed.; New York: Random House, 1958), I, 166–68.
62. Joseph E. Brown to Jefferson Davis, June 21, 1862, in *Official Records*, Ser. IV, Vol. I, 1160–61.

ever citizens saw the justice of their government's cause. Finally he complained that the congress passed the exemption act as a favor, not a right. With superficial courtesy and cutting effect, Brown assured the president that his resistance to conscription stemmed from no personal feelings but solely from principle.[63]

Davis replied to Brown's assertions on July 10, 1862, in a short letter. Defending himself against complete identification with Hamilton, Davis pointed out that although the congress was the judge of what measures were necessary and proper, obviously it was not the only judge. The courts could test any law, and in a southern government each state undeniably had the final right to decide whether its powers had been usurped. Davis did not hesitate, however, to indicate that there was a great gulf between his view and Brown's. At the close of his letter he wrote: "I cannot share the alarm and concern about State Rights which you so evidently feel, but which to me seem quite unfounded."[64]

This controversy continued throughout the life of the Confederacy. Brown continued to take sniping shots at Davis, who rarely defended himself publicly after the major exchange of letters. When the congress in September, 1862, passed the second conscription act, extending the maximum eligible age from thirty-five to forty-five, the Georgia governor grew livid. Thundering that this act utterly destroyed the state's militia and left Georgia defenseless against a possible slave uprising, Brown charged that the congress' action "strikes down" the state's "sovereignty at a single blow": "No act of the government of the United States prior to the secession of Georgia struck a blow at constitutional liberty, so fell, as has been stricken by the conscription acts." After obtaining resolutions in support of his protest from the Georgia legislature, Brown nevertheless agreed in this instance to call out no one between eighteen and forty-five for the state militia who had been enrolled in Confederate service.[65]

63. Joseph E. Brown to Jefferson Davis, June 21, 1862, in Candler (ed.), *Confederate Records of Georgia*, III, 252, 253, 258–59, 268, 280–81.

64. Jefferson Davis to Joseph E. Brown, July 10, 1862, *ibid.*, III, 285–86.

65. Joseph E. Brown to Jefferson Davis, October 18, 1862, and December 29, 1862, *ibid.*, III, 299, 301–302, 317.

Brown's fiery protests gave courage to other advocates of states' rights. Perhaps his arguments inspired the Charleston *Mercury* to fall in line on conscription, for the South Carolina journal steadily changed its position. Originally the *Mercury* had endorsed the draft and even criticized Jefferson Davis for being too slow to adopt the necessary measure. But in the spring and summer of 1862 editor Rhett discovered that he could talk out of both sides of his mouth. While advocating an extension of conscription to all men between forty-five and fifty years of age, the *Mercury* publicized a statement by Governor John Letcher of Virginia that the draft was unconstitutional, even if one could not oppose it during the war. By the end of 1862 the *Mercury* quoted at length from Linton Stephen's bitter assault on conscription: "The essence of Conscription is the right to take away the fighting men of the States against the will of both the citizens and the States. It is the right, make what you will of it, to coerce sovereign States. . . . Conscription . . . is . . . the very embodiment of Lincolnism, which our gallant armies are today resisting."[66]

South Carolina, with the *Mercury* providing support, did not lag far behind Georgia in opposing the conscription laws. The Palmetto state did not attack the concept of conscription but instead concentrated on its execution. Insisting that all men whom state law exempted from the militia should also be exempt from Confederate service, leaders from South Carolina demanded that overseers, in particular, stay on their plantations. Although the first conscription act did not allow this exemption, South Carolinians felt that the supremacy of Confederate law, made explicit in the constitution, did not apply. Judge Benjamin Dunkin, a member of the South Carolina Supreme Court, gave the War Department a lecture on constitutional theory. The South Carolina convention, Dunkin argued, had passed the exemption for overseers, and any state convention, as the embodiment of state sovereignty, possessed higher authority than congress. To give added stress to his theoretical points, Judge

66. Charleston *Mercury*, March 31, 1862, p. 1, April 3, 1862, p. 1, July 30, 1862, p. 1, May 7, 1862, p. 1, December 10, 1862, p. 1.

Dunkin warned that an attempt to enroll overseers would meet resistance.[67]

The secretary of war decided not to force this confrontation and instead referred the dispute to the congress, which soon exempted one white man on each plantation of twenty or more Negroes. But the issue arose again because South Carolina objected to the enrollment of other men covered by state law. After the governor and executive council announced their intention to issue a "countervailing order" against a Confederate conscription officer, President Davis entered the fray in an attempt to calm the state's leaders. Pointing out that the courts were open and existed to resolve such disputes before they became confrontations, Davis argued that the constitution clearly gave the congress the power to declare war and raise armies:

> If a State may free her citizens at her own discretion from the burden of military duty, she may do the same in regard to the burden of taxation, or any other lawful duty, payment or service. In other words, the assertion of such a right on the part of the State is tantamount to a denial of the right of the Confederate Government to enforce the exercise of any delegated power and would render a Confederacy an impracticable form of Government.[68]

In such cases, however, Jefferson Davis avoided a showdown between the Confederate and state governments by taking the disputes into the courts. Moreover, since the congress had never established a Confederate supreme court, Davis went into the state courts and sought a judgment from the highest state tribunal. Assuring South Carolina's governor and executive council that he would release any soldier whose claim to exemption was judged valid, Davis expressed "full confidence" that the law was constitutional. He also steered the

67. Judge Benjamin Dunkin to Secretary of the Treasury C. G. Memminger, May 23, 1862, in Letters Received, Confederate Secretary of War, RG 109, NA, Microcopy M 437, Roll 60, pp. 1101–1107.

68. C. G. Memminger to Secretary of War George Randolph, May 29, 1862, in Letters Received, Confederate Secretary of War, RG 109, NA, Microcopy M 437, Roll 60, pp. 1097–1101; Jefferson Davis to the Governor and Executive Council of South Carolina, September 3, 1862, in Rowland (ed.), *Jefferson Davis*, V, 335.

thorny conflict with Georgia toward resolution in the courts. Writing Senator Benjamin Hill of Georgia, the president said that he relied "on the decision of the Supreme Court of Georgia to remove the difficulties." [69]

As he predicted, Davis won all his court tests. Georgia's supreme court held unanimously that the conscription act was constitutional. As the decision was read, some spectators applauded so heartily that the chief justice had to call for order. Courts in South Carolina and Virginia also found in favor of the central government, and similar decisions supporting conscription came down from tribunals in Alabama, Texas, Florida, and Mississippi. [70]

These decisions and their popularity indicated that Davis did not stand alone against his critics. Despite understandable discomfort about such strong steps as the suspension of *habeas corpus*, conscription, and impressment, most southerners recognized the need for a vigorous central government. They also noticed that the administration's critics seldom offered practical alternatives. Conscription had been necessary to keep an army in the field. As Secretary of War Seddon admitted in an official report nine months after the adoption of the draft, "the spirit of volunteering had died out." Recognizing these facts, the Richmond *Enquirer* greeted conscription with calm approval. The paper described the measure as "extremely advantageous, if not indispensable, to the public interests. That consideration silences all objections to it as a present policy. . . . Our business now is to whip our enemies and save our homes;—we can attend to questions of theory afterwards." [71] In northwest Georgia, the Rome *Weekly Courier* sounded the same kind of realistic note, which no doubt weighed heavily in many people's minds. "Talk about State Rights," the *Courier* said, "when there are no rights, civil or reli-

69. Jefferson Davis to the Governor and Executive Council of South Carolina, September 3, 1862, Davis to B. H. Hill, October 23, 1862, and Davis to Zebulon Vance, November 1, 1862, in Rowland (ed.), *Jefferson Davis*, V, 334–37, 358–59, 362–63.

70. Jno. B. Weems to George Randolph, November 12, 1862, in *Official Records*, Ser. IV, Vol. II, 177; Jefferson Davis to A. H. Kenan, November 11, 1862, in Rowland (ed.), *Jefferson Davis*, V, 368; Moore, *Conscription and Conflict*, 170, 298.

71. James Seddon to Jefferson Davis, January 3, 1863, in Letters Sent by the Confederate Secretary of War to the President, RG 109, NA, Microcopy M 523, Roll 1, pp. 91–99; Richmond *Enquirer*, April 18, 1862.

gious, of person or property, left to any one, unless we succeed in this contest."[72] On rare occasions, a few states voluntarily cooperated without standing on privilege, as when the Alabama and Virginia legislatures declared that all state militia officers were subject to conscription. These states recognized that the need for the men was far greater in the field than at home, and even Governor Brown clamored for prompt and vigorous Confederate action when his state faced invasion.[73]

Davis won the congress' approval for his war measures and eventually put them into operation, but the opposition never subsided completely. From time to time it cropped out again, both in old and in new places. South Carolina continued to guard the exemptions of overseers, and Georgia's Joe Brown briefly found a new issue when General Bragg prepared to seize the state railroad in order to move arms and ammunition. Even Florida's chief executive, who often supported the Richmond administration, declined to cooperate with Davis' request that the states pass laws to encourage the planting of food crops instead of cotton.[74] Then the fall elections of 1862 in North Carolina supplied a new adversary for Jefferson Davis in the person of governor elect Zebulon Vance. Sensing the strong dissatisfaction over the war in his state, Vance wasted no time on courting the Richmond government. Almost immediately he declared his unalterable opposition to suspension of the writ of *habeas corpus*, and in March, 1863, he protested the conscription of justices of the peace, constables, and town police. Vance never went as far as North Carolina's Judge Richmond Pearson, who denounced conscription as unconstitutional and issued writs of *habeas corpus* for virtually all who sought them, but North Carolina's governor surely caused Davis much concern and aided the states' rights opposition.[75]

72. Rome (Ga.) *Weekly Courier*, May 16, 1862, p. 3.

73. *Official Records*, Ser. IV, Vol. II, 213, 880–81, and Joseph E. Brown to James Seddon, August 10, 1863, pp. 753–54. See Chapter V herein, pp. 136–38.

74. *Official Records*, Ser. IV, Vol. II, 864–66; Candler (ed.), *Confederate Records of Georgia*, III, 329–31; Rowland (ed.), *Jefferson Davis*, V, 489; John Milton to Jefferson Davis, April 15, 1863, in *Official Records*, Ser. IV, Vol. II, 487–89.

75. Zebulon Vance to Jefferson Davis, March 31, 1863, in *Official Records*, Ser. IV, Vol. II, 464–65; Richard E. Yates, *The Confederacy and Zeb Vance* (Tuscaloosa, Ala.: Confederate Publishing Company, Inc., 1958), 45–47, 53–57.

Thus the conflict over the extent of central power in the Confederacy continued and could not be stilled. Its effects are difficult to measure, though they were substantial. One study of federalism in the Confederacy has provided a partial, numerical measure of the effect of states' rights opposition. According to Curtis A. Amlund, the states held a total of 25,892 men out of the armies on the grounds that they were essential for state government. North Carolina with 14,675 exempted employees and Georgia with 8,229 supplied approximately 92 percent of the total. Actually, as supplementary reports from the Conscription Bureau made clear, the total number of men withheld was at least 30,060, and the number of exempted state employees in North Carolina was probably even larger than reported.[76] Whether Governors Vance and Brown were defending principles which they considered vital or merely combining states' rights with a grand opportunity to dispense political patronage, their actions denied the southern army a significant number of men. Nevertheless, Amlund's study cogently argues that these potential troops would not have changed the outcome of the war.[77]

The rise of disputes over the central government's power signaled a breach between the administration and part of the articulate, politically active planter class. Dedicated to independence, Jefferson Davis was a revolutionary, a man who was determined to reach his goal even if circumstances required unpalatable measures and unsettling changes. Many planters, on the other hand, revealed that their primary interest was in maintaining the status quo in a more narrowly conceived war. They balked at painful sacrifices and interference with their slave property, and some came to regard the Confederacy as their enemy. Resentment of the Richmond government and personal

76. Curtis Arthur Amlund, *Federalism in the Southern Confederacy* (Washington: Public Affairs Press, 1966), 103; *Official Records*, Ser. IV, Vol. II, 851, 866–70, 894, 976–79, 1112.

77. Amlund, *Federalism in the Southern Confederacy*, 105. Recently Thomas B. Alexander and Richard E. Beringer have shown that Confederate congressmen took many limitations of states' rights in stride and reacted strongly only when many constituents were involved. See Thomas B. Alexander and Richard E. Beringer, *The Anatomy of the Confederate Congress: A Study of the Influences of Member Characteristics on Legislative Voting Behavior, 1861–1865* (Nashville: Vanderbilt University Press, 1972), 303.

animosities toward Davis became so great that a few large slave-holders undoubtedly fought more effectively against the Confederate president than they did against the Federal army. Because the planters were powerful men with great influence, their disaffection was equivalent to the loss of several times that number of fighting men.

Dissatisfaction with Davis' government had an especially profound effect on some prominent southerners because they had entered the war with reluctance and misgivings. Those who never attained the heights of enthusiasm for the cause naturally lost hope and despaired more quickly than a fiery secessionist like Robert Barnwell Rhett. A few Confederates left positions in the United States government which had perfectly suited their tastes. Mary Boykin Chesnut noted that Captain D. N. Ingraham's heart was "torn in twain" because the United States navy had been "his supreme affection, his first thought and duty." John A. Campbell had greatly enjoyed his seat on the Supreme Court, but resigned "for a cause that he is hardly more than half in sympathy with." When Mrs. Chesnut saw his family in Warrenton, Virginia, in July, 1861, she wrote, "There they wander disconsolate, just outside of the gates of their paradise." Judge Campbell rendered faithful service to the Confederacy as assistant secretary of war, but in the case of Vice President Alexander Stephens lingering feelings for the old Union may have combined with resentment of Davis to negate any positive contribution which he might have made. In the first days of the new nation, Mrs. Chesnut twice "had it out" with Stephens and accused him of "looking back." She noted that "fears for the future, and not exultation at our successes, pervade his discourse." A year later she had concluded that he was "half-hearted clear through."[78]

Stephens was not the only leading Confederate who lacked an unquenchable determination to see the war through to success and independence. Mrs. Chesnut found latent defeatism in many Confederate politicians. One evening in May, 1861, she talked with Virginia's R. M. T. Hunter and South Carolina's William Porcher Miles,

78. Chesnut, *Diary*, 105, 76, 46, 217.

both important members of the congress, and with the president of South Carolina's secession convention. Although these men were not "without hope exactly," Mrs. Chesnut discerned that they "are not sanguine. . . . They are agreed in one thing; it is worth while to try a while, if only to get away from New England."[79] One Georgia woman from a prominent family wrote that her father's "judgment told him that secession must inevitably be a failure, in any case."[80] Acknowledging that the world was against the South on slavery, many older slaveholders felt that the United States could have defended slavery, but that the Confederate States could not. Senator Chesnut's father predicted that the "world will not tolerate a small slave power." From the early days of the war some Confederates felt that they could go back to the United States and keep their slaves. Mrs. Chesnut gave one example: "John De Saussure says he means in case of trouble to take refuge under the Federal Flag with his cotton and his Negroes; and he is fool enough to think they will let him keep them."[81]

The states' rights controversy gave such men a means of venting their anger and malaise on Jefferson Davis. Not only was the states' rights issue a cause of complaint in itself, it also focused unspecific resentments and fed on disappointments. As the Confederacy's problems grew worse and the people's burdens became heavier, politicians less imbued with Davis' nationalism could use the rhetoric of states' rights to arouse various kinds of anger.[82] Thus states' rights became a useful tool for any politician who wanted to rise on the falling fortunes of the South. The southern people had to express their frustrations, and as morale fell and war weariness grew with each defeat, the ambitious politician saw that the states' rights issue could concentrate this general malaise and yield political dividends. At-

79. *Ibid.*, 51.

80. Eliza Frances Andrews, *The War-Time Journal of a Georgia Girl, 1864–1865*, ed. Spencer Bidwell King, Jr. (Macon: Ardivan Press, 1960), 279.

81. Chesnut, *Diary*, 161, 165, 160.

82. John B. Robbins made this point in relation to the criticism of the suspension of the writ of *habeas corpus*. Robbins, "The Confederacy and the Writ of *Habeas Corpus*," 97–101.

tacking the central government became a basic device for all politicians who wanted to stay afloat as the ship of state foundered.

Thus, in taking measures necessary to wage a great war, Davis had
to pay a price in loss of support. Initially the price was small compared to the gain. But as the war progressed the cost of his programs
became larger. In the controversy over states' rights Davis lost the
constructive energies of part of the planter class. Moreover, as the
argument continued, it disseminated reasons for dissatisfaction to
other elements of the population. This fact was important, because
the states' rights issue, although it did not cause nonslaveholders to
turn against the Confederacy, may have given impetus to a separate
process which did. Even as he fought with Governor Brown over
conscription, Jefferson Davis had already, for independent reasons,
begun to lose the support of a great many of the South's yeoman
farmers.

4

The Quiet Rebellion
of the
Common People

Even at the bright beginning of the Confederacy, there was a submerged element of discontent. Evidence coming from prominent officials, newspapers, and ordinary citizens in 1861 shows that in almost every state a small minority opposed and obstructed the southern nation. Despite the steady progress of events toward disunion and strong community pressures against dissent, some men from nonslaveholding regions of the South refused to welcome the advent of the Confederacy or to contribute their energies to the establishment of a southern nation.

One of the earliest signs of this attitude came from aristocratic South Carolina, the first state to secede. In May, 1861, the former United States senator James Chesnut, Jr., worried about the fact that the sandhill men, small farmers who worked the rather poor land in the rolling hills between Camden and Columbia, were saying "this is a rich man's war" and that they would have to bear the brunt of combat while the wealthy enjoyed positions of command. To allay these feelings and demonstrate that the planter class was ready to make sacrifices, Chesnut gave his nephew some advice: "Let the gentlemen set the example; let them go into the ranks." Mary Boykin Chesnut noted that young John Chesnut became a "gentleman private" but "took his servant with him all the same."[1]

Serious indications of dissatisfaction among those who held few or no slaves also appeared in Georgia. The northern part of the state

1. Mary Boykin Chesnut, *A Diary from Dixie*, ed. Ben Ames Williams (Sentry ed; Boston: Houghton Mifflin Company, 1949), 54.

94

was hilly and largely unsuited to plantation agriculture, and from this region had come the strongest opposition to secession. After the state convention took Georgia out of the Union, an editor in the northwestern town of Rome urged his readers to join together and put their divisions behind them. Three months later, in May, 1861, this editor addressed some "Important Words to the Disaffected" and warned that unless these complaining citizens showed more loyalty, their neighbors would ostracize them as Tories. Despite the arguments and threats of the newspaper, however, discontent among the nonslaveholding farmers continued to simmer. Even the Confederacy's encouraging victory at Bull Run in the summer failed to unify Georgians behind the cause, and as the fall elections approached, some ordinary citizens began to calculate how their interests diverged under wartime conditions from those of the slaveholders. One citizen addressed this public letter to the candidates of Floyd County:

> Please give your views concerning our present condition—about the war, and the cause of the war . . . and our present condition of taxation for the support of the war. Is it right that the poor man should be taxed for the support of the war, when the war was brought about on the slave question, and the slave at home accumulating for the benefit of his master, and the poor man's farm left uncultivated, and a chance for his wife to be a widow, and his children orphans? Now, in justice, would it not be right to levy a direct tax on that species of property that brought about the war, to support it?

Within a few days the editor of the Rome *Weekly Courier* formally apologized for printing this letter and lamented that it might promote class division. Apparently, however, the perception of different class interests had an independent basis, for the *Courier*'s subsequent efforts to eliminate dissent proved as unsuccessful as previous attempts.[2]

Early dissatisfaction with secession also appeared in Virginia, where unionists in the western part of the state began a political movement which led to the formation of the separate state of West

2. Rome (Ga.) *Weekly Courier*, January 25, 1861, p. 2, May 3, 1861, p. 1, September 27, 1861, p. 3, October 4, 1861, p. 1.

Virginia.[3] In Bedford County, which was in the Blue Ridge Mountains, a similar lack of enthusiasm for the Confederacy manifested itself. According to the report of a committee of alarmed citizens, a "low, treacherous" set of men "positively & absolutely refuse[d] to muster" and said "that they [would] not serve unless *drafted*." By the end of the year these conditions had not abated, for a subcommittee of the Virginia House of Delegates approached Secretary of War Judah Benjamin about the need to remove from the state borders and areas near enemy lines all those who were disloyal or who maintained "an unpatriotic neutrality."[4] Events such as these led the editor of the Richmond *Examiner* to warn on July 19, 1861, that the establishment of loyalty and popular support was a major problem for the Confederacy: "Loyal as the great mass of our people are . . . there is yet no doubt that the South is more rife with treason to her own independence and honour than any community that ever engaged before in a struggle with an adversary."[5]

The mountain regions of the South were especially prone to disaffection since most farmers who lived there owned few or no slaves and lived an independent style of life completely removed from the cotton economy. Eastern Tennessee quickly became a hotbed of opposition to the Confederacy, and the unionism of the farmers there laid the foundation for a persistent loyalty to the Republican party which has long impressed political scientists.[6] In North Carolina the Blue Ridge mountains gave the western part of the state a topography and economy similar to those of eastern Tennessee. Admitting that Tennessee unionists were having some influence in the western border counties and that "a few are disaffected," North Carolina's governor called on the secretary of war in November, 1861, for aid in suppressing treason. Even on the eastern shore of North Caro-

3. James G. Randall and David Donald, *The Civil War and Reconstruction* (2nd ed.; Boston: D. C. Heath and Company, 1961), 236–42.

4. Jno. Huddleston, Grief Adams, John Beard, and others to Jefferson Davis, July 12, 1861, and Andrew Hunter to Judah Benjamin, December 13, 1861, in Letters Received, Confederate Secretary of War, in Record Group 109, National Archives, Microcopy M 437, Roll 5, pp. 351–52, and Roll 20, pp. 1232–34.

5. *Daily Richmond Examiner*, July 19, 1861, p. 2.

6. See V. O. Key, Jr., *Politics, Parties, and Pressure Groups* (4th ed.; New York: Thomas Y. Crowell Company, 1958), 267–69.

lina, however, there were some signs of trouble. According to the report of a loyal citizen, Bertie County, at the head of Albemarle Sound, was "infested by Torys & disloyal persons." Although this county contained a large number of slaves, the concerned citizen who wrote the War Department explained that there were "but few men of wealth compared to the number of nonslaveholding persons."[7]

Florida in the 1860s had its share of plantations and slavery, but many parts of this sparsely populated state seemed only slightly changed from the days of the frontier. The testimony of Florida's governor himself indicated that organized opposition to the Confederacy existed in that state during the early stages of the war. Writing to President Davis in September, 1862, Governor John Milton reminded the chief executive "that in Florida a very large minority" was "opposed to secession, and in many parts of the State combinations existed to adhere to and maintain the United States Government, and even now in some portions of the State there are men who would eagerly seize any opportunity that promised success to the United States."[8]

The people of northern Alabama also had shown a strong tendency to oppose secession, and some writers have tried to explain this fact by the region's proximity to Tennessee. Certain other facts, however, were important in determining the attitudes of northern Alabama's Tories. Although slaves composed 45 percent of the state's population, they were mainly concentrated in the cotton-growing areas of south Alabama.[9] Most disaffection in Alabama arose either in the northern part of the state or in three wiregrass counties in the southeast, where the soil was marshy and unsuited to cotton culture. Almost from the day of secession, unionists in certain northern coun-

7. Henry T. Clark to Judah Benjamin, November 16 and 18, 1861, in *The War of the Rebellion: A Compilation of the Official Records of the Union and Confederate Armies* (130 vols.; Washington: Government Printing Office, 1880–1901), Ser. I, Vol. LII, Pt. II, 209–210, hereinafter cited as *Official Records*; B. A. Capehart to the Secretary of War, September 20, 1861, in Letters Received, Confederate Secretary of War, in RG 109, NA, Microcopy M 437, Roll 10, pp. 363–64.
8. John Milton to Jefferson Davis, September 23, 1862, in *Official Records*, Ser. IV, Vol. II, 92–93.
9. William Stanley Hoole, *Alabama Tories: The First Alabama Cavalry, U.S.A., 1862–1865* (Tuscaloosa, Ala.: Confederate Printing Company, Inc., 1960), 8–10.

ties tried to fly the United States flag, argued with volunteers, and organized to protect their homes and their right of free speech. Some of these men expressed a determination to resist an "unconstitutional Course" by the South. Worried loyalists wrote the governor for aid, and a reliable political leader who had the trust of the people in north Alabama agreed to visit and calm the area. In October, 1861, in an address to the legislature, Governor A. B. Moore claimed that the acts of the United States had united all Alabamians and driven away whatever dissatisfaction once existed over secession. Continuing troubles in northern Alabama proved Moore wrong, however, and eventually this disaffection led to the formation of the First Alabama Cavalry, U.S.A., a white regiment composed of approximately two thousand men who served with General Sherman in Georgia.[10]

Discontent appeared at an early date in Arkansas, where loyal citizens discovered a secret peace society in November, 1861. This organization flourished in six counties in the north-central part of the state, which had apparently opposed secession to the end, and the governor wrote President Davis that as many as 1,700 citizens were members. An historian's careful study of census and tax records has demonstrated that the identifiable members of the peace society were nonslaveholders and poor and that they came from a rather impoverished part of the state which had only 3.8 slaves for every 100 whites. Apparently these men intended to stay at their homes, protect their families, and exercise their right to express their opinions, but harsh suppression of the peace society drove some of them into the United States army.[11]

These various manifestations of disaffection did not pose an immediate threat to the Confederacy during the first year of the war. The overwhelming majority of southerners loyally supported their new government, and even among those who protested only a small number actively supported the Union against the Confederate States.

10. Hugh C. Bailey, "Disaffection in the Alabama Hill Country, 1861," *Civil War History*, IV (1958), 183–93; *Official Records*, Ser. IV, Vol. I, 697–711.

11. Ted R. Worley, "The Arkansas Peace Society of 1861: A Study in Mountain Unionism," *Journal of Southern History*, XXIV (1958), 445–56. The ratio of slaves to whites in the entire state was 34 to 100.

During the entire war no southern state, with the exception of Tennessee, furnished more than a few white regiments for the Federal armies.[12] Those who refused to aid the Confederacy almost always regarded themselves as southerners, though they disapproved of their region's political and military course. Their characteristic stance was one of neutrality as they sought to protect their families from both armies and to carry on their lives as normally as possible. Thus the widespread signs of lack of identification with the Confederacy's cause did not portend a large-scale defection of nonslaveholders into the Federal army. They were, instead, forewarning of the possibility of a quiet rebellion which could cost the Confederacy dearly. Entangled in a tremendously destructive war fought on southern ground, the Davis administration faced the prospect of losing the support of increasing numbers of its citizens unless it could strengthen popular morale.

The dynamics of the southern class system played a major role in the disaffection of many common people in the Confederacy. Among historians there has been considerable controversy about the nature of this class system. Frank Lawrence Owsley argued at length against certain misconceptions of the structure of southern society, particularly against the notion that there were only three classes—the wealthy planters, the oppressed slaves, and the poor whites. Instead, Owsley maintained, the society was complex, and both the slaveholding and the nonslaveholding categories contained many different levels and gradations of income. Striving to rehabilitate the image of the nonslaveholding white, Owsley emphasized that these people were not the offscourings of southern society, but rather an independent, landowning group with its own way of life. Contrary to the view that the successful planters drove southern yeomen onto poorer mountain soil, Owsley suggested that residents of the hilly portions of the South consciously chose these areas because they were familiar with their climate and soil, just as planters who migrated within the South tended to settle on lands similar to those

12. Hoole, *Alabama Tories*, 15.

they had left. Relying on grazing and hunting to supplement the products of their small farms, the nonslaveholding southern yeoman led a self-reliant, respectable life.[13]

Owsley had insisted that class feelings were not strong in southern society. The "plain folk" of the Old South, as Owsley called them, neither opposed slavery nor felt that opportunity was denied them. Possessing a self-respect which came from economic independence, the yeomen shared many social and familial ties with planters. Even in black belt areas, as Owsley and his wife demonstrated, some non-slaveholders cultivated their farms, just as predominantly nonslave-holding regions contained an occasional plantation. Basing his analysis on these facts and on the simplistic observation that the political domination of the planter class necessarily rested on pursuasion rather than coercion, Owsley underestimated the amount of class awareness and tension in southern society.[14]

Another distinguished historian, David Donald, came closer to the truth when he wrote that the antebellum South was a "paradoxical world . . . devoted to the principles of democracy and the practice of aristocracy."[15] The vast differences of wealth and income in the society were too great to be ignored, and many individuals realized that predictable differences of power accompanied the gradations of wealth. But southern society contained democratic forces which coexisted with its aristocratic pretensions. Jacksonian democracy had been a potent force in politics, and the dogma which extolled the common man was as prevalent as the formula of states' rights. Southern aristocrats wisely tried to conceal their conviction of superiority when they dealt with less wealthy whites, for the operating principles of their society held that all citizens were equal.

To a great degree, white racism provided the cement which held the paradoxes of southern society together. Defenders of slavery combined racism with democratic values by developing an argument which emphasized the natural equality of one race and the natural

13. Frank Lawrence Owsley, *Plain Folk of the Old South* (Baton Rouge: Louisiana State University Press, 1949), Chaps. 1 and 2.
14. *Ibid.*, Chaps. 4 and 5.
15. David Donald, "The Southerner as a Fighting Man," in Charles Grier Sellers, Jr. (ed.), *The Southerner as American* (Chapel Hill: University of North Carolina Press, 1960), 87.

subjection of the other. According to this reasoning, all men were equal, but blacks were not men. The South's social ideology was that of a "Herrenvolk democracy," a system in which one segment of society can be exploited because by definition it is outside of the group, while those who belong claim to practice democracy among themselves.[16] A long line of southern political leaders echoed the words of John C. Calhoun: "With us, the two great divisions of society are not the rich and poor, but white and black; and all the former, the poor as well as the rich, belong to the upper classes, and are respected and treated as equals." Near the close of the antebellum period, one proslavery apologist, George Fitzhugh, advanced the thesis that slavery was the perfect labor system and should be applied everywhere, even in situations in which whites would have to enslave men of their own race. No politician, however, dared to adopt Fitzhugh's heretical idea, and the Virginia theorist himself soon returned to the familiar principles that all white men were equal and that all blacks were inferior.[17]

This emphasis on the equality of all white men, from the proprietor of the grandest plantation to the owner of the meanest farm, truly did stimulate the small farmer's sense of his own dignity, and here lay important consequences. The ideology that aristocratic politicians disseminated to protect their property always had the potential of a two-edged sword, for it could also serve as an instrument for the common farmer to defend his interest and pride. Sometimes in situations which galled the pretentious aristocrats, ordinary southerners insisted on the marks of respect and equal treatment to which the ideology of white-man's democracy entitled them. With noticeable acerbity, Mary Boykin Chesnut related in her diary an incident which illustrated the poor man's willingness to use his opportunities to claim an equal place:

We went to one of Uncle Hamilton's splendid dinners, plate, glass, china, and everything that was nice to eat. In the piazza, when the gentlemen

16. George M. Fredrickson, *The Black Image in the White Mind: The Debate on Afro-American Character and Destiny, 1817–1914* (New York: Harper & Row, 1971), 61; Pierre Van den Berghe, *Race and Racism: A Comparative Perspective* (New York: Wiley, 1967).
17. Quoted by Donald in "The Southerner as a Fighting Man," 74; Fredrickson, *Black Image*, 65–68.

were smoking after dinner, in the midst of them sat Squire MacDonald, the well-digger. He was officiating in that capacity at Plain Hill, and apparently he was most at his ease of all. He had his clay pipe in his mouth, he was cooler than the rest, being in his shirt sleeves, and he leaned back luxuriously in his chair tilted on its two hind legs, with his naked feet up on the bannister. Said Louisa—"Look, the mud from the well is sticking through his toes! See how solemnly polite and attentive Mr. Chesnut is to him!"[18]

The South's doctrine of equality for white men fed an already powerful tradition of individualism. Living in a rural environment which in many places was still almost a frontier, southerners developed an assertive sense of themselves and of their rights. The experience of being dependent on no one ill prepared people to accept discriminatory treatment, social injustices, or military discipline. One of the first indications that the individualism of the common southerner could produce problems for the Confederacy appeared in the army. Southern troops during the Civil War were notoriously lacking in discipline. In one of many editorials preaching the need for rigid obedience in the army, the Charleston *Mercury* criticized "the volunteer [who] seems to feel that, having done as he pleased in coming he should do as he might prefer whilst staying. . . . We speak of the volunteer familiar to us all—the man who thinks it humiliating to obey."[19]

The organization of the Confederate armies reinforced the soldiers' resistance to military discipline, for the congress wrote into law the requirement that troops could elect all but their highest-ranking field officers. Confederate commanders protested continually about the destructive effect which this system had on discipline, but the Richmond administration was powerless to change it, for as David Donald has noted, "though militarily indefensible, the system was politically necessary."[20] Adjusting themselves to this reality, some practical newspaper editors adopted another method of dealing with the unsatisfactory relations between officers and men. They abandoned the

18. Chesnut, *Diary*, 143.
19. Charleston *Mercury*, May 6, 1862, p. 1.
20. Donald, "The Southerner as a Fighting Man," 79.

hopeless task of advising the private soldier to be obedient to his superiors and instead publicized letters highly critical of officers who gave peremptory or insulting orders to their men. Such editors enjoyed poking fun at the pretensions of commanders. Almost with glee one newspaper in hilly northwest Georgia, an area of few slaves, reported that while on guard duty "one of our 'boys'" failed to salute a general. When the officer demanded an explanation, the sentinel merely replied, "Oh, h_ll, General, that's played out." To emphasize the common soldier's triumph over pompous military behavior, the newspaper added, "The General rode on." Similarly, a South Carolina journal delighted in the fact that a private on sentry duty made his general mark time when the commander forgot the password. Distaste for the regimentation of military life has been characteristic of American soldiers in every war, but "southern soldiers never truly accepted the idea that discipline is necessary to the effective functioning of a fighting force."[21]

Thus the sturdy sense of individual worth which ameliorated class tensions among whites before the war had a dysfunctional effect in the Confederate army. By resisting a form of discipline which negated the official social standard of equality among all white people, nonslaveholding soldiers reduced the efficiency of the Confederate fighting machine. These yeomen farmers who filled the ranks as privates were neither disloyal to the South nor motivated by a desire to aid the United States. They simply were determined not to submit to treatment which they regarded as insulting, high-handed, or unjust. Although regional identification strongly influenced their actions, stubborn individualism and an insistence on one's social position proved to be the more powerful, controlling factors. In the Confederate army, experience demonstrated that in some situations the dynamics of the class system could weaken the war effort.

This was a significant fact, for the unaccustomed routine of army life was only one of many changes which war imposed on the South. The many others—including shortages of basic commodities, ram-

21. Rome (Ga.) *Weekly Courier*, January 17, 1862, p. 3, October 17, 1862, p. 2; Edgefield (S.C.) *Advertiser*, August 20, 1862, p. 1; Donald, "The Southerner as a Fighting Man," 74–75.

pant inflation, increased taxation, impressment, and a breakdown of the transportation system—all contributed to widespread economic disruption and suffering. These developments placed heavy demands on the mechanisms of interclass unity and tested the devotion of the ordinary nonslaveholder to his country's cause. There was a limit to every southerner's endurance, and yeomen farmers reached theirs quickly when they felt that the war only served the interests of the slaveholder while it injured their own. Similarly, injustices which bore on the common people or discrimination in favor of the wealthy eroded the loyalty of the nonslaveholding majority on whom the Confederate government depended. These ordinary southerners did not go over to the opposing side, but they often withdrew from active participation in the battle for independence and went home to protect their families. This kind of quiet rebellion, sparked by a sense of exploitation and injustice, helped to cripple the Confederate war effort, and only the knowledge that the wealthy classes were making sacrifices equal to those of the poverty-stricken nonslaveholders might have been able to avert it.

Economic difficulties for the ordinary southern citizen arose at an early date due to the war's powerful impact on civilian life. With astonishing rapidity many items of everyday use appreciated in price and became unattainable or dearly purchased luxuries. As one newspaper in upland South Carolina described the situation, salt was "high and hard to get," oats at $1 "and on the rise," eggs scarce, and "shoes and hats . . . away up yonder." The shortage of salt forced southerners to extract small residues of this necessary seasoning from the soil of the smokehouse floor. Butter also grew scarce, and for sugar most families had to turn to sorghum as a substitute. Faced with a shortage of flour, southern women relied on rice or corn meal more extensively in baking and used white potatoes to make pie crusts. Additional items that were in short supply included almost every variety of spice, vinegar, baking soda, and fodder for animals. Many Confederates sorely missed coffee, since before the end of 1861 this popular beverage had almost disappeared. In the last three and a half years of the war all but the wealthiest southerners drank various unsatisfactory substitutes for the real thing. Parched corn, rye, wheat, okra seed, sweet potatoes, chicory, or blends of these, took the place of coffee or stretched treasured hoards of the dark brown beans. Struggling to obtain many basic commodities, people rejoiced when they were able to purchase a much-sought-after item or received a useful gift from a friend. J. B. Jones, a War Department clerk, happily noted in his diary for November 6, 1863: "My wife, today, presented me with an excellent undershirt, made of one of her dilapidated petticoats. A new shirt would cost $30."[22]

Ironically, the initial enthusiasm for volunteering created some of the shortages which plagued the common people. Artisans played a vital role in the South's predominantly rural society and many families depended on the skills of a local craftsman who served the needs of a whole county. The rush of volunteers at the beginning of the war deprived numerous areas of essential or nearly essential services, and usually conscription only aggravated the problem. Frustrated by serious disruption of their local economies, hundreds of citizens from all parts of the Confederacy sent petitions to the Richmond administration. These petitions, filed with the correspondence of the War Department, provide graphic illustrations of the practical difficulties and economic distress which war brought to isolated rural communities.

In September, 1861, William B. Mason and forty-five other residents of Newport, Virginia, in the Allegheny Mountains, wrote to Jefferson Davis and explained their need for a tanner. Asking the president to arrange for the discharge of their local tanner, who had been called into the militia, these citizens complained that they would soon run out of shoe leather. Other counties and states encountered the same problem and made similar requests, often with the support and confirmation of their congressmen or state representative.[23] Nor

22. Edgefield (S.C.) *Advertiser*, September 24, 1862; Mary Elizabeth Massey, *Ersatz in the Confederacy* (Columbia, S.C.: University of South Carolina Press, 1952), 63–68, 70–74; J. B. Jones, *A Rebel War Clerk's Diary*, ed. Howard Swiggett (2 vols.; New York: Old Hickory Bookshop, 1935), II, 90.

23. William B. Mason and forty-five others to Jefferson Davis, received September 20, 1861, in Letters Received, Confederate Secretary of War, in RG 109, NA, Microcopy M 437, Roll 10, pp. 160–62. See also Roll 23, pp. 523–26, Roll 25, pp. 398–404, and Roll 44, pp. 44–51.

were the tanners the only craftsmen whom southern communities needed to maintain the activities of daily life. Twenty-nine citizens of Rockingham County, Virginia, wrote the secretary of war early in 1862 and asked for the detail (that is, the assignment) of their cabinet-maker to his workshop. These people did not want the craftsman to supply them with furniture but with a more basic item—coffins. Georgians, South Carolinians, and residents of other states made pleas for the exemption of their physicians. Clearly the army needed doctors, but many isolated communities worried about the prospect of facing the sickly season without any medical assistance.[24] Potters, millers, wheelwrights, and other artisans also rendered valuable service to their communities, for many ordinary items such as buckets and barrels quickly became scarce during the war. The governor of Alabama attempted to obtain the discharge of a man who ran a wool-carding machine, for without the man's assistance his neighbors could not turn their supply of raw wool into cloth.[25] Almost invariably the War Department, taking the position that legal exemptions did not apply to men already in the army, turned down such petitions.

Undoubtedly the Confederate officials reasoned that citizens left at home would have to do without convenient but nonessential items during the war. To many southerners, however, the presence of craftsmen who were in the army seemed vital. The blacksmith, for example, fulfilled a particularly important role in many cases as the individual who repaired farm tools and implements. Scores of petitions sought the release of smiths, such as that from a group of citizens from Patrick County, Virginia, who unsuccessfully argued that their blacksmith would "render more good Service as a Smith at home than he would in the Confederate army." A similar fate awaited

24. Archibald Holland to George W. Randolph, March 27, 1862, in Letters Received, Confederate Secretary of War, in RG 109, NA, Microcopy M 437, Roll 50, pp. 644–47, and P. P. Butts and others of Thomaston, Georgia, to the Secretary of War, June 5, 1862, Roll 34, pp. 1–2. See also Roll 39, pp. 1914–17, Roll 47, pp. 1226–31, Roll 63, pp. 976–80, and Roll 66, pp. 754–60.

25. Massey, *Ersatz in the Confederacy*, 136–37; J. G. Shorter to James Seddon, December 8, 1862, in Letters Received, Confederate Secretary of War, in RG 109, NA, Microcopy M 437, Roll 73, pp. 802–805. See also Roll 40, pp. 1245–47, Roll 80, pp. 193–98, and Roll 92, pp. 100–101.

the plea of a group of Alabamians who felt that men fighting in the field deserved to know that their families at home would be able to raise their crops. This Alabama petition begged for consideration of "the distressed Condition of this our Section of Country on account of being left entierly Destitute of any man that is able to keep in order any kind of Farming Tules, Such as the few aged Farmers and families of Those that is gone to defend there rites is Compeled to have to make Support With."[26]

Probably a portion of such petitions were designed to liberate some soldier who did not want to remain in the army. Occasionally documents which reached the War Department revealed that the soldier himself had initiated the petition, and two men who claimed to be operating a tannery necessary to the community virtually admitted that they had only recently established their tan yard. One conscript from Tennessee tried to strike a bargain with the government by saying that he would put three shoe-peg machines into operation if the conscription officers did not enroll him. Miles Botts, a gunsmith and member of the Twelfth Virginia Regiment implicitly revealed his attitude toward military life: "Having been informed that the government is in want of gunsmiths and that being my trade I would like very much to be detailed."[27] On the other hand, many areas of the South suffered from a shortage of skilled workmen, and undoubtedly most petitions expressed a real need.

For thousands of southern families the most crucial problem was the loss of one man: the husband, father, and breadwinner. While editors and proslavery propagandists boasted that the war would demonstrate the great value of slaves, who could work the fields while white men fought, nonslaveholding families confronted a severe

26. Citizen of Patrick County, Virginia, to the War Department, March 23, 1863, and Citizens of Dale County, Alabama, to the Secretary of War, March 15, 1863, in Letters Received, Confederate Secretary of War, in RG 109, NA, Microcopy M 437, Roll 84, pp. 912–14, and Roll 110, pp. 1000–1002.

27. M. J. Marley and E. G. Westcott to the Secretary of War, May 17, 1862, W. J. Andrews to the Secretary of War, October 26, 1862, and Miles Botts to Judah Benjamin, received January 8, 1862, in Letters Received, Confederate Secretary of War, in RG 109, NA, Microcopy M 437, Roll 60, pp. 1183–87, Roll 30, pp. 1291–92, and Roll 20, pp. 1781–82.

shortage of labor. As the Edgefield, South Carolina, *Advertiser* observed, "The duties of war have called away from home the sole supports of many, many families. . . . Help must be given, or the poor will suffer." On most one-man farms, the wife had performed a full complement of chores and cared for the children while her husband cultivated the land. When the men from such farms went into the army, the women left behind had more work to do than any single individual could manage. Even if a family owned a few slaves, the wife frequently found it difficult to supervise the slaves effectively. Tied down by six small children, one Georgia woman found that the slaves brought her more worry than comfort, and she protested to Secretary of War Seddon, "I can't manage a farm well enough to make a suporte." Aged parents and widowed mothers often sought the discharge of their sons as did a Virginian who wrote, "If you dount send him home I am bound to louse my crop and cum to suffer. I am eaighty one years of adge." [28] A tone of desperation crept into many of these pleas for the exemption or discharge of the family provider, as it did in a letter from Elizabeth Leeson to Secretary of War Seddon in July, 1863: "I ask in the name of humanity to discharge my husband he is not able to do your government much good and he might do his children some good and thare is no use in keeping a man thare to kill him and leave widows and poore little orphen children to suffer while the rich has aplenty to work for them . . . my poor children have no home nor no Father." [29]

These examples did not represent isolated cases of hardship. In every part of the South newspapers described the terrible suffering among soldiers' families and called upon more fortunate citizens to "Relieve the Destitute" or "Think of the Poor." Little more than a year into the war the Atlanta *Daily Intelligencer* reported that "want

28. Edgefield (S.C.) *Advertiser*, March 5, 1862; Mrs. L. Bonnel to Secretary of War Seddon, May 4, 1864, and Joseph B. Bowles to John Letcher, September 12, 1861, in Letters Received, Confederate Secretary of War, in RG 109, NA, Microcopy M 437, Roll 120, pp. 508–510, and Roll 10, pp. 163–64.

29. Elizabeth Leeson to James Seddon, July 22, 1863, in Letters Received, Confederate Secretary of War, in RG 109, NA, Microcopy M 437, Roll 100, pp. 664–66. See also Roll 10, pp. 1227–33, Roll 30, pp. 982–85 and 1501–1505.

and starvation are staring thousands in the face. . . . Around fireless hearths many will be the cries of cold and hunger." State governors appealed to Confederate authorities and emphasized in the strongest terms that the government had to take some steps to alleviate the condition of the common people. In March, 1863, for example, Governor Vance of North Carolina, a state which had many areas with few slaves, wrote that conscription had swept off "a large class whose labor was, I fear, absolutely necessary to the existence of the women and children left behind." South Carolina's Governor M. L. Bonham reported in June, 1864, that there were almost no men left at home in the state's nonslaveholding regions. Although the officials of South Carolina usually showed great concern for the safety of Charleston, in this instance Bonham urged the secretary of war not to call up three regiments of state troops for service in Charleston. The worried governor predicted that if the Confederate government took the troops, "there will be a great suffering next year, and . . . possible starvation."[30]

As if to aggravate the serious situation on many southern farms, the Confederate government felt compelled to resort to a system of supplying its armies which Secretary of War Seddon admitted was "the sorest test of [the people's] partiotism and self sacrificing spirit." Seizing needed suppies by impressment, Seddon conceded, was "a harsh, unequal, and odious mode of supply." Hard-pressed Confederate commanders had to requisition supplies from the surrounding region, and since all areas of the Confederacy did not feel the war equally, some citizens gave more than their share to the army. Those who lived near major roads or railway connections always received closer attention from impressment officers than farmers who lived in relatively inaccessible locations. As the lines of the conflicting armies shifted back and forth, some southerners even found that both armies took their food or livestock. Motivated by concern for public morale and agricultural productivity, an Alabama resident warned Secretary

30. Atlanta *Daily Intelligencer*, September 4, 1862; Zebulon Vance to Jefferson Davis, March 31, 1863, in *Official Records*, Ser. IV, Vol. II, 464–65; M. L. Bonham to James Seddon, June 2, 1864, in *Official Records*, Ser. I, Vol. XXXV, Pt. II, 519–20.

Seddon that there was "great complaint among the people" about the army's seizure of work oxen, mules, milk cows, and heifers large enough to have calves. When Confederate officers impressed food in a nonslaveholding area of Georgia which had suffered through a drought the previous summer, Governor Joseph E. Brown alerted Davis that "If this continues the rebellion in that section will grow, and soldiers in service will desert to go to the relief of their suffering families."[31]

The War Department tried to avoid abuses of impressment by disciplining its troops, but reports arrived of property taken in a "grossly illegal manner," and the governor of Florida complained that troops had seized the last milk cows from starving families of soldiers. In Mississippi in 1864 "the most scandalous outrages" took place according to Seddon, who also condemned the "lawless conduct of sabaltern officers." Yet, even had all Confederate troops respected farmers' rights, in many instances the central government would not have been able to pay for the provisions which it impressed. Commissary agents who did pay for meat or grain offered far less than the market price and occasionally even less than the owner's cost. Expressing a position frequently taken by southern newspapers, the Richmond *Examiner* declared that although impressment might be necessary, the compensation paid by the government was too low.[32] Even the passage in March, 1863, of a bill which allowed farmers to appeal to three appraisers, chosen jointly by the farmer and the impressment agent, failed to remove the widespread discontent over the prices paid for impressed goods.

31. James Seddon to Jefferson Davis, November 26, 1863, in Letters Sent by the Confederate Secretary of War to the President, in RG 109, NA, Microcopy M 523, Roll 1, pp. 120–35; David Anderson, Jr., to James Seddon, May 11, 1863, and W. M. Byrd to James Seddon, March 22, 1864, in Letters Received, Confederate Secretary of War, in RG 109, NA, Microcopy M 437, Roll 80, pp. 431–35 and Roll 120, pp. 280–84; Joseph E. Brown to Jefferson Davis, February 18, 1863, in Allen D. Candler (ed.), *The Confederate Records of the State of Georgia* (6 vols.; Atlanta: Chas. P. Byrd, 1910), III, 328.

32. Preston Pond, Jr., to Henry Allen, May 8, 1864, in *Official Records*, Ser. IV, Vol. III, 398–400, John Milton to James Seddon, January 26, 1864, pp. 45–48, James Seddon to Lt. General R. Taylor, September 27, 1864, pp. 688–90, Charles Taylor to Major R. W. N. Noland, January 6, 1865, pp. 1005–1006, and John Breckinridge to Jefferson Davis, February 18, 1865, p. 1094.

The destruction of property which frequently accompanied the encampment of troops proved costly and galling to ordinary southerners. Soldiers ruined crops, slaughtered animals, and tore up fencing and dismantled outbuildings in order to obtain firewood. William R. Ashton of Virginia wrote to President Davis in August, 1862, and lamented that his "whole place [was] perfectly desolated. . . . The work of destruction could not have been more complete if the troops had been sent for no other purpose than to destroy." One woman asserted that the troops which had camped on her land even had the nerve to "catch up the fowls before my eyes" and shot two of her slaves who tried to protect her property. Commenting on such cases, the Richmond *Enquirer* reported in August, 1862, "We often hear persons say, 'The *Yankees cannot do us any more harm than our own soldiers have done.*'" Partisan rangers, who had an ill-defined freedom of action, caused so many complaints that the secretary of war recommended that the government abolish and disband all units. Cavalry detachments enjoyed the same notorious reputation and evoked this eloquent denunciation from North Carolina's Governor Vance:

> If God Almighty had yet in store another plague worse than all others which he intended to have let loose on the Egyptians in case Pharoah still hardened his heart, I am sure it must have been a regiment or so of half-armed, half-disciplined Confederate cavalry. Had they been turned loose among Pharoah's subjects, with or without an impressment law, he would have become so sensible of the anger of God that he never would have followed the children of Israel to the Red Sea! No, sir; not an inch![33]

These kinds of bitter experiences caused the Confederate government to lose the loyalty and support of many of its poorest citizens.

33. William R. Ashton to Jefferson Davis, August 23, 1862, and Mrs. Judith Watkins to James Seddon, March 5, 1863, in Letters Received, Confederate Secretary of War, in RG 109, NA, Microcopy M 437, Roll 30, pp. 989–92 and Roll 90, pp. 533–35; *Daily Richmond Enquirer*, August 22, 1862, p. 2; James Seddon to Jefferson Davis, November 26, 1863, in Letters Sent by the Confederate Secretary of War to the President, in RG 109, NA, Microcopy M 523, Roll 1, pp. 120–35; Zebulon Vance to James Seddon, December 21, 1863, in *Official Records*, Ser. IV, Vol. II, 1061–62.

Frequently, sheer economic privation drove nonslaveholding southerners to the edge of despair and robbed them of enthusiasm for the
war. These common citizens felt that while they owed the duty of
military service to the government, the Confederacy also owed them
the right to live. Pressing this logic on President Davis, local officials
from Taylor County, Florida, asked that fifteen or twenty potential
conscripts be allowed to remain at home to care for eighty or one
hundred soldiers' families "who are generally very destitute. . . . If
this petition is not granted . . . in our humble opinion the women
and children of our county are bound to come to suffering if not starvation." Both newspapers and government officials who were sta-
tioned close to the people reached the same conclusion: "When our
brave and true men, shall hear that their wives and little ones are
actually suffering for bread, they will naturally become restless and
dissatisfied, and mutiny in our army will result, as naturally and as
certainly as gravitation."[34]

As unbearable economic difficulties brought thousands of southerners to the breaking point, the specific complaint varied. The imposition of the tax-in-kind drove a tax assessor in Georgia to exclaim,
"This is a very pore County of peopl and most all of the working Class
of the cuntry is in the army and ther [are] Famileys in Scores that
has not a year of corn." Inexorably rising prices compelled one
woman to write the secretary of war anonymously and demand, "Tell
me how can a poor man live—but worse than that a widow with
some five or six children or a poor soldiers wife?" The prospect of
short crops, decayed fencing, and inadequate pay for their husbands
led women in Miller County, Georgia, to pour out their complaints
in an anonymous petition which closed with a lengthy, strongly
worded threat:

> An allwise god . . . will send down his fury and judgement in a very
> grate manar [on] all those our leading men and those that are in power

34. Petition from officials in Taylor County, Florida, to Jefferson Davis, August 11,
1863, in *Official Records*, Ser. IV, Vol. II, 839–40; Rome (Ga.) *Weekly Courier*, April 11,
1862, p. 1; W. S. Keen, Provost Marshal of Allegheny County, Virginia, to the Secretary of
War, April 2, 1863, in Letters Received, Confederate Secretary of War, in RG 109, NA,
Microcopy M 437, Roll 110, pp. 1045–47.

ef thare is no more favors shone to those the mothers and wives and of those hwo in poverty has with patrootism stood the fence Battles. . . . I tell you that with out some grate and speadly alterating in the conduckting of afares in this our little nation god will frown on it and that speadly.[35]

Perhaps the height of desperation was reached by a Virginia woman who could no longer stand her own "deplorable" condition or "the wail of the widows and orphans, the poor and oppressed." In October, 1864, she asked for a sixty-day furlough for her husband so that she could journey to Washington and see the leaders of the United States. Hoping that she could "penetrate those hard hearts," she asked, "Do you believe a *Lady* could do anything with them?"[36]

But economic hardship was not the only cause of disaffection. Class resentments played an even more critical role in alienating the yeomen from the cause of the Confederacy. During the war tensions and bitterness of the southern class system surfaced strongly, as southerners of slight or modest means looked up from their daily struggle to stay alive and saw that many wealthy individuals seemed to enjoy the position of a privileged class. The feeling that all classes were not sharing equally in the sacrifices of the war and that rich slaveholders were escaping their burdens turned many small farmers and nonslaveholders away from the Richmond government. Believing in their own worth and in their right to equal treatment as citizens of a democracy, the common people could not stomach the favoritism and special consideration which allowed some members of the planter class to avoid danger and continue to make profits. In an ironic change of circumstance, the rhetoric of white democracy that the planter class had used before the war to defend its power justified many nonslaveholders in the decision to withdraw their

35. A. Dean to James Seddon, November 28, 1863, "A Lady" to James Seddon, received August 18, 1863, and Petition from women of Miller County, Georgia, to the Secretary of War and the President, September 8, 1863, in Letters Received, Confederate Secretary of War, in RG 109, NA, Microcopy M 437, Roll 90, pp. 351–53 and Roll 80, pp. 700–705 and 776–80.

36. Mrs. R. H. Hinolin to Secretary of War Seddon, October 27, 1864, *ibid.*, Roll 130, pp. 730–32.

support from the Confederacy. Resentment of injustices and class discriminations pushed discontent over the threshold of action and thus contributed fundamentally to the failure of Confederate nationalism.

Although Jefferson Davis hoped that war would knit southerners together, the gap between the classes widened, as many upper-class southerners seemed totally unable to imagine what life was like for the common people. Economic difficulties affected almost everyone, but the adjustments required of each social class were on different orders of magnitude. Even Mary Boykin Chesnut, usually a keen and sensitive observer of people and events, was slow to appreciate the sacrifices which the poor had to make. Although many southern yeomen ran out of coffee in the summer of 1861, not until January 29, 1862, did Mrs. Chesnut record with amazement in her dairy that some people parched rye and drank it instead of coffee. As the war dragged on and conditions worsened, she continued to fill pages with accounts of the dinner parties she attended and lists of the fine dishes which she was served. Young ladies from the planter class still enjoyed their flirtations and parties, and although the war eventually forced them to turn their gowns inside out, this regrettable necessity scarcely affected their scale of values. Life for them was still a game, and although their parents felt the war more deeply, the upper class sacrificed luxuries while poorer Confederates faced a grim struggle for existence. The relatively carefree life-style of the upper class in the midst of war and poverty did not pass unnoticed by the common people. The Rome, Georgia, *Weekly Courier* expressed the feelings of mountain whites when it stated in October, 1862, that "there is one mode that would work most successfully in bringing down the prices of everything, and that is for the wealthier classes to practice, for awhile, the rigid self-denial that the poor are compelled to practice."[37]

The feeling against class favoritism arose at a very early date in the

37. Chesnut, *Diary*, 187, 255–57, 364, 366–67, 288; Eliza Frances Andrews, *The War-Time Journal of a Georgia Girl, 1864–1865*, ed. Spencer Bidwell King, Jr. (Macon, Ga.: Ardivan Press, 1960), 71, 76, 53, 95; Rome (Ga.) *Weekly Courier*, October 31, 1862, p. 1.

war and increased as conditions worsened. Perhaps the first situation which stirred angry feelings of discrimination among nonslaveholders was an apparent inequality in the acceptance of volunteers. Since volunteers for three years or the duration of the war exceeded the Confederacy's supply of arms, the government decided to accept and arm only long-term volunteers. To increase the size of the forces, however, Davis' administration made an exception and allowed companies that could arm and equip their own men to enter the service for only twelve months. This created an unfair difference in treatment, because in effect the price of being a patriot was higher for the common man than for the rich man, three times higher to be exact. Only men from the wealthier classes could afford to form twelve-months units.[38]

Yet the small farmers and nonslaveholders most needed a short enlistment, for they could ill afford to leave their homes for an extended period. In May, 1861, James Phelan, a Confederate senator from Mississippi, advised Jefferson Davis that "the idea of an indefinite absence or a protracted absence is not eagerly embraced by the comparatively lethargic masses of our rural population" as compared to "the pride of intellect, position, and education." William Brooks, who had presided at Alabama's secession convention, described a similar situation in Perry County, where the majority held no slaves. Nonslaveholders there had adopted "the belief that nothing is now in peril in the prevailing war but the title of the master to his slaves," and they had "not unfrequently declared that they will 'fight for no rich man's slaves.'" After some well-placed men succeeded in "partially" changing these sentiments and raised 250 to 300 soldiers from the hill-county population, the government announced its regulations that barred this unit from serving except for three years. These "poor laboring men, who own no slaves and live in non-slaveholding communities" naturally compared their lot to that of "the slaveholders [who] can enter the army and quit it at the end of twelve months."

38. A. T. Bledsoe, Chief of the Bureau of War, admitted that this policy had created "no little dissatisfaction in the country." A. T. Bledsoe to John B. Sale, June 17, 1861, in *Official Records*, Ser. IV, Vol. I, 380.

Concluding with the remark "I leave you to imagine the consequences," Brooks urged Davis to change the War Department's
policy.[39]

The adoption of conscription in 1862 exacerbated this problem
rather than relieving it. The Confederate Congress did not enact a
levee en masse but rather a system much like the twentieth century's
selective service. In order to maintain essential civilian activities,
the congress exempted such categories as state and Confederate officials, transportation workers, miners, factory operatives, some teachers, and some apothecaries, in addition to the physically unfit. Perhaps the common people would have accepted this system if the
government had administered it with rigid equity, but examples of
favoritism appeared in almost every community, and the system itself allowed a method of escape from military service for any man
with sufficient means. These exemption laws infringed a basic sense
of fairness and equity and aroused much outrage. P. A. Wellford, a
captain and assistant commissary of subsistence, recognized that the
people would only accept measures which were both "necessary and
uniform," and he wrote wisely when he declared that "to this latter
condition even more importance is attached than to the other. . . .
The neglect of this rule has been a greater cause of dissatisfaction and
complaint than all the other acts of the Government combined."[40]

Inequities in the administration of the conscription and exemption
laws produced disastrous results for the Confederacy. Judge Robert S.
Hudson warned Jefferson Davis that the incompetency, favoritism,
and laxness of conscription officers caused much of "the real and admitted disloyalty, discontent, and desertions" in Mississippi. Striking
the same note, an anonymous correspondent from Georgia charged
that "its a notorious fact if a man has influential friends—or a little
money to spare he will never be enrolled." In October, 1862, a Virginian who added the caption, "A Poor man," beneath his signature
made the often-heard complaint that many men who came home on

39. James Phelan to Jefferson Davis, May 23, 1861, and William M. Brooks to Jefferson
Davis, May 13, 1861, *ibid.*, 352–53 and 318–19.
40. For the text of this exemption act, see Candler (ed.), *Confederate Records of Georgia*, III, 201–202; P. A. Wellford to Brigadier General I. M. St. John, February 24, 1865, in
Official Records, Ser. IV, Vol. III, 1113–14.

short furloughs were still at their homes "well & hearty" more than three months later, and that other healthy soldiers had contrived to obtain discharges.[41]

Some eligible conscripts, aided by friendly doctors, managed to escape service through rulings of the exemption boards. Virginia's Governor John Letcher found that an appalling number of men were able to obtain certificates of disability at the beginning of that state's system of conscription, and complaints from other states were of the same character. Perhaps men from all classes sought exemptions from service, but poor men often felt that only the rich, who had better connections, succeeded. Robert H. Whitfield, a congressman from Virginia, suggested to Secretary of War Seddon in March, 1864, that the exemption boards may have ruled unjustly. "There is much complaint," Whitfield wrote, "and if what I hear is true, the public interest, and common justice to the poor and uninfluential demand investigation."[42]

One of the greatest causes of discontent was the system of substitution. In 1862, the Rome, Georgia, *Weekly Courier* propounded its concept of the principle on which the South's revolution depended: "*All classes of the community MUST do their share of the fighting*, the high, the low, the rich and poor, and those who have *the means MUST pay the expense*, as those who have not the means cannot pay." Soon, however, it seemed to many yeomen farmers that the wealthy were using their great means not to finance the war but to buy their way out of it. Under conscription the War Department allowed men to furnish substitutes, who agreed to serve in place of others for a price. Some newspapers like the Richmond *Examiner* openly defended this controversial system. Arguing that certain people were more valuable to society as citizens than as soldiers, the *Ex-*

41. Robert S. Hudson to Jefferson Davis, October 5, 1863, in *Official Records*, Ser. IV, Vol. II, 856–58; A Friend to the Confederate Government to the Secretary of War, September 3, 1862, and William R. Allen to George Randolph, October 25, 1862, in Letters Received, Confederate Secretary of War, in RG 109, NA, Microcopy M 437, Roll 30, pp. 1058–59 and 1386–87.

42. *Official Records*, Ser. IV, Vol. I, 1021; "A Soldier" to the Secretary of War, August 30, 1863, and Robert H. Whitfield to James Seddon, March 1, 1864, in Letters Received, Confederate Secretary of War, in RG 109, NA, Microcopy M 437, Roll 80, pp. 746–48 and Roll 120, pp. 116–20.

aminer arrogantly asserted that "this ability to pay the commutation is, in most cases, the best proof of the citizen's social and industrial value." Whatever the defects of the *Examiner*'s argument, many citizens did possess ample ability to pay. One anonymous writer charged that some men had paid up to $5,000 for a substitute, and another man who adamantly defended substitution confirmed this claim by admitting that some contracts reached the sum of $6,000. In 1864 Mary Boykin Chesnut recorded an acquaintance's admission that his grandson had "spent a fortune in substitutes. Two have been taken from him, and two he paid to change with him when he was ordered to the front. He is at the end of his row now, for all able-bodied men are ordered to the front. I hear he is going as some general's courier."[43]

Some Confederate officials recognized at an early date that the policy of allowing substitution represented a grave error. In August, 1862, Secretary of War George Randolph reported to Davis that substitution had "led to great abuses. The procuration of substitutes has become a regular business." Indeed, substitutes had become a commodity, whose price J. B. Jones recorded in his diary as an index of inflation. Making what he called a "moderate estimate," the assistant adjutant general of the Confederacy declared that there were 50,000 able-bodied conscripts who had employed a substitute. The total may have been considerably higher, although a group of high-ranking officers from the Army of Tennessee probably exaggerated when they placed the number in excess of 150,000. In any case the large number of substitutes constituted what Bell Wiley has called "a shameful reflection on Confederate patriotism." Realizing that most substitutes deserted, the government gradually restricted the privilege over the vehement protests of many wealthy southerners, but it was

43. Rome (Ga.) *Weekly Courier*, October 24, 1862, p. 3; *Daily Richmond Examiner*, January 31, 1862, p. 2; [?] to James Seddon, January 29, 1864, and [?] to the Secretary of War, December 10, 1863, in Letters Received, Confederate Secretary of War, in RG 109, NA, Microcopy M 437, Roll 118, pp. 114–17 and Roll 80, pp. 1028–33; Chesnut, *Diary*, 415. The statement that two substitutes had been "taken from him" refers to the fact that conscription laws drafted some men who were serving for others and that the congress abolished substitutions at the beginning of 1864.

not until the beginning of 1864 that the congress finally abolished this demoralizing and counter-productive system.[44]

For some men the abolition of substitution represented only a greater challenge to their ingenuity. President Davis himself expressed concern over the large number of men who managed to find employment at depots and supply offices. Numerous letters from anonymous citizens, some of whom signed with a phrase such as "A looker on injustice," complained about the robust young men who filled "bombproof" offices in the expanding Confederate bureaucracy such as quartermasters, commissaries, clerks, or warehouse workers. One Virginian named J. M. Radford warned Seddon that such facts created dangerous feelings among the common people:

> It is impossible to make *poor* people comprehend the policy of putting the able-bodied, healthy, Mr. A. in such light service as collecting tithes and money *at home*, when the well known feeble & delicate Mr. B.— who is a poor man with a large family of children depending on him for bread—is sent to the front. . . . I beseech you to be warned of the coming storm—the people will not *always* submit to this *unequal, unjust* and partial distribution of favor and wholesale conscription of the *poor* while the able-bodied & healthy men of property are all occupying *soft places*.[45]

Support for this conclusion came from many other sources. For example, a correspondent from Louisiana asserted that the large number of staff appointments which went to inexperienced but well-placed

44. George Randolph to Jefferson Davis, August 12, 1862, in *Official Records*, Ser. IV, Vol. II, 42–49; Jones, *A Rebel War Clerk's Diary*, II, 219; Assistant Adjutant General Samuel W. Melton to James Seddon, November 11, 1863, in *Official Records*, Ser. IV, Vol. II, 944–52; *Official Records*, Ser. IV, Vol. II, 670–71; Bell Irvin Wiley, *The Life of Johnny Reb: The Common Soldier of the Confederacy* (New York: Bobbs-Merrill Company, 1943), 127. In the United States men were allowed to provide substitutes all through the war, and until July 2, 1864, they could avoid service simply by paying a fee of $300. Over 86,000 paid their fee and gained the privilege of staying home.

45. Jefferson Davis to Robert E. Lee, August 2, 1863, in Dunbar Rowland (ed.), *Jefferson Davis: Constitutionalist; His Letters, Papers, and Speeches* (10 vols.; Jackson, Miss.: Little & Ives Co., 1923), V, 583–84; "A looker on injustice" to James Seddon, July 10, 1863, and [?] to the War Department, September 10, 1862, in Letters Received, Confederate Secretary of War, in RG 109, NA, Microcopy M 437, Roll 80, pp. 623–24 and Roll 30, pp. 1060–61; also J. M. Radford to James Seddon, October 17, 1864, in Letters Received, Confederate Secretary of War, in RG 109, NA, Microcopy M 437, Roll 140, pp. 110–14.

young men fed the impression that "'this is a war for the rich man.'"
One of Jefferson Davis' staunch supporters, a senator from Mississippi, warned the president that apparently "nine tenths of the young-
sters of the land whose relatives are conspicuous in society, wealthy,
or influential obtain some safe perch where they can doze with their
heads under their wings." A group of citizens from North Carolina
who protested the excessive number of railway conductors in their
area deplored the fact that "there is no exemption for the honest
Farmer, the bone and sinew of the country."[46]

The honest farmer, who received no exemption, grew particularly
angry when he discovered that prosperous slaveowning planters were
entitled to stay home. In its first exemption law the congress made
no provision for overseers or managers of slaves, and the Davis administration refused to allow conscripted managers of plantations to
stay at home. But the congress bowed to an avalanche of protests
from planters and state officials and in October, 1862, authorized the
exemption of one white man for every twenty Negroes under his control. Almost immediately this statute, notoriously called the "twenty
nigger law," created resentment among the Confederacy's small farmers. One congressman warned the government that "never did a law
meet with more universal odium than the exemption of slave-owners.
. . . Its influence upon the poor is most calamitous, and has awakened a spirit and elicited a discussion of which we may safely predict
the most unfortunate results. . . ." The general assembly of the state
of North Carolina formally protested the "unjust discrimination" of
this law and other exemptions for the rich and called on the congress
to repeal such provisions "at the earliest possible day." Although the
War Department recognized the dire effect of the law, the congress
enacted only mild measures to restrict the exemption of overseers.
Conscription officers found that planters gladly paid a $500 tax im-

46. I. D. Allen to the Secretary of War, April 3, 1863, in Letters Received, Confederate
Secretary of War, in RG 109, NA, Microcopy M 437, Roll 80, pp. 480–88; James Phelan to
Jefferson Davis, December 9, 1862, in *Official Records* Ser. I, Vol. XVII, Pt. II, 788–92;
"Many Citizens" to James Seddon, received July 6, 1863, in Letters Received, Confederate
Secretary of War, in RG 109, NA, Microcopy M 437, Roll 80, pp. 603–606.

posed on overseers in May, 1863, and Colonel T. P. August of the
conscription bureau lamented that the tax was not much higher, since
it would have been an assured source of revenue.[47]

Issues such as the "twenty nigger law" opened a breach between
the planter class on the one hand and the small farmers and nonslaveholders on the other. There were many cases of individual planters who aided their poorer neighbors, and private charity expanded
greatly in a vain effort to relieve suffering before conditions overwhelmed it and government had to assume a welfare role. But there
were other wealthy planters who reacted to the stresses of war by
selfishly trying to maintain their customary style of life. Criticizing
such men, the Edgefield, South Carolina, *Advertiser* asked in regard to the Confederacy's soldiers, "What would sooner make them
falter than the cry from their families, 'We are suffering yet those
holding the purse-strings and property will not help?'" Some of the
best-known leaders of the South foolishly defied public opinion and
refused to make the kinds of gestures which could have unified the
people and created the feeling that all classes were pulling together.
At a time when the Augusta *Constitutionalist* and the Charleston
Mercury were urging planters to give up cotton and raise food crops
to supply the soldiers' families, Georgia's Robert Toombs stubbornly
devoted a large fraction of his lands to cotton, despite the protests of
local groups.[48]

When needy yeomen encountered such indifference to their plight
among the wealthy, they felt great frustration and anger. A rebuff at
the hands of well-fed slaveowners drove many hungry mothers almost to distraction. With evident bitterness one woman protested

47. James Phelan to Jefferson Davis, December 9, 1862, in *Official Records*, Ser. I, Vol.
XVII, Pt. II, 790; *Public Laws of the State of North Carolina passed by the General Assem-
bly at its Session of 1862–1863* (Raleigh: W. W. Holden, Printer to the State, 1863), 49;
James Seddon to G. J. Pillow, September 23, 1863, and Colonel T. P. August to Colonel
G. W. Lay, August 10, 1863, in *Official Records*, Ser. IV, Vol. II, 848–49 and 761–63.

48. Edgefield (S.C.) *Advertiser*, July 30, 1862; Charleston *Mercury*, February 1, 1862,
p. 1 (which also quotes the Augusta *Constitutionalist*); Rome (Ga.) *Weekly Courier*, June 20,
1862, p. 1, and July 4, 1862, p. 1.

the "great injustice" of poor men having to serve in the army "whilst the rich man who has never handled a plow or hoe is left to luxuriate and hoard up all he can get his hands on." Another mother of three, who suffered from consumption and was already in need of food in March, 1862, wrote Jefferson Davis, "It is folly for a poor mother to call on the rich people about here there hearts are of steel they would sooner throw what they have to spare to their dogs than give it to a starving child." Then, revealing that her anger extended to and included the government which allowed her to suffer so much, this woman closed with a threat: "If I and my little children suffer [and] die while there Father is in service I invoke God Almighty that our blood rest upon the South." This woman's attitude was one of the signs that economic privation, combined with a conviction that the government allowed injustice and favoritism, was turning many common people away from the Confederacy.[49]

One condition above all others evoked the most complaints of injustice and demands that the government act to relieve the suffering of the people. As shortages appeared and prices soared, people all over the South condemned speculation and extortion, which some felt had caused the problem and which others knew aggravated it. In a period of steadily rising prices, some merchants probably heard the accusation that they were profiteering when in fact rising costs merely had driven up the price. But there were undoubtedly thousands of speculators and an even greater number of citizens who contributed to shortages and high prices by hoarding. The fever affected everyone to some extent. Mary Elizabeth Massey, an historian who has made a valuable study of the problem of shortages in the Confederacy, found that speculation began as soon as the Federal navy established its blockade around the Confederate coast. Speculators bought up stocks of scarce items such as salt, bacon, and leather, and a clique of a half-dozen men obtained control of the Con-

49. Virginia Berry to James Seddon, April 29, 1864, and Almira P. Acors to Jefferson Davis, March 23, 1862, in Letters Received, Confederate Secretary of War, in RG 109, NA, Microcopy M 437, Roll 120, pp. 469–72 and Roll 29, pp. 167–69.

federacy's two nail factories. Prosperous individuals ensured their future comfort by purchasing the entire stock of a store, as did a man in North Carolina and a family in Louisiana. According to the Richmond *Enquirer*, one Confederate bought and hoarded seven hundred barrels of flour, and one planter brought in wagon-loads of supplies until "the lawn and paths looked like a wharf covered with a ship's loads." The governor of Florida informed the Davis administration in June, 1862, that observation had convinced him that some southern businessmen had formed partnerships with men in Havana and New York and were making heavy profits by exchanging cotton for salt, coffee, dry goods, and other articles. Other correspondents warned the War Department that speculators planned to take their profits out of the country if they could obtain a passport.[50]

The governors of the states frequently condemned extortioners and threatened action against them. Before the end of 1861, Alabama's Governor A. B. Moore issued a proclamation denouncing speculators, and the governor of Tennessee spoke out at the same time in an address which the Charleston *Mercury* and other papers quoted. Zeb Vance, urging that the North Carolina convention reconvene to act against extortioners, lamented that "the cry of distress comes up from the poor wives and children of our soldiers . . . what will become of them.?"[51] Joining in the universal but ineffective denunciation of speculation, the Richmond *Examiner* declared, "This disposition to speculate upon the yeomanry of the country . . . is the most mortifying feature of the war." Later the *Examiner* asserted that "native Southern merchants have outdone Yankees and Jews. . . . The whole South stinks with the lust of extortion." When all else failed to have any effect, the Rome, Georgia, *Weekly Courier*

50. Massey, *Ersatz in the Confederacy*, 17, 20–21; John Milton to George Randolph, June 25, 1862, in *Official Records*, Ser. IV, Vol. I, 1173; [?] to the Secretary of War, November 13, 1863, in Letters Received, Confederate Secretary of War, in RG 109, NA, Microcopy M 437, Roll 80, pp. 934–36.
51. *Official Records*, Ser. IV, Vol. I, 697–711; Rome (Ga.) *Weekly Courier*, November 8, 1861, p. 2 (quoting the Charleston *Mercury*); Zebulon Vance to Weldon N. Edwards, September 18, 1862, in *Official Records*, Ser. IV, Vol. II, 85–86.

quoted the Bible against extortioners. Other journals worried about the effect which heartless speculators would have upon the poor. The Lynchburg, Virginia, *Republican*, feared that "the poor of our own town and country will be unable to live at all," and the Atlanta *Daily Intelligencer* wrote that because of speculation, "want and starvation are staring thousands in the face."[52] Citizens' meetings, resolutions against extortion, and even a widespread resort to barter all proved in vain, and bitterness grew over the fact that some prosperous men increased their fortunes during a period of general suffering. A newspaper from the mountain region of Georgia asked, "Can it be possible that the Southern planter, the synonym of nobility and benevolence, can hear the accounts of the desperate battles, the heroic deaths . . . of his gallant countrymen, and then turn away and ingloriously revel amidst his comfort and wealth, and extort upon his government and his people, for the necessaries of life.?"[53]

In their anger against speculators, some soldiers banded together and vowed vengeance on extortioners when peace came or as soon as they returned home. A more common reaction of many soldiers brought immediate aid to their families. In the words of an anonymous Virginian, "what man is there that would stay in the armey and no that his family is sufring at home?" A friend of Jefferson Davis advised the Confederate president in October, 1863, that speculators had been "the cause of thousands of good men leaving their posts and going home to look after their familys." Nor was the reaction against extortion limited only to the men in the armies. An enrolling officer in the mountain areas of South Carolina reported to his superiors that previously loyal civilians were sustaining the deserters in that district. These civilians, the agent noted, "if they do not proclaim hostility to our cause, urge that it is lost because of the specu-

52. Quoted in the Rome (Ga.) *Weekly Courier*, October 18, 1861, p. 1; *Daily Richmond Examiner*, July 22, 1862, p. 2; Rome (Ga.) *Weekly Courier*, January 10, 1862, p. 3; quoted in the Rome (Ga.) *Weekly Courier*, November 22, 1861, p. 2; Atlanta *Daily Intelligencer*, September 4, 1862.
53. *North Carolina Whig* (Charlotte, N.C.), October 22, 1861; Spartanburg (S.C.) *Carolina Spartan*, May 1, 1862; Rome (Ga.) *Weekly Courier*, July 25, 1862, p. 1.

lations and extortions so rampant throughout the land. . . . They swear by all they hold sacred that they will die at home before they will ever be dragged forth again to do battle for such a cause."[54]

Thus class resentments turned many southerners away from the Confederacy. One of the most damaging ways in which southerners withdrew their support from the new nation was to leave the armies. The knowledge that loved ones were suffering at home while others profited gave many soldiers whatever moral justification they needed to desert, and the common man's strong sense of individualism made him bold enough to defy any who would stop him. Many other factors, such as the tedium of camp life, resentment of discipline, failure to receive pay and equipment, and poor medical care, contributed to desertions, but in a large number of cases concern for one's family was paramount. Mrs. Chesnut told of a woman in a "cracker bonnet" who squalled to her husband as they dragged him off, "You desert again, quick as you kin. Come back to your wife and children. Desert, Jake! Desert agin, Jake!" Both state and Confederate officials realized that despairing letters from home played a catalytic role in inducing soldiers to desert.[55]

From the first days of the war there was a small trickle of deserters, but the Confederate government did not show serious concern until the summer of 1862. About the first of that year there were approximately 259,000 men present out of a total enrollment of 327,000. (A portion of the absent always represented those on forlough or sick leave.) Six months later, despite the adoption of conscription, only

---

54. Rome (Ga.) *Weekly Courier*, December 19, 1862, p. 2; [?] to James Seddon, February 9, 1863, in Letters Received, Confederate Secretary of War, in RG 109, NA, Microcopy M 437, Roll 80, pp. 126–30; H. Hinds to Jefferson Davis, October 11, 1863, in Rowland (ed.), *Jefferson Davis*, VI, 59–60; Jno. D. Ashmore to Major C. D. Melton, August 7, 1863, in *Official Records*, Ser. IV, Vol. II, 771–73.

55. Wiley, *Johnny Reb*, Chap. 8; Harry N. Scheiber, "The Pay of Confederate Troops and Problems of Demoralization: A Case of Administrative Failure," *Civil War History*, XV (1969), 226–36; Chesnut, *Diary*, 512; C. D. Melton to John S. Preston, August 25, 1863, in *Official Records*, Ser. IV, Vol. II, 769–70; B. M. Edney to James Seddon, August 18, 1863, in Letters Received, Confederate Secretary of War, in RG 109, NA, Microcopy M 437, Roll 90, pp. 775–76.

224,000 were present of a total force which had remained almost the same. Reacting with alarm to the downward trend of these figures, Secretary of War Randolph dispatched a confidential circular to every state governor on July 17, 1862. In this letter Randolph admitted that the weakness of the Confederate armies was affecting strategy and called on the state executives to use their powers to arrest stragglers and deserters and send them back to their posts. In September, 1862, the War Department reported that it had employed provost marshals to keep order and stem desertion. Davis' administration also took steps to weed out incompetent officers on the assumption that they contributed to "the vast amount of stragglers which now paralyze our Army and defeat all attempts to re-enforce it."[56]

According to Confederate reports, these measures had a beneficial effect, for in April, 1863, the army had 360,000 men present out of a total of 498,000. This marked the high point of Confederate military strength, however. From the spring of 1863 through the end of the war, the curve of army returns plunged downward while that of desertions rose steeply. In June, 1863, the acting chief of the Bureau of Conscription reported that desertion was increasing "with the determination to avoid and even resist future service." Armed bands of deserters now existed in every one of the Atlantic states and elsewhere besides. The defeats at Gettysburg and Vicksburg in July, 1863, represented severe blows to morale and led many soldiers and civilians to conclude that the war was hopeless. In an intradepartmental communication of July 25, 1863, the assistant secretary of war, John A. Campbell, recommended an amnesty for those absent and wondered aloud whether "so general a habit" as desertion should be considered a crime. Campbell estimated that 40,000 or 50,000 men were AWOL and that as many as 100,000 were evading duty in some manner.[57]

Liberal furloughs and a proclamation of amnesty, however, failed

56. *Official Records*, Ser. IV, Vol. I, 822, 1176, and Vol. II, 7; George W. Randolph to Jefferson Davis, September 3, 1862, in Letters Sent by the Confederate Secretary of War to the President, in RG 109, NA, Microcopy M 523, Roll 1, pp. 59–60; George W. Randolph to Ed. Sparrow, September 29, 1862, in *Official Records*, Ser. IV, Vol. II, 97–98.

57. *Official Records*, Ser. IV, Vol. II, 530, 607–608, 674.

to reverse the trend, and a Virginian notified the government that part of the continual stream of deserters from Lee's army was stopping at poor people's houses to "croak about the war, and tell of their hardships,—& that it is useless to fight the Yankees any longer." Admonitions to the public from newspapers and orders to all local commanders to arrest deserters, stragglers, and absentees had little effect. Facing up to the gravity of the situation, the secretary of war reported to Davis on November 26, 1863, that "the effective force of the Army is generally a little more than a half, never two-thirds, of the numbers in the ranks." Even after allowing for absences due to sickness, Secretary Seddon still concluded that one-third of the army was absent without permission.[58]

Ella Lonn, the authority on desertions from both armies during the Civil War, asserted that harsh measures by the Confederate government slowed desertions in the winter of 1863–1864. Even so, at the end of 1863 army returns showed only 278,000 men present out of 465,000, and by the middle of 1864 this total had plummeted to 195,000, while the total enrollment in the armies had dropped to 316,000. The stream of desertion, which widened in 1863, had become a virtual flood. Hundreds of men left the armies every day, even the army of Robert E. Lee. At the end of the war, official Confederate returns showed only 160,000 soldiers present in the armies out of a total of 359,000, and only 126,000 men were ready for duty.[59]

These figures amply justify Lonn's conclusion that there was "an overwhelming amount of desertion in the Confederacy, revealing the important part this factor played in the ultimate failure of the South to achieve independence." All authorities agree that most de-

58. Jefferson Davis to Robert E. Lee, July 28, 1863, in Rowland (ed.), *Jefferson Davis*, V, 579; General Orders No. 109, August 11, 1863, Record Group 109, National Archives, Microcopy T 782, Roll 1, p. 176; [?] to the Secretary of War, August 10, 1863, in Letters Received, Confederate Secretary of War, in RG 109, NA, Microcopy M 437, Roll 80, pp. 683–84; Charleston *Mercury*, August 18, 1863, p. 1; General Orders No. 116, August 31, 1863, RG 109, NA, Microcopy T 782, Roll 1, p. 188; James Seddon to Jefferson Davis, November 26, 1863, in *Official Records*, Ser. IV, Vol. II, 995.

59. Ella Lonn, *Desertion During the Civil War* (New York: Century Co., 1928), 25–27; *Official Records*, Ser. IV, Vol. II, 1073 and Vol. III, 520; Lonn, *Desertion*, 27–29; *Official Records*, Ser. IV, Vol. III, 1182.

sertion came from the poorer classes of society.[60] Since the South could not achieve nationhood without an army, the decision which common soldiers made with their feet sealed the fate of the Confederacy. The large desertions from the southern armies represented an overall judgment by the common people on Jefferson Davis' policies. The action of thousands of soldiers proved that his government had failed to meet their needs and build the kind of morale necessary to endure a long and difficult struggle. Large-scale desertions were a tangible indication of Davis' inability to provide conditions which would promote the spirit of Confederate nationalism.

Southerners who were not in the army also expressed their declining morale and dissatisfaction with the state of the nation. Urban dwellers suffered almost as greatly as the soldiers, for the towns and cities of the Confederacy swelled in population during the war but received inadequate supplies of food as a result of the breakdown of the transportation system. In Charleston, South Carolina, and other urban centers residents organized "free markets" and various charities through which the poor could obtain food or clothing cheaply. Swiftly rising inflation injured everyone, but especially the government employees who had to live on fixed salaries. The diary of J. B. Jones contains many references to his struggle to keep himself and his family fed and clothed. Such conditions contributed to the food riot in Richmond in April, 1863, which President Davis himself had to calm. Although many of the rioters seemed more intent in looting than on obtaining food, there was no doubt that the shortage of food was real and serious. Other food riots in Atlanta and Macon, Georgia, Salisbury and High Point, North Carolina, and Mobile, Alabama, demonstrated the extent of urban suffering.[61]

Civilians in the rural South likewise showed their inability to tolerate the deteriorating conditions of life. To fight impressment which

60. Lonn, *Desertion*, v, 123–24; Wiley, *Johnny Reb*, 145–46.
61. Charleston *Mercury*, November 22, 1862, pp. 1 and 2; Jones, *A Rebel War Clerk's Diary*, II, 9; William J. Kimball, "The Bread Riot in Richmond, 1863," *Civil War History*, VII (1961), 149–54; Emory M. Thomas, *The Confederacy as a Revolutionary Experience* (Englewood Cliffs, N.J.: Prentice-Hall, Inc., 1971), 103–104.

might take away the small supplies they had left, Confederate citizens sometimes resorted to concealment or removal of their threatened property. As Major S. B. French noted, "In all the States impressments are evaded by every means which ingenuity can suggest, and in some openly resisted. In North Carolina our receipts are insignificant, and in Georgia and Alabama we are unable to purchase corn for want of money." Commissary agents found that the nation's farmers, when they would provide food to the government, refused to accept certificates of credit and government bonds as payment, which was required by law. Moreover, the conscription officers who came to localities to induct men into the army increasingly discovered that no one was around to be drafted. In 1864 Senator Herschel Johnson advised Jefferson Davis that "the disposition to avoid military service is . . . general."[62]

By far the most convincing evidence of the common people's alienation from their government and its cause, however, was the steady growth of disaffected areas.[63] In state after state yeoman discontent reached such proportions that certain districts welcomed deserters and fell under the dominant influence of those who wanted to withdraw from the war. The majority of the population in these areas had reached its limit of endurance and hoped to relieve its suffering by ceasing to cooperate with the central government. Through persistent resistance and occasionally violent opposition, disaffected southerners frustrated the purposes of Confederate authorities. Not only did such obstruction remove human and material resources from the war effort, but it also depressed morale in other parts of the South.

Alabama had one of the most persistent and serious problems of disaffection in the Confederacy, and the locus of resistance was in the nonslaveholding northern and southeastern portions of the state. The secretary of war learned as early as January 19, 1862, that a few

62. Major S. B. French to Colonel L. B. Northrop, September 15, 1864, and James Seddon to Howell Cobb, September 15, 1864, in *Official Records*, Ser. IV, Vol. III, 653–54 and 644–45; Herschel Johnson to Jefferson Davis, 1864, in Jefferson Davis Papers, Duke University.

63. Georgia Lee Tatum, *Disloyalty in the Confederacy* (Chapel Hill: University of North Carolina Press, 1934), 4–13.

hundred Union men were organizing into companies in two northern counties. Resistance to conscription later arose in several areas,
notably Randolph County, and at least one enrollment officer died
violently in the course of his duties. In October, 1862, Senator Clement C. Clay, Jr., wrote his friend Jefferson Davis that "the disloyal
stand in open defiance of constitutional authority" in northern Alabama. When Governor John Gill Shorter took office in 1862 these
difficulties continued, and open resistance flared up for the first time
in the southeastern, wiregrass region of the state. In Shorter's words,
the southeastern counties near the coast served as "the common retreat of deserters from our army, tories, and run-away negroes." State
authorities and Confederate officials continued to worry about deserters, and finally in the summer of 1863 the army ordered General
Gideon Pillow to track down and arrest all the men who were skulk-
ing from the service. Pillow reported that there were 6,000 to 10,000
deserters in the mountains of north Alabama, and his vigorous efforts resulted in the capture of many of them, but the problem did
not disappear.[64]

Similar demoralization appeared in Mississippi, especially after
Federal forces threatened and then penetrated large parts of the state
in 1862 and 1863. Along the Mississippi River respected planters
lost heart and raised large cotton crops for sale to the United States,
while the central and northern sections of the state filled up with deserters. One loyal citizen urged lenient treatment of deserters in
three southeastern counties because the inhabitants were "very illit-
erate persons," which was another way of saying that people there
were poor, nonslaveholding, small farmers who lived quite apart
from the economy and social environment of the planters. According
to a commissioner under the impressment law, favoritism and inefficiency in conscription and the presence of many healthy men in

64. *Official Records*, Ser. I, Vol. VII, 840 and Vol. XV, 939, 946–48; *Official Records*,
Ser. IV, Vol. I, 1149, and Vol. II, 87, 207–208, 141, 253–56, 258, 419–20, 603–604, 680–81,
and 853–54. See also Bessie Martin, *Desertion of Alabama Troops from the Confederate
Army: A Study in Sectionalism* (New York: Columbia University Press, 1932), Chaps. 2 and 3.

"bomb-proof" jobs in the commissary and quartermaster departments increased popular discontent.[65]

Georgia's leaders encountered the same kinds of problems, and again the mountain region of the state was the focal point of disaffection. In July, 1862, the provost marshal at Atlanta reported that hundreds of deserters were passing through the city and that many local citizens were trading with the United States and discounting Confederate currency. By 1863 the number of deserters had swelled to the point that Governor Brown issued two proclamations on the subject and ordered the arrest of disloyal men in northeast Georgia who had armed themselves and were "in rebellion . . . robbing loyal citizens." General Pillow estimated that 25,000 to 30,000 men liable to duty had evaded conscription in Georgia.[66]

In Florida and South Carolina the areas of disaffection did not seem to be as large as in most other states, but the extent of the people's demoralization caused deep concern. Illegal trade with the enemy occurred frequently in Florida, with its immense coastline, and Governor Milton felt that it was his duty to inform the central government in October, 1863, that deserters and other malcontents had combined in "various parts of the state" to support "reconstruction of the United States Government." South Carolina's deserters gathered in the mountainous regions of the state near North Carolina and robbed local inhabitants to satisfy their needs. The commandant of conscripts for the Palmetto state sketched a vivid picture of the nature of discontent in August, 1863. Pointing out that serious disaffection existed only in the hill counties, he said: "The people [there] . . . are poor, ill-informed, and but little identified with our struggle. They have been easily seduced from their duty. .' . . The tone of the people is lost; it is no longer a reproach to be known as a de-

65. *Official Records*, Ser. I, Vol. XXIV, Pt. I, 505, and Ser. IV, Vol. II, 681–82; E. Barksdale to Jefferson Davis, July 29, 1863, in Rowland (ed.), *Jefferson Davis*, V, 580–82; Will. Wren to Jefferson Davis, August 12, 1863, in *Official Records*, Ser. IV, Vol. II, 708; Jno. W. C. Watson to General S. Cooper, August 4, 1863, in *Official Records*, Ser. I, Vol. XXIV, Pt. III, 1043–44.

66. *Official Records*, Ser. IV, Vol. II, 9–10, 360–61, 639–41, 680–81.

serter; all are ready to encourage and aid the efforts of those who are avoiding duty."[67]

By the end of 1862 reports of straggling and desertion in Virginia arrived at the War Department. One correspondent from a county bordering North Carolina and the Blue Ridge wrote that his area was "infested with these stragglers & they are beginning to be very bold in their depradations. [*sic*]." Again the mountainous areas proved to have the greatest amount of disaffection, and in such counties the authorities had almost no recourse because deserters often outnumbered the loyal militiamen who could be called out to suppress them. After visiting nine mountain counties in the summer of 1863, J. E. Joyner wrote that "the people seem completely demoralized, and this state of things exists to a great extent among the best citizens. They think and say we are whipped and are bound to be overrun and subjugated. . . . A good many deserters are passing the various roads daily . . . they just pat their guns and defiantly say, 'This is my furlough.'" Joyner added that the deserters, determined to stay out of the army, were organizing to prevent arrest. Conscription officers acknowledged that these facts had "long since been known . . . but the evil continues on the increase."[68]

Probably North Carolina had the greatest amount of disaffection among its people, although toward the close of the war Georgia's leaders, intentionally or not, promoted a similar degree of discontent in that state. North Carolinians had shown a marked reluctance to secede, and when Zebulon Vance assumed the governor's chair in 1862 he took special pains to foster the delicate sense of loyalty to the Confederacy among the mountain population. Arguing to Davis that "the opinions and advice of the old Union leaders must be heeded with regard to the government of affairs in North Carolina or the worst consequences may ensue," Vance sought to have native

67. *Official Records*, Ser. IV, Vol. II, 879–80, 741, 769–70; J. C. Burgess to James Seddon, received July 15, 1864, in Letters Received, Confederate Secretary of War, in RG 109, NA, Microcopy M 437, Roll 120, pp. 870–71.

68. [?] to James Seddon, December 2, 1862, in Letters Received, Confederate Secretary of War, in RG 109, NA, Microcopy M 437, Roll 30, pp. 1565–67 (see also Roll 110, pp. 529–33 and Roll 80, pp. 625–27); *Official Records*, Ser. IV, Vol. II, 721–22.

North Carolinians execute the conscription laws and command troops from the state. As early as November, 1862, Vance used militia to arrest deserters, but their numbers grew steadily, and in 1863 Confederate commanders complained that the desertion of North Carolina troops had assumed uniquely dangerous proportions.[69] Despite the governor's energetic efforts and the repeated dispatch of Confederate troops, the western part of North Carolina effectively ceased to be a contributing part of the Confederacy and sheltered thousands of men from the army. Tax collections stopped, officials did not dare to enforce conscription, and opponents of the Confederate authorities overawed whatever loyal citizens remained in the region. John A. Campbell, the assistant secretary of war, did not exaggerate when he declared that "the condition of things in the mountain districts of North Carolina, South Carolina, Georgia, and Alabama menaces the existence of the Confederacy as fatally as either of the armies of the United States."[70]

Nor were conditions any better in the Trans-Mississippi South. Large-scale evasion of the draft in 1862 illustrated the extent of public despondency in Louisiana, and that state's governor warned Jefferson Davis in December, 1862, that unless the government sent back Louisiana troops to defend their state, the citizens might demand the secession of Louisiana from the Confederacy. Conditions in much of Arkansas had never been good and deteriorated rapidly. In Texas a clash emerged in the legislature between the rich planters and the non-cotton interests. The planters successfully barred restrictions on cotton planting, laws allowing impressment of their slaves, and impressment of foodstuffs to aid soldiers' families. This defense of narrow class interests damaged morale and led W. P. Ballinger, a prominent political leader, to confide to his diary that se-

69. *Official Records*, Ser. IV, Vol. II, 146–47, 180–90, and Ser. I, Vol. LI, Pt. II, 702, Vol. XXV, Pt. II, 746–47, and Vol. XVIII, 860–61.

70. *Ibid.*, Ser. IV, Vol. II, 460–61, 732–34, and Ser. I, Vol. XXIX, Pt. II, 676; B. M. Edney to James Seddon, August 18, 1863, and Thompson Allen to James Seddon, November 12, 1863, in Letters Received, Confederate Secretary of War, in RG 109, NA, Microcopy M 437, Roll 90, pp. 775–76 and Roll 80, pp. 955–56; *Official Records*, Ser. IV, Vol. II, 786.

cession had been "the work of political leaders" without the strong support of "the *mass of the people* without property." He feared "a reaction against the leaders of the Revolution & the Slaveholders."[71]

Throughout the western Confederacy, according to its historian, Robert L. Kerby, the "mood approached despair" by the beginning of 1863. Speculation plagued that area as viciously as it did the rest of the South, and desertion, resistance to authority, and the growth of peace societies seemed to be even more prevalent than they were east of the Mississippi. In July, 1863, President Davis had to ask the commanding general, Kirby Smith, whether the rumor that the Trans-Mississippi Department might secede was true. That event did not occur, but possibly because people were too exhausted to express their feelings in formal political action. Two years before the end of the war, according to Kerby, "the common folk were tired of fighting; they simply wanted the boys to come home."[72]

Thus throughout Jefferson Davis' new nation, the conditions of life for the common people deteriorated, and at the same time class resentments sapped the loyalty of nonslaveholding soldiers and civilians. By 1863 this combination of declining morale and growing disaffection had become President Davis' number one domestic problem. The key to this grave situation was governmental action—bold, decisive governmental action in the form of concrete, practical steps to relieve the suffering of the people. Responsible authorities had to demonstrate that they cared and could make a difference in the conditions of life. This responsibility rested mainly with President Davis and the executives of the states, and their responses to the challenge had a crucial influence on the future of Confederate nationalism. The differing manners in which Jefferson Davis and Georgia's Joseph E. Brown responded to the plight of the common people revealed much about the weakness of Confederate nationalism and the strength of state particularism.

71. Robert L. Kerby, *Kirby Smith's Confederacy: The Trans-Mississippi South, 1863–1865* (New York: Columbia University Press, 1972), 23, 29–30, 36–39, 55–56, 63–64, 87–95; Nancy Head Bowen, "A Political Labyrinth: Texas in the Civil War—Questions in Continuity" (Ph.D. dissertation, Rice University, 1974), 84–87, 89–90, 140–41.
72. Kerby, *Kirby Smith's Confederacy*, 23, 29–30, 36–39, 55–56, 63–64, 87–95.

5

Leadership and Loyalty–
Jefferson Davis, Joseph E. Brown,
and the Common People

War brings many changes, and with stunning rapidity the Civil War visited mass poverty upon the South. For the first time in their experience, many families of small farmers lost the ability to provide for themselves, and since private charity could not meet the huge needs created by war, the yeomen became dependent upon government. This was a fundamental change which produced swift and remarkable alterations in traditional patterns of behavior. In the rural, agricultural South, prevailing social and political values had stressed individual independence, local ties, and a government of limited responsibilities. Suddenly need compelled people to reach beyond their local communities, and old values crumbled as southerners called upon the government for aid.[1]

The existence of widespread suffering, though disturbing, presented an important opportunity to the Confederate government. By providing relief to destitute southerners, the central government could establish a direct connection with the people and make its presence real to them. At the beginning of the war, the Confederate government was a distant and abstract entity, little more than an idea to which people gave their loyalty. The economic difficulties of the people promised to make their image of the Confederacy more

---

1. See, for example, Sallie Robertson to John Breckinridge, February 20, 1865, in Letters Received, Confederate Secretary of War, in Record Group 109, National Archives, Microcopy M 437, Roll 150, pp. 660–62. One of the greatest causes of distress was uncontrollable inflation. In Richmond a dollar in gold bought $2.50 in Confederate Treasury notes in September, 1862; $3.00 in December, 1862; $20.00 in December, 1863; and $70.00 before the end of the war.

concrete. On the one hand, the government could prove that it was responsive to its ordinary citizens and win their gratitude and deepened loyalty. Or, on the other hand, the reaction of Richmond officials could fall short and have the effect of diminishing the faith that southerners originally placed in their leaders.

State governments faced the same challenge and opportunity as did the Confederacy. People struggling with poverty were likely to give their support to those leaders who effectively demonstrated concern. For many politicians, this situation represented a golden chance to further their own goals, whether these harmonized with or obstructed the program of the Davis administration. Thus, the response of the central government and of the states to the problems of the common people had vital significance for Confederate nationalism. In the differing reactions of Jefferson Davis, president of the Confederacy, and Joseph E. Brown, one of the most adroit state leaders, lay one key to the fate of the southern nation. For in practice, people's search for aid often led them to support either those who believed in Confederate nationalism or the proponents of an obstructive state particularism.

The traditional political values of the South had prescribed a limited role for the central government and primary reliance upon state and local authorities. The war, however, upset this established pattern just as it did many others. To direct a conflict which quickly reached unprecedented size, the Confederate government had to expand its authority in many areas. Under Jefferson Davis' strong leadership, the central government unhesitatingly assumed the task of directing the southern war effort.

Although strident opposition to Davis' policies arose, on the whole people accepted his leadership and the government's assumption of major new powers. In the early days of the war, even some newspapers that have been remembered as the administration's fiercest critics argued that the times demanded effective rather than constitutional action. For example, the *Daily Richmond Examiner*, which later endorsed conscription, declared on May 8, 1861, "We need a Dictator" and predicted that "usurpations" would be seen as "patriotism" in the future.[2] Still more significant was the fact that many southerners wanted the central government to go further and undertake more responsibilities than it already had. J. L. M. Curry, an Alabama congressman and ally of Davis, was one of those who believed that extraordinary circumstances required bold measures. Impatient with the voluntary program to restrict cotton production in 1861, Curry recommended that the congress impose on every farm in the South a ban on the cultivation of cotton during the war. In Curry's view, "'the common defence and general welfare' require[d] the *speedy* adoption of this measure."[3]

Among prominent men, Curry's viewpoint was somewhat unusual, for most southern leaders had learned their political principles in the states' rights school, and strict-constructionist thinking made them cautious. Ideology meant less, however, to the common people of the Confederacy. Their prime need was immediate economic assistance, and they did not hesitate to seek or accept it whenever it was offered. Indeed, a majority of the common people may have welcomed and even desired an aggressive expansion of the central government's role. Many seemed to expect that the Davis administration would exercise far more authority than it ever claimed.

By the thousands, letters from the South's small farmers poured into the government bureaus in Richmond. This flood of correspondence demonstrated that the southern people did not hesitate to turn to the central government, with its extensive responsibilities and powers. Most letters simply stated the writer's problem and asked the authorities to grant some specific relief, such as the exemption of a husband or son. But a few revealed something about

2. John Brawner Robbins has argued convincingly that states' rights did not constrict the central government from taking vigorous steps to prosecute the war and that Confederate nationalism received substantial support even from the states. His study is a necessary corrective to the view that states' rights caused the defeat of the Confederacy. See John Brawner Robbins, "Confederate Nationalism: Politics and Government in the Confederate South, 1861–1865" (Ph.D. dissertation, Rice University, 1964).

3. J. L. M. Curry to Judah Benjamin, December 26, 1862, in Letters Received, Confederate Secretary of War, in RG 109, NA, Microcopy M 437, Roll 20, pp. 1034–36. Curry apparently was recalling the wording of the United States Constitution, for neither the provisional nor the permanent Confederate Constitution contained the phrase, "general welfare."

the people's political values and showed that some ordinary southerners wanted the Richmond administration to ignore states' rights,
reach into their communities, and use its powers to provide help.
Relief, not political principles, was paramount in the minds of these
writers, and since the Confederate government had a great capacity
to act, they hoped that it would respond to their needs.

Repeatedly the War Department received letters which showed
misunderstanding of the government's relationship to railroad companies. Although Davis had boldly recommended Confederate aid
in the construction of certain new lines, his government left control
of the railways in the hands of their private owners. Even in the latter part of the war when central control seemed imperative and the
congress had authorized such action, the administration shied away
from public management. To many citizens, however, government
operation of the railroads seemed so logical that they thought that it
was already in effect. Numerous letters asked the War Department
to grant a license for the transportation of goods or send information
about government regulations. Some correspondents assumed that
government regulations of transportation included roads as well as
railways. To these inquiries the War Department replied that it did
not control transportation facilities or "interfere with the management of Railroads beyond securing for the Government the prompt
transportation of its freight."[4]

Control over the economy seemed even more logical to ordinary
southerners who were in need. In February, 1862, the War Department took a first step in this direction when it seized corn from the
hands of distillers in Richmond. A Virginia congressman who visited
his constituency at this time noted the enthusiastic reaction: "I have
found the People from Richmond to this place proclaiming with one
Voice as it were that the Government has taken a step in the right
direction in seizing the grain in the hands of that Mammoth distill-

4. James Seddon to Congressman W. W. Clapp, April 21, 1863, in Letters Sent, Confederate Secretary of War, in Record Group 109, National Archives, Microcopy M 522, Roll
7, p. 35.

ery." He added that they wanted this policy extended to "all things which enter in to the Consu[m]ption of our Army and the families." A Georgian who read in his newspaper about the seizure of corn promptly wrote to the War Department and urged that the Confederacy take the same step in his state and county in order to avert a shortage of bread. When news of the War Department's action reached a remote town in upland South Carolina, its newspaper thought that a general crackdown on distilling was underway and added, "God grant it may be done."[5] Such action by the central authorities seemed neither unconstitutional nor oppressive because it was necessary.

Other initiatives by the government won similar strong approval. When the War Department impressed saltpeter from speculators and refused to pay the exorbitant price, several newspapers in Georgia carried an article bearing the caption WELL DONE! WELL DONE![6] The Spartanburg, South Carolina, *Carolina Spartan* hoped that the Confederate impressment law would be used to shake loose provisions from "all those who have locked up their corn cribs and smoke houses against their friends and neighbors." Even martial law had its champions. The *Atlanta Daily Intelligencer* applauded the system of price regulation established under military rule in Mobile and New Orleans and declared that unless other measures brought relief, "we shall bless the day when martial law shall relieve us from the intolerable oppression which monopoly and extortion have brought upon us." Outrage at rising prices also led the *Richmond Examiner* to urge the Confederate government in December, 1862, to pass a law against speculation.[7] Probably most common people would not have

5. Fayette McMullen to John Letcher, February 17, 1862, in Historical Society of Pennsylvania; H. Hall to Judah Benjamin, February 21, 1862, in Letters Received, Confederate Secretary of War, in RG 109, NA, Microcopy M 437, Roll 50, pp. 174–75; Edgefield (S.C.) *Advertiser*, March 12, 1862, p. 1.

6. See the Atlanta *Daily Intelligencer*, February 16, 1862, for a description of "the article going the rounds of the press."

7. Spartanburg (S.C.) *Carolina Spartan*, April 9, 1863; Atlanta *Daily Intellingencer*, April 6, 1862, and April 2, April 4, and November 7, 1862; *Daily Richmond Examiner*, December 1, 1862, p. 2.

objected to an active central government which was working to help them. In their demands for relief, the poor formed a constituency for enlarging the role of the Confederate government.

Faced with widespread suffering among its citizens, the Confederacy did make an effort to help. In addition to its attempts to limit the harmful effects of troop movements and harsh government policies, the Davis administration took a few positive steps. For example, it sought to shield the civilian economy from the drain of resources into the army. Salt was an essential but scarce item, and rather than compete for the inadequate civilian supply, the army worked to develop new sources of salt for its own use. An important mine was discovered in Louisiana, and in response to letters from Mississippi's governor, Jefferson Davis allowed state contractors and private entrepreneurs to work the vein of rock salt along with the army and thus increase production. Declaring that he was "deeply conscious of the necessity existing for a vigorous prosecution of this work, and [was] endeavoring to secure to the country the full benefit to be derived from it," Davis arranged military protection for all the workers at the mine.[8]

When shortages of food and fuel developed throughout the country, the central government gave special consideration to charitable organizations whenever possible. On behalf of a committee of ministers, for example, who were trying to obtain wood and coal for the poor of Richmond in December, 1862, Secretary of War Seddon wrote to the president of the Richmond and Danville Railroad and urged him to do whatever he could to further the ministers' goal. As the Confederacy's transportation system deteriorated, delays in shipping army supplies increased, and eventually the War Department had to stop supporting private shipments on the railroads. But officials did grant other privileges to charities. In 1863, for example, Secretary Seddon assured the Columbus (Georgia) Relief Associa-

8. Jefferson Davis to John Pettus, September 25, 1862, and October 25, 1862, in Dunbar Rowland (ed.), *Jefferson Davis: Constitutionalist; His Letters, Papers, and Speeches* (10 vols.; Jackson, Miss.: Little & Ives Co., 1923), V, 344, 360–61.

tion that he would exempt from impressment all articles which the association purchased for the poor and the families of soldiers.[9]

After initially lending support to charity, the Confederacy gradually became more deeply involved in the provision of food to the needy. Congressional enactments on impressment and the tax-in-kind created a structure through which the central government could furnish food cheaply to local officials. The impressment law of March, 1863, established a board of assessors in each state which determined the prices to be paid for goods taken from merchants or entrepreneurs. Every two months the assessors published a list of these prices, which were below the level of the market, and people who needed to buy tended to look upon the government prices as a fair value. After the congress passed the tax-in-kind law in April, 1863, destitute counties trying to feed their poor often asked to buy back at government prices part of the food collected as tax. Initially Secretary Seddon resisted this idea, but within a month he yielded and started making government supplies available for civilian relief. Asking only that the authorities of Carroll County, Georgia, for example, certify the necessity of obtaining food from the tax-in-kind, Seddon authorized the quartermaster in that state to sell bread at assessors' valuation and assured the officials that the War Department was not indifferent to their conditions.[10] Assistant Quartermaster General Larkin

9. James Seddon to Lewis E. Harvie, December 12, 1862, and James Seddon to Hines Holt, April 22, 1863, in Letters Sent, Confederate Secretary of War, in RG 109, NA, Microcopy M 522, Roll 5, p. 181 and Roll 7, pp. 36–37.

10. M. L. Bonham to James Seddon, October 8, 1863, and James Seddon to M. L. Bonham, October 16, 1863, in *The War of the Rebellion: A Compilation of the Official Records of the Union and Confederate Armies* (130 vols.; Washington: Government Printing Office, 1880–1901), Ser. IV, Vol. II, 863–64 and 875–77, hereinafter cited as *Official Records*; James Seddon to William E. Draughon, November 27, 1863, and James Seddon to W. W. Merrill, January 22, 1864, in Letters Sent, Confederate Secretary of War, in RG 109, NA, Microcopy M 522, Roll 8, p. 148, and Roll 9, pp. 277–78. E. Merton Coulter has incorrectly asserted that "although . . . state and local governments aided relief, the Confederate government never dared to venture into that field." The present author feels that the Confederate government's efforts in this area were inadequate, but Davis' administration certainly was involved in relief. See E. Merton Coulter, *The Confederate States of America, 1861–1865* (Baton Rouge: Louisiana State University Press, 1950), Vol. VII of 10 vols., in Wendell Holmes Stephenson and E. Merton Coulter (eds.), *A History of the South*, 424.

Smith drew up regulations authorizing this aid in all the states, and the Confederacy supplied some aid to the poor under this system at least until the fall of 1864.[11]

The passage of the new exemption law of February 17, 1864, extended the scope of the Confederacy's relief activities. To allay some of the popular discontent over the exemption of overseers, Congress added the requirement that planters who wanted to retain their overseers agree under bond to provide the government each year with surplus food in the ratio of one hundred pounds of bacon and one hundred pounds of beef for each able-bodied slave. The government had the right to purchase this meat at assessors' prices, and the planter also had to pledge to sell surplus grain and provisions to the government or to soldiers' families at the same prices. In addition this act gave the president and his secretary of war broad discretionary authority to exempt or detail individuals "on account of public necessity, and to insure the production of grain and provisions for the army and the families of soldiers." Under this law the Confederate government assumed a responsibility for providing food to the poor. In August, 1864, the War Department instructed its commissaries to purchase no more than half of the surplus from bonded agriculturalists "and to leave the remainder for the persons who purchase on behalf of the families of soldiers." County relief agents looked to the government to supply food for the poor from this source, and disabled veterans or soldiers' wives rejoiced when they received permission to purchase food from the bonded farmers.[12]

11. Confederate States of America. War Department. Communication from the Secretary of War (transmitting a report by the Assistant Quartermaster General in charge of the tax-in-kind, Larkin Smith), January 19, 1864, Library of Congress; "Instructions to be observed by officers and agents receiving the tax in kind," March 29, 1864, Library of Congress; receipt dated 30 September 1864 for ten thousand bushels of corn from the "Tax in Kind for the use of the indigent soldiers families of Randolph County," Alabama, in the Compiled Service Records of Major Geo. W. Jones, Controlling Quartermaster for Alabama, Compiled Service Records of Confederate General and Staff Officers, & Nonregimental Enlisted Men, in Record Group 109, National Archives, Microcopy 331, Roll 143.

This aid, though welcome, probably was not of sufficient scope and quantity to supply civilian needs. Larkin Smith's regulations limited the amount of food which could be sold to any county to the amount which that county had furnished in tax. Therefore, the aid would not offset any decline in production or compensate for poor harvests.

12. General Orders of the Confederate Adjutant and Inspector General's Office, No. 26, March 1, 1864 and No. 69, August 27, 1864, in Record Group 109, National Archives, Mi-

In a limited number of cases the Richmond administration acted more directly to help poor, nonslaveholding families. Rather than encouraging planters to produce a surplus which would be drawn upon for the poor, the government occasionally exempted men from service so that they could go home and farm their own land. In December, 1862, Governor Vance asked the president to exempt the mountainous Tenth Congressional District of North Carolina from further calls for troops in order to avert suffering and starvation, and Davis agreed to enroll only a reserve force which could remain at home. Distressed areas in other states occasionally received similar consideration when the military situation permitted, and once President Davis intervened with Mississippi's governor on behalf of two hundred state militiamen who needed to return home to plant their crops. The exemption act of May 1, 1863, gave Confederate officials another means to alleviate individual cases of poverty, for one clause of that act authorized the president to grant exemptions "in districts . . . deprived of white or slave labor indispensable to the production of grain or provisions" and when required by "justice, equity, and necessity." According to Assistant Secretary of War John Campbell, that power had "rarely been used with reference to the cases of owners of plantations. It has generally been applied to the condition of those who were destitute, or those who have furnished, to the army several members, leaving *one* to take care of the families & fortunes of the remainder."[13] Apparently the Davis administration continued to grant this type of exemption under the subsequent law of February 17, 1864. As a general rule, only large producers obtained exemptions to raise provisions under the 1864 act, but a ledger of agricul-

crocopy T 782, Roll 1, pp. 46–55 and 301–302 for 1864; William M. Hannah to the Secretary of War, and James Rivers to James Seddon, November 4, 1864, in Letters Received, Confederate Secretary of War, in RG 109, NA, Microcopy M 437, Roll 130, pp. 351–55 and Roll 140, pp. 178–80.

13. Zebulon Vance to Jefferson Davis, December 19, 1862, in *Official Records*, Ser. IV, Vol. II, 246–48 and Vol. III, 845–47; Jefferson Davis to John Pettus, April 4, 1863, in Rowland (ed.), *Jefferson Davis*, V, 468; James M. Matthews (ed.), *Statutes at Large of the Confederate States of America, Third Session, First Congress, 1863* (Richmond: R. M. Smith, 1863), 158–59; James A. Campbell to W. P. Chilton and David Clopton, January 29, 1864, in Letters Sent, Confederate Secretary of War, in RG 109, NA, Microcopy M 522, Roll 7, pp. 41–42.

tural details in Virginia revealed that a small proportion of the bonded farmers probably were poor men. This record book described the reason for their exemption as "Care of Private Necessity." Their bond was small, and only if they produced a surplus did they have to furnish food to the government.[14]

The administration of these exemption laws undoubtedly gave a small amount of relief to the South's poverty-stricken yeomen, and Jefferson Davis' government also showed some sensitivity to the charge that certain statutes were unjust. Substitution provoked strong resentment among the common people, who could not afford to buy their way out of military service, and the War Department also found that it brought only unreliable, undesirable men into the army. In the fall of 1862 the War Department started to restrict the privilege of substitution, and at the end of 1863 Secretary Seddon, despite bitter protests from the wealthy, urged the immediate repeal of the law. After Davis included that recommendation in his address to the congress on December 7, 1863, the lawmakers bowed to public pressure and abolished the hated practice. Tardy as this action was, it nonetheless showed greater sensitivity in the Davis administration than in the Lincoln government, for the United States never abolished substitution and until the last ten months of the war allowed any draftee to purchase his exemption from service by paying three hundred dollars.[15]

14. "Agricultural Detail Book, Virginia, 1864–1865," Record Group 109, Chap. I, Vol. 236, National Archives. Of the 454 cases enumerated in this ledger, 17 were noted "Care of Private Necesity," and several more which did not have this description carried such small bonds that the individuals involved probably were small farmers.

15. Asbury A. Adams to George Randolph, September 13, 1862, in Letters Received, Confederate Secretary of War, in RG 109, NA, Microcopy M 437, Roll 30, pp. 1108–1109; John A. Campbell to R. R. Collier, December 23, 1862, and James Seddon to John Gibson, December 23, 1862, in Letters Sent, Confederate Secretary of War, in RG 109, NA, Microcopy M 522, Roll 5, pp. 209–210 and 212; E. Dargan to the Secretary of War, September 26, 1863, in Letters Received, Confederate Secretary of War, in RG 109, NA, Microcopy M 437, Roll 90, pp. 186–87; James Seddon to Jefferson Davis, November 26, 1863, in Letters Sent by the Confederate Secretary of War to the President, in Record Group 109, National Archives, Microcopy M 523, Roll 1, pp. 120–35; James D. Richardson (comp.), *A Compilation of the Messages and Papers of the Confederacy, Including the Diplomatic Correspondence, 1861–1865* (2 vols.; Nashville: United States Publishing Company, 1906), I, 370; *Official Records*, Ser. IV, Vol. III, 11–12; James G. Randall, *Lincoln the President* (4 vols.; New York: Dodd, Mead & Company, 1945–1955), III, 127–30.

Another unpopular statute was the exemption of overseers who supervised at least twenty Negro slaves. Nonslaveholding southerners in great numbers condemned this law as a piece of class legislation which discriminated unfairly in favor of the planters. Recognizing the resentment of this law, Davis attempted to explain its purpose when he traveled to Mississippi in December, 1862. In a speech before the Mississippi legislature, he denied that the congress had intended to favor the rich or draw any distinction between classes. Rather, the reason for exempting overseers was to provide a necessary police force in slaveholding areas and support agricultural production on which both the army and the poor depended. Declaring that all classes had made sacrifices, Davis asserted, according to a newspaper account, that "any law intended to bear unfairly upon the poor, even to a feather's weight, would never have received his signature."[16]

On his return to Richmond, Davis found that the annual report of Secretary of War Seddon expressed deep concern over the unpopularity of the "twenty-nigger law." Davis passed over the sweeping changes in exemptions which Seddon recommended but absorbed part of the spirit of the secretary's report. Sending a message to the congress on January 12, 1863, he declared, "I specially recommend . . . some revision of the exemption law of last session. Serious complaints have reached me of the inequality of its operation from eminent and patriotic citizens whose opinions merit great consideration, and I trust that some means will be devised for leaving at home a sufficient local police without making discriminations, always to be deprecated, between different classes of our citizens." To the detriment of morale, however, the congress reacted slowly and ineffectively to Davis' recommendation. After months of debate, the lawmakers agreed on a bill which retained the exemption and merely limited the possibility that planters would abuse its provisions by hiring new overseers or dividing up their slaves. Subsequent laws which contained some aid for poor families never eradicated the resentment over the exemption of overseers.[17]

16. Rome (Ga.) *Weekly Courier*, January 9, 1863, pp. 1–2.
17. James Seddon to Jefferson Davis, January 3, 1863, in Letters Sent by the Confeder-

The congress' hesitant, partial response to the controversy over exemptions for overseers was symptomatic of the failure of the central government to deal boldly and forcefully with the problems which beset the common people. Although the Confederate government modified some of its laws and tried to succor those in greatest need, its policies failed to measure up to the scope of the problem. For this failure the Davis administration bore primary responsibility. The congress looked to the president for initiative and direction during the crisis, but Davis' government seemed reluctant to act as vigorously to aid the common people as it had often done to prosecute the war. A combination of political pressures, economic theories, and the imperious demands of war held Davis back from a more active approach to the internal problems of the Confederacy.

The administration's policy toward inflation illustrated some of the forces which restrained the central government from acting effectively. Although the uncontrolled escalation of prices threatened every southern household and demoralized the people, the Confederate government acted cautiously, pondered long-term remedies, and eventually allowed the pressing daily demands of the armies to obscure this crucial issue until it was too late to find a solution. The outcry against speculation burst forth loudly in 1861 and increased to the point that Davis himself admitted that "love of lucre" had "eaten like a gangrene into the very heart of the land." Initially Confederate officials made some aggressive attempts to crush speculation at its source in various localities. Generals who encountered profiteering among suppliers of provisions moved with military dispatch to seize the needed commodities. Under the direction of Secretary of War George Randolph commanders were authorized to impress the stocks of speculators and pay only cost for the items taken.[18] This kind of

---

ate Secretary of War to the President, in RG 109, NA, Microcopy M 523, Roll 1, pp. 91–99; Rowland (ed.), *Jefferson Davis*, V, 413; Matthews (ed.), *Statutes at Large . . . Third Session, First Congress*, 1863, 158–59.

18. Richardson (comp.), *Messages and Papers of the Confederacy*, I, 328; George W. Randolph to Ralph Garrell, October 1, 1862, and Randolph to Major General Sam Jones, October 6, 1862, in Letters Sent, Confederate Secretary of War, in RG 109, NA, Microcopy M 522, Roll 5, pp. 65 and 74.

action could not remove all the causes of inflation, but it contributed to a solution and served as a highly visible sign that the government was working to correct injustices and aid the people.

Fear for states' rights, however, raised obstacles to strong government policies. In February, 1862, when the Confederacy seized grain from a distillery in Richmond, the cabinet debated whether to extend this action to other places. Half of Davis' advisers opposed the idea as a "dangerous and unauthorized use of power," and because of the even division it was agreed that the president should merely issue a proclamation urging the states to pass laws against distilling. Later, at the beginning of 1863, Davis discouraged military action against speculators. A variety of factors then entered into his thinking, but the stage had been set by states' rights protests and by the overzealous actions of one of his commanders, General T. H. Holmes, who was in charge of the Trans-Mississippi Department. Holmes's excessive use of martial law and military police had aroused great complaint in Arkansas before he wrote Davis and proposed using military power to enforce a system of fixed prices. Reacting to popular criticism of Holmes, Davis rejected the idea and instructed the general to limit his army's interventions in civilian affairs. The Confederate president feared that the army only aroused opposition when it dealt with civilians, and he had just endured a sustained assault on conscription by Georgia's champion of states' rights, Governor Joseph E. Brown. Apparently believing that the Confederacy could not take on new tasks without angering the states' rights forces, Davis recommended to the state governors that they adopt means to combat inflation and advised General Holmes to leave the job to the states.[19]

Davis also believed, correctly, that the fundamental economic problems of the Confederacy were a major cause of inflation. As he explained to General Holmes, no law against extortion could restrain

19. Thomas Bragg Diary, 1861–1862 (Southern Historical Collection, University of North Carolina), February 15, 1862; Jefferson Davis to T. H. Holmes, January 28, 1863, in Rowland (ed.), *Jefferson Davis*, V, 424–46; Circular Letter to Governors, November 26, 1862, in Allen D. Candler (ed.), *The Confederate Records of the State of Georgia* (6 vols.; Atlanta: Chas. P. Byrd, 1910), III, 305–306.

price rises "where the amount to be sold is too small for the number of consumers." The woeful redundancy of the currency also contributed to inflation, and Davis moved tardily to decrease the amount of money in circulation. Urging a "radical reform of the currency" at the end of 1863, Davis threw his influence against the universal desire for an increase in the pay of soldiers. Long before 1863 it was obvious that eleven dollars per month was utterly inadequate for the families of privates. More than a dozen resolutions from state legislatures demanded a substantial increase in soldiers' pay. Not until the summer of 1864 did the congress finally increase the salary of privates to a modest eighteen dollars per month. Although Davis correctly believed that currency reform was a basic need and that higher expenditures tended to fuel inflation, he greatly underestimated the frustration of the people and overestimated the Confederacy's ability to control prices. In the end no exertions of the Treasury Department could right Confederate finances, and the southern people had to bear what seemed to be indifference on the part of their government.[20]

Since Davis ruled out direct and highly visible interventions in the economy, there were few immediate measures the central government could take. Left to their own devices, desperate southerners developed some original strategies to arrest the rampant inflation. A group in Enterprise, Mississippi, formed a "Confederate Society" which required that all members of the society buy and sell only at reduced prices. Newspapers in distant parts of the Confederacy applauded and publicized the organization's program as a patriotic measure which might have some effect. In a letter to the secretary of the Confederate Society, Jefferson Davis eloquently denounced the evil effects of inflation and wished the group success, but clearly this voluntary organization raised only fragile barriers to the onrushing tide of price increases.[21]

20. Jefferson Davis to T. H. Holmes, January 28, 1863, in Rowland (ed.), *Jefferson Davis*, V, 425; *Official Records*, Ser. IV, Vol. II, 1024–49; Joseph E. Brown to Jefferson Davis, April 14, 1863, in Candler (ed.), *Confederate Records of Georgia*, III, 332–33; Wilfred B. Yearns, *The Confederate Congress* (Athens: University of Georgia Press, 1960), 113.
    21. *Daily Richmond Examiner*, August 28, 1863, p. 2; Charleston *Mercury*, September

Probably one of the greatest reasons for Davis' failure to take bold action on behalf of the common people was the continual atmosphere of military crisis. Often, in fact, the pressing needs of the army required the adoption of measures which aggravated the problems of the poor. Davis' military background and the fact that the existence of the Confederacy depended on military success predisposed him to concentrate on the supervision of the army. As military problems increased and defeats became more numerous in 1862 and 1863, the administration's preoccupation with military affairs naturally intensified. In the final year of the war, as even a cursory perusal of Confederate documents makes clear, the Davis administration felt compelled to subordinate all other programs to a desperate attempt to obtain more men. Despite Davis' general awareness and grasp of the internal problems of the Confederacy, military events remained the focus of his concern.

Thus, as the war approached its end, Davis devoted his energies and those of his government to placing more soldiers in the ranks. A stream of progressively more demanding regulations issued from the War Department in an attempt to scour the country for all available manpower. Davis had always resisted pleas to increase the list of exemptions, and in 1863 he urged the governors to organize exempts into local defense units which could function as a reserve force. To improve conscription the administration established a special bureau to execute the draft and the exemption laws.[22] But no single measure could suffice, and the search for remedies continued. At the end of 1863 the War Department and the president pressed the congress for the power to make all exemptions discretionary, for Davis believed that in every exempted category there were some men who were not needed at home. One year later Secretary Seddon desperately recommended ending all exemptions except for government

---

30, 1863, p. 1; Jefferson Davis to J. W. Harmon, September 17, 1863, in Rowland (ed.), *Jefferson Davis*, VI, 40–41.

22. Jefferson Davis to Zebulon Vance, November 29, 1862, and Jefferson Davis to J. J. McRae, June 13, 1863, in Rowland (ed.), *Jefferson Davis*, V, 380, 519; Robert E. Lee to Jefferson Davis, July 27, 1863, and Davis to Lee, July 28, 1863, in *Official Records*, Ser. I, Vol. XXVII, Pt. III, 1040–1041 and Ser. I, Vol. LI, Pt. II, 741.

officers and making details in the few cases absolutely essential for production. In preparation for the last crisis, the government required all detailed men to organize in reserve units during the summer of 1864, and in October General Orders Number 77 revoked all but a handful of details and sent the men into full-time duty in the field.[23]

These measures were the last resort of a dying government, for after a point the recruitment of troops damaged the productive capacity of the economy, which was equally essential to the war effort. Moreover, many of the steps taken to bolster military strength sapped civilian support by making conditions worse for the common people. Every detailed man whom the government called from his farm into the ranks represented one less man to supply food for hungry soldiers' families. Frequently reserves had to go on active duty during planting or harvesting time, when their labor was vital for the crops. Inevitably, as the task of supplying the army became more difficult, measures to relieve the civilian population suffered. The War Department refused requests to furnish meat from the tax-in-kind for soldiers' families, and an act of the congress in February, 1864, authorized the government to take as much as one-half of any family's annual meat supply. An attempt by Virginia to furnish cotton cloth and yarn to her poor foundered because the Confederacy had exclusive contracts with all the available factories.[24] Each of these developments was certain to anger those who were battling against economic disaster.

23. *Official Records*, Ser. IV, Vol. II, 944–52, 1024–49; James Seddon to Jefferson Davis, November 26, 1863, in Letters Sent by the Confederate Secretary of War to the President, in RG 109, NA, Microcopy M 523, Roll 1, pp. 120–35.

24. Susan Robinson and others to Jefferson Davis, October 19, 1864, in Letters Received, Confederate Secretary of War, in RG 109, NA, Microcopy M 437, Roll 140, pp. 165–68; M. L. Bonham to James Seddon, June 2, 1864, in *Official Records*, Ser. I, Vol. XXXV, Pt. II, 519–20; E. Burk to J. F. Johnson, March 5, 1864, in Letters Received, Confederate Secretary of War, in RG 109, NA, Microcopy M 437, Roll 120, pp. 146–48; General Orders of the Confederate Adjutant and Inspector General's Office, No. 39, March 24, 1864, in RG 109, NA, Microcopy T 782, Roll 1, pp. 96–97; A. R. Lawton to James Seddon, July 26, 1864, in *Official Records*, Ser. IV, Vol. III, 556–58.

Without the support of the common people the Confederacy could not survive, and it became increasingly apparent as the war progressed that the government was not meeting the needs of its poorer citizens. Occasionally Davis' administration displayed its concern, but more often government measures made the economic position of the yeomen even more precarious than it already was. The Davis administration labored under severe restraints, but its failure to relieve the suffering of the poor cannot be explained wholly by the pressures of war. There was also a failure of imagination on the part of the government. Measures to aid the common people usually came as an afterthought if at all. Never did the administration adopt a major policy based on the need to win the affections and loyalty of the yeomen on whom the Confederacy ultimately depended.

There were a few officials who saw that vigorous action to aid the poor was vital, and they raised their voices at the highest levels of the government. These men recognized that unless the Confederacy eased privation and ended injustice, all measures to fill the army would fail. The direct, singleminded concentration on army strength was counter productive. In the recommendations of a few highly placed officials, Davis' government had the key to a different strategy for maximizing the war effort, a strategy premised on meeting the needs of the common people.

Secretary of War James Seddon made one vital recommendation in January, 1863. Struck by the tremendous resentment on the part of the poorer classes toward the "twenty nigger law," Seddon realized that there was a basic shortage of manpower on many nonslaveholders' farms. Seddon's concern culminated in a recommendation to the president that the Confederacy should exempt soldiers on whom several helpless dependents relied for food. Much of the complaint about the exemption of overseers, in Seddon's opinion, arose from "mere invidiousness," but he admitted that there was virtue in the argument that, if slaves deserved proper care, nonslaveholding whites did also. Stressing the legitimate needs of many southern families, Seddon wrote: "It would properly relieve the law from much odium and yet only promote equity and the public good, if when, as in cases not infrequently presented, eight or ten helpless whites are dependent on one male friend within the prescribed ages, exemption should be accorded by law."[25]

Seddon's proposal was one of the most important ideas advanced within the Confederate government during the war, for it had the potential of relieving much of the suffering which sapped the loyalty of the common people. Although both desertion and the growth of disaffected areas had advanced quite far by 1863, the adoption of Seddon's idea might have infused new strength and morale into the Confederacy. But Davis never approved the recommendation, although he did ask the congress, after reading the secretary's report, to revise the exemption for overseers. Probably Davis feared the effects of allowing more exemptions from the short-handed army and failed to realize that only a frontal attack on the problems of the non-slaveholding population could avail.

Thus Davis ignored the signposts marking a turning point in his administration. Concentrating too narrowly on military strength, he lost an opportunity to secure the support of common southerners, whose growing disenchantment with the government doomed the Confederacy. As Bell Wiley has written, "the refusal to exempt from conscription nonslaveholding adult males upon whose labor the livelihood of wives and small children was vitally dependent" and the failure to take effective action against speculation were "two of the greatest mistakes of the Confederate government."[26]

Another sensitive Confederate official was Thompson Allen, the commissioner of taxes. Although he held a high office, Allen received reports from tax collectors close to the people and developed a clear understanding of the plight of the South's yeomen. In a report to the

25. Citizens of Jefferson County, Virginia, to James Seddon, received July 13, 1863, and Mrs. Mary Elliot to Jefferson Davis, August 19, 1863, in Letters Received, Confederate Secretary of War, in RG 109, NA, Microcopy M 437, Roll 100, pp. 622–26 and Roll 90, pp. 781–82; *Official Records*, Ser. IV, Vol. II, 287–88. The United States allowed exemptions to those who were the only son of a dependent widow or of infirm parents.

26. Bell Irvin Wiley, *The Plain People of the Confederacy* (Baton Rouge: Louisiana State University Press, 1943), 69.

secretary of the treasury in November, 1863, he described the effect which heavy taxation had on the Confederacy's poorer citizens: "This class of people have a hard struggle to live at best, and the assessment of their little produce and money is found to be irritating, and produces discontent and murmurings against the Government. Numerous appeals have been addressed to the Tax Bureau in behalf of this class, principally by the local tax officers." Believing that the entire structure of the government's taxes needed to be changed, Allen argued that it made little sense to tax poor women and children who struggled to raise a crop, because before the next harvest the government had to support these same people at public expense. Therefore Allen urged the adoption of taxes which in modern terminology would be called progressive. Sales taxes, he noted, should not be increased because they fell on "the consumers, those least able to bear it."[27]

To implement his theories of taxation, Allen proposed a number of exemptions for the poorer classes and steeply graduated taxes on the income of the rich. Although he approved the tax-in-kind, Allen wanted to exempt from the tithe all small farms which produced meat and grain solely for home consumption. As he explained, "The tax under this Section will operate harshly and oppressively on the poor, in many cases. . . . The loss to the Government by such discrimination in favor of the poor and humble in circumstances, would be insignificant, and more than compensated by allowing no reservation [of an untaxed portion] whatever to the more wealthy." To reduce the currency and stimulate the purchase of Confederate bonds, Allen recommended increasing the income tax to 25 percent on incomes over $5,000 and 50 percent on incomes over $10,000. In addition he proposed a tax of 50 percent on the profits of corporations and joint stock companies after allowing them a 25 percent dividend for their stockholders. Acknowledging that his recommendation would arouse criticism, the commissioner of taxes countered that these measures

27. Thompson Allen to C. G. Memminger, November, 1863, in Letters Received, Confederate Secretary of the Treasury, in Record Group 109, National Archives, Microcopy M 499, Roll 2, pp. 418–47.

would keep down speculation and the amassing of wartime fortunes and would force every man to do his part.[28] The congress adopted part of Allen's recommendations when it wrote a new tax bill in February, 1864. The legislators exempted poor families worth less than $500 from the tax-in-kind and established a graduated income tax. The range of this tax, however, was small, as the congressmen apparently decided that the wealthy could bear their share of the burdens without paying the high rates advocated by Allen. Under the congress' statute, the highest tax charged was a rate of 15 percent on incomes over $10,000.[29]

Proposals such as those made by James Seddon and Thompson Allen had the potential to relieve discontent and foster loyalty. Had they been enacted as laws and rigorously enforced, these ideas would have improved the condition of the treasury, alleviated want on many farms, and given the common people of the South a feeling that their government cared about their needs and that the rich sacrificed equally in the war. But Jefferson Davis rejected the secretary of war's proposal, and the congress gave only partial expression to the views of the commissioner of taxes. On the whole the Confederate government put the needs of the army and the preferences of the planter class ahead of the urgent problems of nonslaveholding southerners.

As a result of this failure to address the problems of ordinary citizens, the Confederacy became a source of trouble rather than aid, an unwelcome presence rather than a friend. In many areas the government seemed to do nothing to defend the citizens, yet it constantly demanded more from them. People dreaded the approach of Confederate agents, who swept more men into the net of conscription, impressed property, or appropriated a tenth from meager crops. Even when the central government called out local defense units to defend their homes, these men often sat in camp or marched about ineffectively while their crops withered in the field or their land

28. *Ibid.* The congress allowed farmers to reserve a certain number of bushels of various crops which were not taxed.

29. *Official Records*, Ser. IV, Vol. III, 140–52. Overall, the Confederacy raised only 1 percent of its revenue by taxes.

lay fallow during planting season. To southern yeomen the government's demands for further sacrifice seemed especially galling because the administration wasted much of what it obtained. Transportation breakdowns and administrative inefficiency caused food to spoil at depots and soldiers to go without proper equipment.[30] Thus the Richmond administration became a distant, oppressive force in the eyes of many of the people.

If increasing desertions and rising discontent had not made this fact clear by the fall of 1863, the Davis administration should have learned a lesson from the congressional elections. Incumbents, supporters of the administration, and secessionist Democrats lost ground everywhere to candidates who were not identified with the government and who often had been Whigs. In North Carolina, where eight of the state's ten congressmen became administrative opponents, only one Democrat gained a seat and no original secessionist was elected. But the truly ominous development was that five candidates who ran on a peace platform were victorious. In Georgia voters displayed a wholesale rejection of the men in the congress and elected nine new candidates, eight of whom opposed Davis. Half of Texas' delegation to the second congress was new, and former Whigs and opponents of secession also gained in Mississippi. In Alabama the Whigs unseated the incumbent governor, the state's two senators, and two members of congress. Four victorious congressmen were rumored to be reconstructionists, and the congress unanimously expelled one of them.[31] A disturbed Confederate official reported to

30. Ladies of Goldsboro, North Carolina, to Jefferson Davis, July 30, 1863, and Harriet Strother to Jefferson Davis, February 20, 1864, in Letters Received, Confederate Secretary of War, in RG 109, NA, Microcopy M 437, Roll 100, pp. 681–83 and Roll 140, pp. 753–57.

31. Robbins, "Confederate Nationalism," Chap. 7; Yearns, *Confederate Congress*, 54–59; Thomas B. Alexander, "Persistent Whiggery in the Confederate South, 1860–1877," *Journal of Southern History*, XXVII (1961), 305–329; Thomas B. Alexander and Richard E. Beringer, *The Anatomy of the Confederate Congress: A Study of the Influences of Member Characteristics on Legislative Voting Behavior, 1861–1865* (Nashville: Vanderbilt University Press, 1972), 330. Alexander and Beringer found that the opposition to Davis was composed of an ever-shifting group of members and that the most important determinants of a congressman's voting behavior were the location of his constituency, his stand on secession, and his party (in descending order of importance). The authors inferred that there had been no true commitment to Confederate nationalism in the South in 1861, and they noted that after 1863 voters in interior areas wanted peace and were growing somewhat "populist."

his superiors that the election results in Alabama were indications of "disaffection (to use the mildest possible term)" and that people referred to the opposition as the Peace party. This commandant of conscripts added that representative J. L. M. Curry lost by a large majority "on account of his identification with the Government." Morale had deteriorated so severely that in the second congress, according to W. B. Yearns, "only the nearly solid support from occupied districts enabled President Davis to maintain a majority in Congress until the last days of the nation."[32]

Aided by this atmosphere of discontent with the Richmond administration, Davis' political enemies flourished in the closing years of the war, but it is important to note that they did not offer a solely negative program. Instead, many of the president's opponents in state governments had a solid base of loyal support which they established by ministering to the needs of the people. Although the central government hesitated to attack the widespread poverty and destitution, the states stepped into the void at an early date and distributed food or money to the people. Unlike Confederate officials who forfeited their chance to earn the people's trust, some state leaders took actions which won for them an abundant store of gratitude and loyalty.

The responsibilities which state governments quickly assumed in order to help the needy were unprecedented. Only the extraordinary difficulties occasioned by war could have wrought such a rapid transformation in the nature of southern state governments. As Charles W. Ramsdell has observed, "during less than two years of war . . . the southern people . . . abandoned their habitual laissez-faire concepts of the functions of government." Traditional, restrained state governments turned into expanding, vigorous administrations in response to the outcry from poorer citizens. State officials created a panoply of new laws designed to alleviate suffering and equalize the burdens of war. The development of these laws, in Ramsdell's words, "was remarkable because it represented a complete break with their

32. Major W. T. Walthall to Lt. General G. W. Lay, August 6, 1863, in *Official Records*, Ser. IV, Vol. II, 726; Yearns, *Confederate Congress*, 59.

traditions and their whole political philosophy."[33] But the cause of this transformation was not mysterious. Thousands of the common people of the South were struggling against destitution, and they needed and demanded help.

The first steps taken by states at the outset of the war came as a recognition of the sacrifice that soldiers were making. To save the volunteer and his family from undue hardships caused by service to the country, most state legislatures enacted statutes which protected the property rights of troops in their absence. Legislators in North Carolina, for example, passed a stay law, which suspended the payment of debts; and despite the loud protests of creditors, stay laws won passage in most states. The legislature of Arkansas exempted soldiers from a variety of legal proceedings or requirements, such as creditors' attachments, statutes of limitation, or the need to make a personal appearance in court. With unusual prescience, Arkansas' lawmakers also empowered county courts to use the income from a special tax to aid families of volunteers who were in actual service.[34]

In a short while, these early measures expanded in many new directions. Between November, 1861, and March, 1862, seven states passed relief laws to provide for their poor. Typically these statutes relied upon the county governments to distribute funds raised by a state tax or a special county levy. Within a year these relief measures had proved inadequate, but the states did not give up on their efforts. Mississippi, North Carolina, Georgia, Louisiana, and Alabama took over the responsibility for relief from county authorities, passed appropriations as high as $6 million, and redoubled their search for revenue. Some states shifted from money taxes to the tax-in-kind and distributed food as well as money. The Georgia legislature once purchased 97,500 bushels of corn and specified that it was to go to the poor in sixteen hard-hit northern counties. Since certain essential items were very scarce, state governments also purchased

33. Charles W. Ramsdell, *Behind the Lines in the Southern Confederacy*, ed. Wendell H. Stephenson (Baton Rouge: Louisiana State University Press, 1944), 40, 82.

34. *North Carolina Whig* (Charlotte, N.C.), June 11, 1861, p. 2; Coulter, *Confederate States of America*, 426; *Official Records*, Ser. IV, Vol. I, 350–51, 362–63.

salt, medicines, cloth, and cotton and wool cards for the poor.[35]

Direct relief was not the only manifestation of the states' concern for their poorer citizens. In March, 1862, Arkansas struck out in a new direction and required farmers to shift from cotton to food crops. Alabama and Georgia followed before the year was out, and South Carolina also limited the production of cotton in February, 1863. Distilling attracted much unfavorable attention in the Confederacy because it consumed grain which people needed for bread. Accordingly, many states tried to prohibit distilling in order to conserve food. In 1862 six state legislatures—South Carolina, Virginia, Arkansas, North Carolina, Georgia, and Alabama—passed laws to this effect.[36]

To ease shortages of industrial products, the states also plunged into manufacturing enterprises. Initially most legislatures did not attempt to produce goods themselves but instead offered aid and inducements to private companies to make items needed by the public. Arkansas gave loans and grants of land to would-be manufacturers, and Alabama and Mississippi pledged bonuses to anyone who would make cotton or wool cards needed in making cloth. Texas promised 320 acres of land for every $1,000 invested in machinery to produce iron, textiles, firearms, nitre, sulphur, powder, salt, or oil. When private enterprise responded inadequately to the public demand, the states turned to importing and eventually to manufacturing the commodities themselves. State leaders transformed penitentiaries into textile mills, carpenters' shops, and machine shops, and prisoners learned how to make shoes and clothing. Governor Henry Allen of Louisiana displayed special ingenuity and established state-run turpentine stills, an iron foundry, and plants for making baking soda, castor oil, and medicines.[37]

The state governments also moved against the evil which most en-

---

35. Ramsdell, *Behind the Lines*, 25, 62–67; *Acts of the General Assembly of the State of Georgia Passed in Milledgeville at the Annual Session in November and December, 1863; also Extra Session of 1864* (Milledgeville: Boughton, Nisbet, Barnes & Moore, 1864), 8, 67; May Spencer Ringold, *The Role of the State Legislatures in the Confederacy* (Athens: University of Georgia Press, 1966), 80.

36. Ramsdell, *Behind the Lines*, 34–37.

37. Ringold, *Role of the State Legislatures*, 48–52.

raged ordinary southerners: speculation. Seven states passed laws against extortion and speculation, in response to strong popular sentiment. North Carolina and Florida prohibited the exportation of essential goods, while other states passed ordinances against monopoly and excessive profits. Often these laws were too vague, sometimes the courts proved too lenient, and, in general, laws against speculation proved impossible to enforce.[38] Nevertheless, the leaders of the states attempted to solve the problem.

Southerners received vast amounts of relief through their state governments, and even when certain measures fell short of success they were usually appreciated. The leaders of the states demonstrated a lively concern for their citizens and considerable energy in working to help those in economic difficulty. Naturally these actions by elected officials stimulated feelings of gratitude and loyalty among hard-pressed yeoman farmers. By reaching out to help, state leaders tapped the springs of loyalty which Confederate authorities were never able to find. The state governments seemed close, sympathetic, and supportive, whereas the Confederate government appeared to be distant, indifferent, and oppressive.

Of all the state governors, one stood out as the most vigorous, determined, and effective defender of the common people. That man was Georgia's Joseph E. Brown, and, not coincidentally, he was also one of Jefferson Davis' most powerful opponents. Blessed with the ability to appeal both to planters and to yeomen, Brown was a puzzling figure, as principled as he was unscrupulous, and as hostile toward the Davis administration as he was toward the United States. Often the Georgia executive attacked Davis for something which he himself had also done, and in the postwar period this advocate of secession transformed himself into a Republican and led the Radical forces in the state. Brown was combative, ambitious, and crafty. His guiding principle may have been simply to stay in power, but no one can deny that he was a consummate politician. In that department he ran rings around the less imaginative, austere Confederate president. Despite his defects in character, Brown held the trust of the

38. *Ibid.*, 73–77.

people throughout his Confederate career and won reelection for a third term as governor in 1861 and a fourth in 1863.

The southern yeomen were not as ideological as the planter class, and they supported Brown not because he was fighting for states' rights but because he was standing up for their interests. Brown's appeal to the common people took two forms: his harping on the themes of Jacksonian democracy and his offers of tangible relief such as food and clothing. Georgia's nonslaveholders and small farmers remembered that Governor Brown helped them, and this alone influenced them to reciprocate with their ballots at the polls. But Brown also convinced many Georgians that the Richmond administration had never learned to cherish the common people. He persuaded them that the Confederacy threatened their welfare and their liberties and that he had to oppose the Davis administration in order to defend the people. With impressive skill this Georgia politician cultivated backing for himself against the Confederacy not by calling on the people to oppose the national government but simply by asking them to speak out for their own welfare. Functionally, however, this was often equivalent to opposing the aims of the Richmond administration.

Brown's opportunity to gain the people's affection arose from their need. One sign that hard times had arrived even by 1861 was the fact that newspapers in nonslaveholding areas of Georgia kept close watch on proposals to aid the poor and lamented the shortages of essential items. Salt had particular importance since it served as a preservative for meats, and farmers could hardly do without it. In December, 1861, the Rome, Georgia, *Weekly Courier* reported that, "the Salt question, in this section at least, is assuming a greater magnitude than even the war." The usual price of this commodity was about fifty cents per sack, and the *Weekly Courier* understandably reported that "complaints were loud when it was $10 per sack, but the howls, now that there is none, is terrific."[39] Something had to be done.

39. Rome (Ga.) *Weekly Courier*, December 13, 1861, p. 3.

Governor Brown did not disappoint the citizens in Rome and other parts of Georgia. With swift and decisive actions he moved to relieve the shortage and obtain a supply of salt for those who needed it most. On November 20, 1861, he ordered the state's commissary general to seize all salt that was selling at more than five dollars per sack for the use of state troops and telegraphed the mayor of Augusta to seize two thousand sacks that were about to be shipped out of the state. From the legislature he sought a law authorizing him to impress essential items, though he later opposed Confederate impressments. At the same time the governor arranged to manufacture salt in Virginia on state account and transferred funds from other projects to pay for this activity until the legislature made a specific appropriation. Both the state-owned railroad and other Georgia railways carried salt free of charge.[40]

Even before the salt from Virginia arrived, Brown managed to find some supplies for poverty-stricken areas, and one can imagine the galvanizing effect of this advertisement, which appeared in the Rome, Georgia, *Weekly Courier* on January 3, 1862:

Salt, Salt!

I have a lot of Salt sent to Rome by Gov. Brown for distribution to soldiers' wives, and destitute widows—½ bushel each, at $1.25 per half bushel. After they are supplied, poor people will be entitled to ½ bushel each.

C. A. Smith, Agent

Neighboring regions of South Carolina shared in the excitement and rejoiced that Georgia's governor was finding a way to alleviate the salt problem. In Edgefield, South Carolina, an editor quickly reprinted this notice and commented: "Bless that man Brown." Later Brown made such distributions a regular practice and furnished salt to soldiers' families on at least three occasions. Giving first consideration to those least able to pay, Georgia's energetic executive gave one-half bushel to widows and parents of dead soldiers and allowed

40. Louise Biles Hill, *Joseph E. Brown and the Confederacy* (Chapel Hill: University of North Carolina Press, 1939), 113–15.

soldiers' families to purchase a half bushel for $1.00. After these Georgians were supplied, heads of families could purchase a bushel for $4.50. During the war the state supplied about six pounds of salt per capita per year.[41]

Shortages of clothing also developed due to the blockade, since the South previously had imported most of its cloth. Before cotton, which was in abundant supply, could be spun into cloth, one had to card it in order to untangle the fibers. There were few cards in Georgia or other states, but Brown established a factory in the penitentiary and, according to his biographer, Louise B. Hill, "swept the state clean of sheep, goat, deer, and dog skins, and of wire and tacks, and sent an agent to Europe to procure more of these raw materials to be used in the manufacture of cards." By March, 1863, the state factory had produced 1,777 pairs of cards and later achieved a capacity of 100 pairs per day. When this supply failed to meet the demand, Brown recommended an appropriation of $1 million to use in obtaining more cards from Europe. Once again the governor gave preference to the poorest citizens and arranged to supply soldiers' families and those on relief first.[42]

Georgia's men in service also enjoyed the special attentions of their tireless governor. At first the states had to clothe their own troops, but Brown insisted that Georgia continue this practice after the central government was ready to assume the task. Sending agents throughout the Confederacy and into Europe, Brown bought blankets, clothing, shoes, and other supplies. With great success he chartered steamers in 1864 which ran the blockade and exported $5 million worth of cotton to exchange for military supplies. Thanks to the thorough and energetic actions of their governor, Georgia's troops were better clothed and supplied than those of any other state, with the possible exception of North Carolina, where Governor Vance accomplished feats rivaling those of Brown.[43]

41. Rome (Ga.) *Weekly Courier*, January 3, 1862, p. 1; Edgefield (S. C.) *Advertiser*, January 8, 1862; Hill, *Joseph E. Brown*, 114–15.

42. Hill, *Joseph E. Brown*, 116–17.

43. *Ibid.*, 118–19. For a description of Governor Vance's import program, see Richard E. Yates, *The Confederacy and Zeb Vance* (Tuscaloosa, Ala.: Confederate Publishing Company, Inc., 1958), Chap. V.

Through all of Governor Brown's activities ran a characteristic concern for those in the most difficult circumstances. In addition to giving first consideration to the poor in the distribution of salt and cotton cards, Brown sought other ways to relieve the suffering of the state's humblest citizens. He asked the legislature in November, 1862, to grant a bounty of one hundred dollars for the family of each soldier whose taxable property was less than one thousand dollars. To pay for this appropriation, the governor suggested drawing on the income of the state-owned railway, raising freight rates, and enacting a special tax on the incomes of speculators. Brown believed that since "the poor have generally paid their part of the cost of this war in military service, exposure, fatigue and blood, the rich, who have been in a much greater degree exempt from these, should meet the money demands of the Government." Therefore he also asked the legislature to relieve soldiers from the poll tax and allow them a thousand-dollar exemption on the property tax.[44] These actions strengthened the governor's reputation as a friend of the common man and a champion of his interests in troubled times.

Brown's fight against distilleries illustrated the way in which his vigorous defense of the interests of the poor could convert even longtime opponents. The editor of the Rome, Georgia, *Weekly Courier* opposed Brown in every election and often launched stinging criticisms of the pugnacious executive. At the beginning of the war the *Weekly Courier* denounced Brown's lack of cooperation with Confederate authorities and thereafter ridiculed the state militia as a collection of draft dodgers or poked fun at the governor's huge corps of exempted state officials. When Brown issued a proclamation against illegal impressments in October, 1863, however, this hill-country paper published a brief word of praise. The distillery issue accelerated the growth of warm feelings on the part of the *Courier* toward its habitual opponent.[45]

In the fall of 1863, the shortage of food in the Rome area was acute,

44. Rome (Ga.) *Weekly Courier*, November 21, 1862, p. 4; Candler (ed.), *Confederate Records of Georgia*, II, 761; Hill, *Joseph E. Brown*, 120.
45. Rome (Ga.) *Weekly Courier*, May 16, 1862, p. 3, June 27, 1862, p. 3, January 23, 1863, p. 1, March 6, 1863, p. 1, October 2, 1863, p. 1.

so acute that on November 12 the *Weekly Courier* ran a headline asking, WHAT SHALL WE DO FOR SOMETHING TO EAT? After the paper's editor learned that some citizens in north Georgia were making whiskey for the Confederate army, he strongly condemned the practice and stressed that the scarcity of corn made distilling intolerable. Governor Brown, who had been fighting the distilleries since early in 1862, entered the fray at the requests of three local judges and declared that he had issued no licenses to allow distilling. Even the Confederate government needed a license, according to Brown, whose willingness to oppose the Richmond administration was well known. On this issue the *Weekly Courier* showed warm appreciation for Brown's attitude, and although the newspaper continued to criticize its old antagonist, Brown's opposition to distilling probably won him many friends among the common people.[46]

Brown was a master of the rhetoric which exalted the common people and portrayed himself as their protector. The ordinary citizens in a democracy, Brown asserted, made the greatest contributions, and therefore he was determined to stand up for their interests. When Howell Cobb, with good reason, attacked Brown in May, 1864, for obstructing the Confederacy's war effort, the feisty governor replied by praising the people's noble sacrifices, stressing his aid to them, and making this thrust at Cobb's considerable wealth: "I am perfectly willing that the hardy, wayworn veterans of Georgia who are kept in the front, and have no comfortable office, and no command in the rear, who left their wives and little ones to defend your large inheritance, as well as their own log cabins . . . shall judge whether . . . I have indeed been their friend, or, as you would intimate, only their 'pretended friend.'" Finally he pointed out that, unlike Cobb, he had started life as a poor man and earned his wealth. On another occasion Brown countered the attacks of critics by boasting to a Confederate general that "the Governor and Legislature of your State whom you denounce have appropriated for this year nearly $10,000,000 to feed and clothe the suffering wives, and widows, and

46. *Ibid.*, November 12, 1863, p. 3, November 20, 1863, p. 1, November 27, 1863, p. 1.

orphans, and soldiers, and to put shoes upon the feet and clothes upon the backs of soldiers themselves, who are often destitute."[47]

By his aggressive battles for the interests of ordinary Georgians, Joe Brown won the loyal support of many poorer citizens. In addition to this following he had a claim on the loyalty of many planters, who saw his championing of states' rights as a defense of the basic purposes of the southern nation. Brown's political genius enabled him to blend these two appeals into one and go beyond a reliance on separate issues for different groups of the electorate.[48] He managed, in the context of the war and the expanding role of the central government, to fuse states' rights and Jacksonian ideology, to make states' rights seem the necessary instrument for serving the common man. By picturing the Confederate government as a threat to the common people, Brown made states' rights relevant to the daily problems of Georgia's nonslaveholders and farmers and bound them to his administration rather than to the national government.

Frequently the governor pointed out that the Confederacy did not help the ordinary people but instead left them in suffering or worsened their condition. Georgia's soldiers, Brown said, relied upon the state because they "cannot get supplies from the Confederate government." Nor did the Confederacy provide for the civilian population, since "the helpless families" of soldiers "were dependent upon the action of the Governor and Legislature for bread." Brown's resistance to illegal impressments spotlighted the way in which he tried to protect the people from Confederate policies that threatened their welfare.[49] Soldiers who wanted a furlough knew that Brown was their protector. Throughout Georgia people contrasted the actions of the Confederate government, which continually demanded more men, more money, or more food, with those of Joe Brown,

47. Joseph E. Brown to Howell Cobb, May 20, 1864, and Brown to Brigadier General Anderson, May 2, 1864, in *Official Records*, Ser. IV, Vol. III, 431–39, 372–75.

48. The author owes the inspiration for his interpretation of Governor Brown's politics to Horace Montgomery's studies, particularly *Howell Cobb's Confederate Career* (Tuscaloosa, Ala.: Confederate Publishing Company, Inc., 1959), 117–18, and *Cracker Parties* (Baton Rouge: Louisiana State University Press, 1950), 200–210 and 235–38.

49. *Official Records*, Ser. IV, Vol. III, 372–75, and Ser. IV, Vol. II, 943–44.

who gave money, food, and other forms of support to the people.

These facts contributed to Brown's great popularity, which he strengthened by arguing that the Confederacy threatened not only people's livelihood but also their freedom. To hard-pressed Georgians Brown taught that the Davis administration's heavy demands were unconstitutional and illegal. Not only had the central government forgotten the people, but it was also trying to establish a despotism over them. Conscription had elicited the first charges of usurpation from Brown, and the suspension of the writ of *habeas corpus* reawakened his ire. He hotly denied that the congress had the power to "authorize the President to arrest the people and send them in irons to the islands or dungeons of other States, and confine them at his pleasure. . . . This is not the constitutional liberty which so many Georgians have died to defend. He who possesses this control over the personal liberties of the people has in his hands the powers of a monarch, call him by what name you may."[50] Thus Georgia's governor claimed to defend both the basic rights of the people and their material interests from Confederate encroachments. One task merged into the other, and each of his many feuds with the central government had both symbolic and practical significance. In addition to defending the principle of states' rights, Brown's protests aimed at winning some privilege for Georgia's troops or some benefit for her civilian population.

Thus, to many Georgians, the Confederate States became an enemy, and the state government a friend. The Confederacy forfeited its chance to gain the people's gratitude and loyalty and instead brought only trouble. The state won that loyalty by helping when the people most needed assistance and promoting social justice among the classes. Although Brown was the most adroit and articulate state leader, the same conditions existed elsewhere and the same process was underway. While the Confederacy was losing its hold on the people's devotion, state governments were earning increased popularity through service to their citizens. As a result of its weakened

50. *Ibid.*, Ser. IV, Vol. III, 372–75.

political position, the Richmond administration often failed to obtain full cooperation from the states. Some politicians interfered to protect their constituents, while others used quarrels with the Davis administration to further their own goals. Governor Brown, secure in the knowledge that he had the support of his citizens, did not hesitate to impair the war effort and promote what amounted to a separate foreign policy in 1864. When Jefferson Davis came into conflict with Joseph Brown, Confederate nationalism was the loser and a narrow, self-serving conception of states' rights was triumphant. As the common people, driven by need, turned away from the Confederacy, they often turned toward state leaders who frustrated Confederate nationalism.

The growing influence of state leaders like Brown indicated that Jefferson Davis had a diminished capacity to inspire the people, but the Confederate president tried nevertheless to retain southerners' loyalty through an appeal to ideology. To counter the serious decline in morale which by 1863 was painfully evident, he stressed the goals of the South's cause and painted a dark picture of the enemy. Davis' use of ideological themes revealed his estimate of the state of morale and the kind of appeals which could stimulate new efforts from the people. The changing emphasis in his pronouncements was a sign both of plummeting enthusiasm and of the difficulties which strong executive leadership encountered in relation to Confederate ideology.

6

In Search
of an
Ideology

On November 2, 1863, Jefferson Davis visited Charleston, South Carolina, the birthplace of secession. All the paraphernalia of a festive occasion were in place—garlands and banners hung along the route and flags fluttered from almost every building. According to one newspaper account, "The streets along the line of procession were thronged with people, anxious to get a look at the President. The men cheered and the ladies waved their handkerchiefs." Arriving at city hall Davis delivered a "brilliant speech" and accepted the greetings of leading men from the Palmetto state. On the surface this reception had all the marks of a familiar southern scene—flags and bunting, politicians in abundance, and states' rights oratory.[1]

Davis' remarks reinforced this impression, for he quickly alluded to John C. Calhoun. Recalling that he had accompanied Calhoun's remains back to Charleston in 1850, Davis invoked the spirit of this stern states' rights theorist to watch over the young southern nation. The Confederate president also acknowledged his debt to Dr. Thomas Cooper, another South Carolinian, whose *Southern Quarterly Review* had inculcated true doctrine in Davis and other young southerners in the 1820s and 1830s. From such words it seemed that a kind of political reunion was taking place, as the Confederacy's leader and the citizens of Charleston joined together to celebrate their common goals. Except for Davis' comments on the military situation and one sharply worded but brief reference to disunity, the

1. Dunbar Rowland (ed.), *Jefferson Davis: Constitutionalist; His Letters, Papers, and Speeches* (10 vols.; Jackson, Miss.: Little & Ives Company, 1923), VI, 73–78.

scene could have taken place early in 1861 rather than in the midst of a costly and divisive war that was not going well for the South.[2]

In reality, however, the character of Davis' visit to Charleston was very different from its appearance. Rather than visiting with his admirers, Davis was plunging into a lion's den. The Rhetts, father and son, attended the public ceremonies but greeted the president with an icy civility which recalled their attacks on his programs, and General P. G. T. Beauregard felt so alienated from his commander-in-chief that he refused to attend a private reception.[3] Although Davis had often spoken of states' rights before, his use of the familiar rhetoric in Charleston represented a brave attempt to concede nothing to his critics. Many events had taken place since the bright days of 1861, and both the fortunes of the Confederacy and Jefferson Davis' position among states' rights leaders had suffered.

The references to states' rights which Davis made on the portico of the city hall masked great changes in Confederate ideology. Under the stress of two and half years of war, Davis had modified the ideological appeals with which he had stirred southerners in 1861. New themes appeared in his addresses in 1862 and 1863, and these made the Charleston speech more atypical than characteristic of his public utterances. This transformation of Confederate ideology possessed great significance because it revealed much about the condition of the southern nation. The alteration of themes reflected drastic changes in morale and internal divisions over Confederate goals. To recapture the flagging enthusiasm of the people, Davis had adjusted his statement of Confederate ideology to accord with his estimate of morale and had sought new arguments capable of reviving the war spirit. The evolution of his ideology also provided evidence of the need to redefine Confederate purpose in the face of vigorous criticism of presidential acts.

At the beginning of the Civil War Davis had framed an ideology which helped unify the different classes and regions of the South.

2. *Ibid.*
3. Hudson Strode, *Jefferson Davis* (3 vols.; New York: Harcourt, Brace and Company, 1955–1964), II, 492.

His success in this task had been one of the greatest achievements of his leadership during the crucial early days of the nation. At a time when many southerners were reluctant to leave the Union, Davis identified Confederate goals with the history and traditions of the United States. The key to the effectiveness of his ideology was its claim that the Confederacy was the true embodiment of American democracy. Since Davis shared with many southerners a lingering affection and loyalty for the government founded by George Washington, he had known how to reach others and lead them toward a new loyalty to the Confederacy. Repeatedly he sounded his main theme: that the new southern nation was the true heir of the founding fathers and existed to continue the work which they had begun.[4] As a supplement to this, he tried to demonstrate that the United States had fallen away from its heritage and become a land of fanaticism, executive usurpations, and tyranny.

Essentially, this was a conservative ideology which made the fewest possible demands on southerners' weak sense of separate nationality. By enunciating these themes, Davis eased the transition from a familiar, well-loved government to an untried new one. Rather than insisting that southerners break with the United States, he merely urged them to transfer their love for the Union to a more worthy object. In the uncertain days of 1861 this ideology proved timely, appropriate, and relevant. It reassured those whom events had forced into war by its stress on the clean hands and peaceful intentions of the South. The Confederacy's expressed devotion to revered traditions strengthened its claim to legitimacy, and Davis' occasional comments on the misdeeds and wartime cruelties of northerners aroused feelings of indignation and defiance.

In 1862 the course of the war posed different and greater challenges for Confederate leadership. Where Davis formerly had sought to create unity, he now had to maintain it in the face of disappointing reverses. Where the direction of events had once been on his side, it now worked against him. The magnitude of the war and the de-

4. See Chapter II herein for greater detail.

feats which southern armies suffered drove home to Confederates the unwelcome fact that they faced a long, grinding, and bloody conflict. Even the occasional southern victories failed to bring peace any closer, and thus the conditions with which Davis had to deal changed. Rather than witnessing an outpouring of enthusiasm for the war such as had occurred in the summer of 1861, the Confederate president battled against signs that the will to fight was waning. Instead of arguing that southerners should preserve their old loyalties, Davis now worried that memories of the United States might stimulate a longing for reconstruction.

Military events in 1862 first brought a series of disappointments and then raised Confederate hopes only to dash them cruelly. January began on a low note occasioned by somber New Year's reflections on the prospects of the war. In substantial numbers southerners initially had believed that the North would not fight or that if a war came it would bring a swift and decisive victory. After the brilliant Confederate success at Bull Run, however, the Union armies did not crumble and disappear. Under the painstaking, professional direction of General George McClellan, a formidable army of a quarter million men took shape in northern Virginia. From July, 1861, to March, 1862, this force augmented its battalions, perfected its organization, and prepared for war. It was obvious that the United States was girding for a long struggle, and as one Confederate soldier remarked in January, 1862, "the vast preparation of the enemy" produced "a more general feeling of despondency prevailing at this time than ever before since the war began."[5]

February brought bad news from the west, where military operations turned on the control of important rivers. The Confederacy had fortifications on three western waterways, and each outpost was a linchpin in the defensive structure which guarded Kentucky and Tennessee. At Columbus, Kentucky, a large garrison watched the

5. J. G. Randall and David Donald, *The Civil War and Reconstruction* (2nd ed; Boston: D. C. Heath and Company, 1961), 209; Edward Younger (ed.), *Inside the Confederate Government: The Diary of Robert Garlick Hill Kean, Head of the Bureau of War* (New York: Oxford University Press, 1957), 23, herinafter cited as *Diary of R. G. H. Kean.*

Mississippi River, while Fort Henry commanded the Tennessee, and Fort Donelson on the Cumberland guarded the approaches to Nashville. Yet within a period of ten days General U. S. Grant, who earned his sobriquet "Unconditional Surrender Grant" during this campaign, drove the southerners out of Forts Henry and Donelson. Albert Sidney Johnston, the ranking Confederate general in the west, had to abandon his Kentucky front and evacuate Nashville, and during the next two months Union forces slowly dislodged the Confederates from Columbus, Kentucky, as well. These reverses dismayed some southerners and disturbed Jefferson Davis, who worried more about their impact on morale than their effect on military operations. To General J. E. Johnston, then commanding in Virginia, Davis commented, "Recent disasters have depressed the weak, and are depriving us of the aid of the wavering. Traitors show the tendencies heretofore concealed, and the selfish grow clamorous for local, and personal, interests." In an "unofficial letter" to Albert Sidney Johnston, Davis urged the unsuccessful general to explain the loss of Fort Donelson and Nashville and try to offset unfavorable newspaper comment. The significance attached to these defeats in the press, Davis feared, had "undermined public confidence and damaged our cause."[6]

If the reaction to Confederate military reverses had not already wakened Davis' concern, a letter from a prominent Alabamian surely would have done so. Judge W. M. Brooks, who had been president of Alabama's secession convention, sent the president a painfully frank letter reciting commonly heard complaints about the administration and its policies. These showed that the people, at least in Alabama, were losing confidence in the ability of their government to conduct the nation's affairs. According to Brooks, it was "credibly said" that the president had "scarcely a friend and not a defender in Congress or in the army," that he had not held a cabinet meeting in

6. Randall and Donald, *The Civil War and Reconstruction*, 202–204; Jefferson Davis to J. E. Johnston, February 28, 1862, and Davis to A. S. Johnston, March 12, 1862, in Rowland (ed.), *Jefferson Davis*, V, 209, 215–16.

four months, that he had adopted a purely defensive policy and kept the generals in leading strings, and that his administration proscribed all men who had not formerly been Democrats. Davis tried to respond constructively to these criticisms and thanked Brooks for his efforts to defend the administration, but the chief executive worried that such criticisms might "succeed in destroying the confidence of the people."[7]

The spring brought added concerns for Davis, who had given close attention to the defense of Richmond. For months southerners had watched the continual buildup of forces under McClellan, and they knew that eventually the United States would send the full shock of these battalions against the Confederate capital. Before these engagements took place, however, the opposing armies in the west fought a major battle on April 6 and 7, 1862. At Shiloh Church, near the Tennessee-Mississippi border, Confederate forces attempted to regain the ground lost in February, but on the second day of fighting Federal troops reinforced General Grant, who drove the southerners back upon Corinth, Mississippi. Although not all southern newspapers saw the fighting at Shiloh as a Confederate defeat, the fall of New Orleans to Union forces on April 29, 1862, could bear no other interpretation. Soon after these events President Davis wrote to the commander in Virginia that he hoped for a "brilliant" victory "which the drooping cause of our country now so imperatively claims."[8]

As Davis knew, the inevitable result of these defeats was growing fear and shrinking confidence among the people. It was becoming apparent that the outmanned Confederacy was unable to defend all of its territory simultaneously. Whenever the government drew troops from one point to concentrate them at another, the residents of exposed areas expressed deep concern for their safety. As early as May, 1862, a petition arrived from citizens in Virginia who formally asked

7. Jefferson Davis to W. M. Brooks, March 13, 1862, in Rowland (ed.), *Jefferson Davis*, V, 216–19.
8. Randall and Donald, *The Civil War and Reconstruction*, 205–206; Jefferson Davis to J. E. Johnston, May 10, 1862, in Rowland (ed.), *Jefferson Davis*, V, 242–43.

permission to take pay from the enemy and trade for the necessities of life if their county was overrun and they could obtain no protection from the Confederate government. At the same time in Arkansas an impression that the central government had abandoned the defense of the state and of the whole Trans-Mississippi Department gained wide acceptance. Davis directed General Earl Van Dorn, who had temporarily moved his forces into Tennessee to oppose United States General Halleck, to issue a proclamation to counter this feeling and to reassure the people that the government was planning for their effective defense. From Louisiana in September, 1862, came a prominent journalist's warning that "a feeling prevails among our people that they have been forgotten or abandoned by the Government for which they suffer," and one month later Governor Vance of North Carolina informed Davis that a similar attitude prevailed in the eastern counties of his state.[9]

Despite these problems, Davis had hopes that developments abroad would soon ensure Confederate independence. From the beginning of 1862 he had favored the idea of offering free trade and other advantages to foreign nations as an inducement to them to break the Union blockade and recognize the southern government. The unanimous disapproval of his cabinet in January influenced Davis to drop this scheme for a while, but he revived it in the spring after Judah Benjamin, his closest advisor, became secretary of state. In April, 1862, Benjamin instructed the southern representative in France, John Slidell, to make Napoleon III an offer of free trade and a cotton subsidy in return for aid to the Confederate cause. Slidell communicated this proposition to the French emperor in July, and Davis expected great results from the plan. On July 6, 1862, he wrote to his wife that "there is reason to believe that the Yankees have gained from England and France as the last extension, this

9. Petition of citizens of Middlesex County, Virginia, May 6, 1862, in Letters Received, Confederate Secretary of War, in Record Group 109, National Archives, Microcopy M 437, Roll 60, pp. 899–907; Jefferson Davis to General Earl Van Dorn, May 20, 1862, in Rowland (ed.), *Jefferson Davis*, V, 248–49; Alexander Walker to Davis, September 13, 1862, in Jefferson Davis Papers, Library of Congress; Davis to Zebulon Vance, October 17, 1862, in Rowland (ed.), *Jefferson Davis*, V, 354–55.

month, and expect foreign intervention if we hold them at bay on the first of August."[10]

Although foreign recognition did not come, August did bring a splendid Confederate victory. At long last, General Robert E. Lee, who had succeeded Joseph E. Johnston as commander of the army of northern Virginia, inflicted a severe defeat on the fumbling General John Pope at Second Manassas. One result of this Union debacle was that Richmond, for the first time in months, was quite safe— the main Union army was in full retreat toward Washington and no other threatening enemy forces operated within one hundred miles of the southern capital. A more important result of the victory at Second Manassas was that General Lee felt encouraged enough to invade the North. Moving into Maryland on September 5, Lee raised Confederate hopes by his advance, which was coordinated with the start of an ambitious campaign in the west. At the end of August forces under the command of Kirby Smith entered Kentucky and General Braxton Bragg led his troops toward that state from Chattanooga, Tennessee. Thus in both the east and the west Confederate armies were on the offensive, a fact which lifted the spirits of the southern people and presented Jefferson Davis with an opportunity to change the terms of the war.[11]

After months of concern about the strength of his country's internal morale, Davis now hoped to take advantage of the reaction which advancing Confederate armies would produce in the North. In directives to the three commanding generals, Davis framed a declaration to the citizens of the invaded areas. Returning to the ideology used in the first year of the contest, he stressed that the Confederacy had no aggressive designs and was fighting only in self-defense and for the right of self-government. All efforts toward peace by the South

10. Thomas Bragg Diary, 1861–1862 (Southern Historical Collection, University of North Carolina), January 6, 1862; Robert Douthat Meade, *Judah P. Benjamin: Confederate Statesman* (New York: Oxford University Press, 1943), 255–56; Jefferson Davis to Varina Howell Davis, July 6, 1862, in Rowland (ed.), *Jefferson Davis*, V, 291.
11. Randall and Donald, *The Civil War and Reconstruction*, 218–20, 407; Archer Jones, *Confederate Strategy from Shiloh to Vicksburg* (Baton Rouge: Louisiana State University Press, 1961), 70–83.

had been rebuffed, and therefore the Confederate government had to make the effects of continued war "fall on those who persist in their refusal to make peace." Davis urged the people of Maryland and Kentucky to exercise state sovereignty and make "a separate treaty of peace" if they could not prevail on the government of the United States. In a bid to disaffected elements in the northwestern United States, the president also declared that the Confederacy was "still ready to adhere" to the principle of free navigation of the Mississippi River.[12]

To Davis' profound disappointment, however, both Lee's advance into Maryland and the combined invasion of Kentucky came to nothing. In an inconclusive battle on September 17, 1862, McClellan stopped Lee near Sharpsburg, Maryland, and although the United States general threw away his opportunities to decimate the southern forces, Lee had to retreat across the Potomac. Similarly, one day after Bragg helped inaugurate a provisional Confederate governor in Kentucky, a sharp contest near Perryville forced the withdrawal of his and Smith's armies into Tennessee.[13]

To Jefferson Davis these reversals indicated that the Confederacy's future was indeed dark. After long months of defeat and disappointment, the South finally had marshaled enough strength to carry the war to the enemy, yet this effort failed completely. Outnumbered and poorly supplied, the South had expended all its energies to no avail, while the United States still had reserves of every kind on which to draw. Expressing his disappointment, Davis told a committee of the congress in October that southerners had entered "the darkest and most dangerous period we have yet had."[14] Undoubtedly many ordinary citizens shared the president's depression.

Thus, during 1862 the course of the war presented a major challenge to Davis' leadership. He had used ideology successfully before in order to strengthen the people's spirit, but the need now was much

12. Jefferson Davis to Generals Robert E. Lee, Braxton Bragg, and E. K. Smith, September 7 (?), 1862, in Rowland (ed.), *Jefferson Davis*, V, 338–39.
13. Randall and Donald, *The Civil War and Reconstruction*, 407; Jones, *Confederate Strategy*, 70–83.
14. Younger (ed.), *Diary of R. G. H. Kean*, 28, 84.

greater. Somehow he had to help southerners regain their determination in the face of disappointment and steel them to overcome the hardships of war. Throughout the conflict Davis tried to accomplish these tasks through ideological appeals designed to strengthen the people's sense of purpose and renew their commitment to independence. His task in 1862 was to find the right combination of appeals which would animate the people.

On a few occasions Davis revived the ideological themes of 1861 and claimed that all hope for constitutional liberty in America rested in the southern nation, which alone had remained true to the original principles of the United States. On February 20, 1862, for example, Davis boasted that in the Confederacy "law has everywhere reigned supreme, and throughout our widespread limits personal liberty and private right have been duly honored." Two days later he completed this implied comparison with the United States by deploring the northern "bastiles filled with prisoners" and the suspension of the writ of *habeas corpus* "by Executive mandate."[15] Davis never completely abandoned this type of argument, for he continued to believe that liberty was more secure in the South than in the North, but the rapid growth of power in his central government created grave problems for such claims.

Only five days after his proud assertion on February 22, 1862, that "there has been no act on our part to impair personal liberty or the freedom of speech, of thought, or of the press," the congress presented him with the authority to suspend the writ of *habeas corpus* and declare martial law. Davis used these powers immediately and during succeeding weeks extended the scope of their operation. Throughout the rest of the war he prodded the congress to renew his power to impose martial law, for he concluded, as had Lincoln, that it was necessary to curtail individual liberties in order to protect the existence of the nation. One month after the first suspension of the writ of *habeas corpus*, Davis proposed another bold abridgment of

15. James D. Richardson (comp.), *A Compilation of the Messages and Papers of the Confederacy, Including the Diplomatic Correspondence, 1861–1865* (2 vols.; Nashville: United States Publishing Company, 1906), I, 217–18, 184, 227–30.

individual freedom when he called for the first national conscription law in the history of America. Not only was the concept itself shocking to many, but the terms of the law also required men who had volunteered for one year's service to remain in their units despite what many regarded as a solemn contract with the government. Shortly after came other vigorous uses of government power, such as heavy reliance on impressment and limitations on the practice of substitution. Davis even argued in December, 1861, and afterwards that the existence of war required temporary government aid to railroad companies, although the constitution explicitly banned such appropriations.[16]

Naturally these actions proved highly controversial. Davis was realistic about the demands of war, and he believed that he needed all the powers which the constitution gave him. At no time did he totally abandon his claim to be a defender of states' rights and individual liberties, and indeed in these areas his record was much better than that of his northern counterpart. But to many advocates of states' rights Davis played the role of a despot. They felt that such strong executive actions threw the whole southern cause into question. With intense anger and stinging attacks they challenged the president's right to speak for the Confederacy in the name of states' rights.

Both the Charleston *Mercury* and the Richmond *Whig* challenged the central government's role in raising an army and favored state leadership. In fact, at the end of 1861 the *Whig* declared its total opposition to an active president, whom it assailed as "an elective king, with an army of dependents and fifty millions of revenue." The suspension of the writ of *habeas corpus* aroused more cries of outrage. Warning that the "struggle for civil liberty never ends," the Richmond *Examiner* demanded an end to martial law in October, 1862, when the first law suspending *habeas corpus* was due to expire. Although this bill was renewed until February 13, 1863, the vocal opposition of such papers as the Charleston *Mercury* and the Richmond *Whig* then made it impossible for the congress to renew the

16. Richardson (comp.), *Messages and Papers of the Confederacy*, I, 185, 205–206; Bragg Diary, February 27, 1862.

suspension in an election year.[17] Opposition to conscription also grew quickly, and both the Richmond *Examiner* and the Charleston *Mercury* moved into the ranks of opponents of the measure.[18] But newspaper criticism seemed paltry compared to the full-scale assault on conscription launched by Governor Brown of Georgia, who charged Davis' government with "bold and dangerous usurpation . . . a rapid stride towards military despotism," and the purpose of striking down state sovereignty "at a single blow." Encouraged by such vigorous assaults, critics of the administration claimed that the president's programs threatened to create "a consolidated despotism."[19]

Thus, during 1862 a torrent of criticism undermined Davis' ability to pose as the defender of states' rights and to identify the Confederacy with the cause of constitutional liberty. Almost every week important segments of the press charged that he had "altogether ignored" or "lost sight of" the fundamental principle of the Confederacy. The harried southern executive even drew fire for referring to the South's confederation of states as a nation.[20] In the face of such attacks, it became increasingly difficult for Davis to employ the major theme of his ideological appeals. No longer could he confidently claim that the Confederacy existed to vindicate states' rights, for such an assertion would have invited instant criticism and placed new ammunition in the hands of his political opponents.

Therefore political considerations impelled Davis to alter his ideological appeal in 1862 and find a new theme to use in building southern morale. The alleged barbarity of the foe—the purposeful cruelty

17. Charleston *Mercury*. September 19, 1861, p. 1; Richmond *Weekly Whig*, September 28, 1861, p.1, November 16, 1861, p. 2, November 30, 1861, p. 3; *Daily Richmond Examiner*, September 25, 1862, p. 2; Richmond *Daily Whig*, March 6, 1863, p. 2, and Charleston *Mercury*, March 12, 1863, p. 1.

18. Initially the *Examiner* supported conscription but later reversed itself. *Daily Richmond Examiner*, January 9, 10, and 12, 1862, August 19, 1862, p. 2 and December 23, 1862, p. 2.

19. Joseph E. Brown to Jefferson Davis, June 21, 1862, and October 18, 1862, in Allen D. Candler (ed.), *The Confederate Records of the State of Georgia* (6 vols.; Atlanta: Chas. P. Byrd, 1910), III, 252, 299; Richmond *Daily Whig*, February 5, 1863, p. 2.

20. *Daily Richmond Examiner*, April 15, 1862, p. 2, and September 11, 1862, p. 2; Richmond *Daily Whig*, October 31, 1863, p. 2.

of the United States army and the uncivilized nature of its warfare—
soon received primary stress in his speeches. From the beginning of
the conflict Davis had used this argument in a secondary capacity,
but now it served as the burden of his message. With increasing fre-
quency Davis turned to this claim as a means to unite the southern
people, strengthen their determination to resist, and prove the justice of the Confederacy's cause.

This theme served Davis' purpose in another way. The stress on
northern barbarity was appropriate to the changed circumstances of
the Confederacy and had a direct relevance to southerners' state of
mind in the second year of the war. Whereas an identification of the
new nation with the traditions of the United States had been effective in the delicate process of secession, Davis' new ideology addressed the fact of continuing bloody conflict. Despite their expecta-
tions, southerners faced protracted war, and Davis sought a way to
gird their morale for the long pull and strengthen their determination to resist.

The former close identification of Confederate purposes with the
traditions and ideals of the United States had lost its usefulness and
had possibly become dangerous. For if the ties between the North
and the South seemed too clear, people were likely to ask whether
the high cost of the war was necessary. Surely, some would reason,
two people who had so many fundamental traditions in common could
find a better way to settle their differences. To prevent the growth
of such feelings, Jefferson Davis had to find some way to make the
South's reasons to fight more compelling. His initial stress on the
Confederacy's bond to the heritage of the United States was no longer
suited to the goal of Confederate independence.

By taking up the theme of northern barbarity, Davis essentially
was attempting to change the South's image of the North. During
more than seventy years of United States history, southerners had
viewed their fellow citizens in the North as part of a common nation,
and this image remained strong. As Kenneth Boulding has observed,
"An enormous part of the activity of each society is concerned with

the transmission and protection of its public image."[21] The image of the North had been mainly a favorable one, and the slow and arduous process of secession demonstrated that many southerners were reluctant to discard their identification with the United States.

This resistance to change is an inherent property of images, both public and private ones. Individuals readily accept information which accords with their existing image, but conflicting data tend to be rejected, even vigorously, and only strong or repeated messages can penetrate one's defenses and produce a modification or overthrow of the accepted view.[22] Considered in terms of this model, the task of southern nationalism was to accelerate the divergence between the image of the Confederacy and that of the United States and to create a separate and distinct image of the South as opposed to the North. Southern nationalists had to convince their fellows that in some way the South was the negation of northern qualities and that no commonality could overcome the differences between them.

Jefferson Davis' stress on the cruelty and savagery of the United States' war effort met this end, for it spotlighted events incompatible with the view that Americans were brothers who shared deep bonds of affection. By harping repeatedly on the alleged purposeful cruelty of the foe, Davis helped tear down the long-established nexus between southerners' images of themselves and of their fellow citizens in the North. The people of the United States could not share any connection with Confederates, Davis argued, because their acts were of such a heinous nature as to deny all kinship. According to Davis' speeches, northerners had a special hatred, a peculiarly bitter animus, toward southerners. The foe refused even to follow the commonly accepted rules of warfare. By dint of repetition this argument put distance between the images of the North and the South and tended to convince Confederates that they were a separate people.

In effect, this new version of Confederate ideology also bypassed Davis' critics. While they charged that the president was destroying

21. Kenneth E. Boulding, *The Image* (Ann Arbor: University of Michigan Press, 1956), 64.
22. *Ibid.*, 12–13.

what was distinctly southern, he showed that no act of the South's leaders could restore the region's identification with the United States. Emergency measures that abridged individual liberty during the crisis could not reduce the Confederacy to a carbon copy of the United States, for an unbridgeable gap separated the two regions. Davis' contention that the Confederacy was the antithesis of the North also implied that independence and not states' rights was the primary goal of the Confederacy. The hostility of the enemy, Davis argued, proved the indispensable need for independence and provided additional reasons to resist.

One of the Confederate president's first protests against specific Union commanders came in the summer of 1862. Accroding to Davis, Major General John Pope ordered the "murder" of Confederate citizens in Virginia on the pretext that they were spies if they remained on their farms in his rear. The chief executive also reacted angrily to the news that one of Pope's brigadier generals, Adolph von Steinwehr, had seized hostages as protection for his soldiers against the attacks of bushwhackers. Writing to Robert E. Lee, the commander of Confederate forces in that area, Davis directed that Pope's officers be denied the treatment due to prisoners of war and threatened to extend Confederate retaliation to enlisted men if the United States' practices continued. The Adjutant and Inspector General's Office directed that Confederate commanders hold Pope's officers in close confinement and cause one "to be immediately hung" for each Confederate citizen "thus murdered by the enemy."[23]

In August, 1862, Davis learned that Major General David Hunter was raising companies of Negro troops in the sea islands. Regarding this as an attempt "to inaugurate a servile war which is worse than that of the savage," Davis lodged a protest with the United States army and threatened to take retaliation as the only way to deter the enemy from such practices. During the same month he told the con-

23. Jefferson Davis to Robert E. Lee, July 31, 1862, and General Orders, No. 54, 1862, issued August 1, 1862, in *The War of the Rebellion: A Compilation of the Official Records of the Union and Confederate Armies* (130 vols., Washington: Government Printing Office, 1880–1901), Ser. II, Vol. IV, 830–31, 836–37, hereinafter cited as *Official Records*.

gress that the enemy was "daily less regardful of the usages of civilized war and the dictates of humanity." Even northern clergymen, he charged, sought to urge "an excited populace to the extreme of ferocity." He specifically condemned General Benjamin Butler, who was widely hated as "Beast Butler" in the South, for issuing an order that women in New Orleans who were discourteous to the Federals should be treated as women of the street. By December, 1862, Davis' anger at Butler had increased to the point that he issued a special proclamation against the Union general, recited his alleged crimes at length, and ordered that Butler be hung as "an outlaw and common enemy of mankind" when captured.[24]

The confiscation acts of the United States Congress heightened southern anger at the North's conduct of the war. In the summer of 1861 Congress had passed a bill providing for the seizure of property which was actually used "in aid of the rebellion." One year later the northern legislators produced a confiscation act which made the first measure seem halfhearted. This new law established stiff penalties for treason and made all southerners subject to the confiscation of their property. Officers of the Confederate government ran the risk of immediate forfeiture of their possessions without warning, while those who supported the rebellion faced similar forfeiture after sixty day's notice. Residence in the eleven "insurrectionary" states constituted evidence of support for the rebellion. In addition the act declared that the slaves of all persons supporting the war were "forever free." Throughout the Confederacy these acts attracted wide notice and aroused resentment.[25]

Southern newspapers actively shared Davis' anger about the North's conduct of the war. The execution of a southern citizen named Mumford, who had torn down a Union flag in New Orleans, occasioned prolonged denunciations in many Confederate newspapers. The Richmond *Enquirer*, which often took the administration's point of view, declared that it was convinced of the Union's

24. Jefferson Davis to Robert E. Lee, August 1, 1862, in *Official Records*, Ser. II, Vol. IV, 835; Richardson (comp.), *Messages and Papers of the Confederacy*, I, 233, 271.
25. Randall and Donald, *The Civil War and Reconstruction*, 283–84, 372.

"extreme malignity towards us," and leading journals in all parts of the Confederacy applauded Davis' attempts to retaliate for alleged northern outrages. In fact, the president's reaction was too cool for many editors, who felt that his reluctance to punish Union prisoners was almost criminal. The Charleston *Mercury*, for example, urged southern generals to take retaliatory action without referring the matter to Richmond, where the administration's supposed timidity always frustrated attempts to gain satisfaction.[26]

Davis did not neglect another possible resource for maintaining morale—the churches. Religion was a powerful force in the South, so much so that the Richmond *Enquirer* speculated that if the churches "had pronounced . . . against us . . . we never could have carried on the war." Moving directly to identify the South's cause with God and enlist the support of the clergy, Davis proclaimed days for nationwide prayer and fasting and urged his countrymen to rejoice or repent in accordance with the outcome of battles. These proclamations appeared at a rate of approximately one every six months, except during 1862, when he three times designated special days for fasting and prayer.[27] Such appeals were the outgrowth of Davis' personal attitudes, for during the war his own religious beliefs deepened, and he seemed to feel that the South's fate was in the hands of Providence.

Southern churchmen responded warmly to Davis' reliance on religion and proved to be the staunchest propagandists for the Confederate cause. As the fortunes of the South declined in 1862, the preachers followed the president's lead in dwelling on Union atrocities and the horrors of life under the depraved Yankees. Clergymen were aware of their role in building morale through sermons and church publications and adjusted their appeals to the probability of a long war by urging the virtue of endurance. According to James W. Silver, who made a lengthy study of the churches and Confederate morale, the church was "the most powerful agency . . . which helped

26. *Daily Richmond Enquirer*, August 8, 1862, p. 2; Charleston *Mercury*, December 6, 1862, p. 1.
27. *Semi-Weekly Richmond Enquirer*, July 14, 1863, p. 1; Richardson (comp.), *Messages and Papers*, I, 103–104, 135, 217–18, 227–28, 268–69, 324–25, 328, 412–14, 564–65, 567–68.

to sustain and elevate the morale of a hard-pressed people." Southern ministers were far more helpful to Jefferson Davis than political leaders and newspaper editors, for unlike these groups the churchmen "unwaveringly supported the administration."[28]

Despite his own efforts and those of religious leaders, however, the Confederate president realized that the will to resist had waned under the shock of 1862's defeats and internal divisions. Many citizens, especially in the west, wrote that Davis' presence would have a salutary effect on morale, and therefore he decided to combine an inspection trip to the newly reorganized western department with an opportunity to revive the spirit of the public. In a letter to Robert E. Lee, Davis mentioned his plans for the western trip and explained, "I propose to go out there immediately with the hope that something may be done to bring out men not heretofore in service, and to arouse all classes to united and desperate resistance."[29] Leaving Richmond early in December, he visited eastern Tennessee, Montgomery and Mobile, Alabama, and Jackson, Mississippi, before returning to the capital almost a month later.

What he found on his journey was not encouraging. From Chattanooga the president sent Secretary of War Seddon some information that was disturbing but could not have been surprising, since the War Department frequently received more detailed reports in the same vein. "The feeling in East Tennessee and North Alabama," Davis wrote, "is far from what we desire. There is some hostility and much want of confidence in our strength." Even before the chief executive left Tennessee, his old friend Senator Clement Clay had conveyed disquieting news about the growing disaffection in Alabama. Writing to his wife, Davis noted that Clay "says the fear of traitors [around Huntsville] is so great . . . that our friends look round to see who is in ear shot before speaking of public affairs."[30] As he trav-

28. James W. Silver, *Confederate Morale and Church Propaganda* (Tuscaloosa, Ala.: Confederate Publishing Company, Inc., 1957), 82, Chap. 3, Preface, and 93.
29. Jefferson Davis to Robert E. Lee, December 8, 1862, in Rowland (ed.), *Jefferson Davis*, V, 384.
30. Jefferson Davis to James Seddon, December 18, 1862, and Davis to Varina Howell Davis, December 15, 1862, *ibid.*, 386, 294–95.

eled farther west, Davis also encountered signs of class resentment
stirred by various government policies, especially the exemption of
overseers and the practice of substitution.

In a few impromptu speeches and one formal address to the Mississippi legislature, Davis adopted an optimistic tone and exhorted
the people to struggle on against the evil Yankees. Before he learned
that Napoleon had declined to pursue the proposal of free trade and
a six-month's armistice without England's support, Davis assured a
crowd in Murfreesboro, Tennessee, that if the South would endure,
European intervention would soon end the war. Later in Mississippi
he predicted that a war of such tremendous magnitude could not last
much longer and, alluding to signs of discontent in the northwestern
part of the United States, said that from that region he looked for "the
first gleams of peace." Before the Mississippi legislature he blamed
the war on "the wickedness of the North" and posed the issues of the
conflict in these terms: "The question is will you be free, or will you
be the slaves of the most depraved and intolerant and tyrannical and
hated people upon earth?" Echoing the tenor of his western speeches,
Davis told a group which welcomed him on his return to Richmond
that the Confederacy's enemy was the foe of religion and humanity,
"the offscourings of the earth." [31]

One of the most striking facts about his tour was that Davis felt the
need to oppose explicitly the idea of reconstruction. After more than
a year and a half of war, some southerners had not lost their identification with the United States and felt that peace and reunion were
preferable to a continuation of destruction. Davis answered this sentiment during his speech to Mississippi's legislators by giving a long
recital of the defects of northern character. "Evil passions," intoler-
ance, and Puritanical fanaticism long had made northerners "infa-
mous," Davis asserted, and he emphatically declared that "under no
circumstances would he consent to re-union." [32]

Davis' words had been necessary, for a desire for reconstruction

31. Strode, *Jefferson Davis*, II, 344; Jackson *Mississippian*, December 27, 1862; *Daily
Richmond Examiner*, January 5, 1863, p. 1; Rowland (ed.),, *Jefferson Davis*, V, 391.
32. Rome (Ga.) *Weekly Courier*, January 9, 1863, p. 1.

was springing up throughout the South, not just in the disaffected hill counties of Mississippi and Alabama. In November, 1862, the Richmond *Examiner* warned against demoralization and admitted that "long after the war had begun, the hope of reconstruction was a latent sentiment in the bosom of the Southern community." The idea that North Carolina was on the verge of seceding from the Confederacy in order to rejoin the Union achieved such wide circulation by the end of 1862 that the state legislature passed a formal resolution denying the "various slanderous reports." The lawmakers of Georgia similarly passed resolutions declaring their determination to fight on to independence, perhaps in the hope that such a declaration would encourage the faint hearted. Florida, too, solemnly resolved that it "will be one of the last [states] to lay down its arms, and in the impending struggle will stand by her sister States."[33]

Adjusting to this dangerous development, Jefferson Davis blended negative and positive predictions in his address to the congress at the start of 1863. He offered promises that the end of the war was near in order to sweeten the bitter part of his message, which was that continued resistance was necessary. Although no acceptable solution through negotiations was visible, Davis expressed faith that the situation would change for the better. As thousands of glum Confederates considered the prospects of the new year, their chief executive hastened to assure them that "we have every reason to expect that this [1863] will be the closing year of the war."[34]

Abraham Lincoln's Emancipation Proclamation demanded some response in this address to the congress, Davis' first speech after the measure took effect. In the light of the problem of Confederate morale, Davis' handling of this subject was very interesting. He sought to use the Emancipation Proclamation as a proof against reconstruction. Arguing that Lincoln's action demonstrated that the Republicans were perfidious and hostile and that southerners had been wise to perceive and resist "approaching despotism," Davis then added

33. *Daily Richmond Examiner*, November 21, 1862, p. 2; *Official Records*, Ser. IV, Vol. II, 378, 233.
34. Richardson (comp.), *Messages and Papers of the Confederacy*, I, 277.

that "this proclamation will have another salutary effect in calming the fears of those who have constantly evinced the apprehension that this war might end by some reconstruction of the old Union."[35] Separation was inevitable, Davis continued, since Lincoln could not retract the measure emancipating black slaves and the South would never accept it.

Still the hopes for an imminent end to the war grew, to the consternation of those who believed that independence was an uncompromisable goal. The Richmond *Examiner* often opposed the administration but firmly shared Davis' determination to achieve independence. Trying to stem the desire for peace, the *Examiner* opposed the idea of a peace conference or convention of the states on several occasions during January, 1863, and on February 2 warned against the damaging effects of the "prevailing sentiment [that] 'we shall have peace in three months.'" Like Davis, the editors of the *Examiner* argued that the northern policy of emancipation rendered all prospects of reconstruction unthinkable, since the South would not accept Negroes as citizens or equals. Yet these arguments failed to effect a transformation in morale, for at the beginning of April the *Examiner* admitted that the Confederacy labored under an atmosphere of "gloom." Sternly the editors declared that southerners had learned that they would have no "peace in 60 days" but "war for life," or at least "years of war."[36]

The Richmond *Enquirer*, whose positions often paralleled the thinking of the administration, undertook a campaign in the spring of 1863 to puncture the hopes of peace and to nerve Confederates for the long pull. Insisting as had Davis that the South would never reunite with the United States, the *Enquirer* attacked the notion that the people of the North were weary of the war. The contrary was true, the paper reported, and even Lincoln's opponents in the northwest, such as Clement Vallandigham, favored reunion and war. Although Vallandigham and other northern Democrats stressed

35. *Ibid.*, 291, 293.
36. *Daily Richmond Examiner*, January 2 and 21, 1863, February 2, 18, and 21, 1863, and April 2, 1863, p. 2.

states' rights and criticized the conduct of the war, the *Enquirer* warned that they refused to accept southern independence. When the demand for peace increased in the summer of 1863, the *Enquirer* suggested that the Confederacy would consider any proposition from the North, but only after it had received recognition as an independent nation. Finally on October 24, 1863, this journal declared that "there will be no peace until the military power of the Yankee nation is entirely broken, and its people so thoroughly sickened of the war that we can exact our own terms." [37]

The longing for peace even threatened the Confederacy's supply of food, for as the spring planting season approached in 1863 some farmers who anticipated an end to the war prepared to plant cash crops like cotton and tobacco in fields which had been devoted to food crops. At the request of the congress, Davis published a special address to the people and warned them that the nation would need another full year's supply of food crops. To cushion the impact of this, he expressed confidence that Vicksburg was safe from Grant's army and asserted that the South's troops were more numerous, better organized, and more thoroughly disciplined, armed, and equipped than ever before. [38]

Up to this point, Confederate leaders had struggled to maintain an acceptable equilibrium in southern morale. Doubts and depression were real, but denunciations of the enemy and appeals to sacrifice still seemed to have some countervailing effect. Into this delicately balanced situation the news of the twin disasters at Vicksburg and Gettysburg crashed like a thunderbolt. Within two days the Confederate army surrendered a strategic point on the Mississippi, where the war had already been going badly, and Robert E. Lee's courageous soldiers met with a bloody defeat in their second attempted offensive on northern soil. The seriousness of these events was undeniable. For thousands of southerners the first week of July turned hope to despair and swept away remaining illusions that the

37. *Semi-Weekly Richmond Enquirer*, May 22, 1863, p. 2, May 29, 1863, p. 2, April 24, 1863, p. 1, May 15, 1863, p. 1, July 24, 1863, p. 2, October 16, 1863, p.2.
38. Richardson (comp.), *Messages and Papers of the Confederacy*, I. 331–35.

South could win the war. After July, 1863, the leaders of the Confederacy had to communicate with a people who knew that their cause was probably lost. Consequently the task of inspiring them to make further sacrifices became immensely more difficult.

Jefferson Davis clearly realized the magnitude of the disasters in July. Although his will was nearly indomitable, his trained military mind could not reject the disturbing results of battle. He admitted to a Confederate senator that the surrender of Vicksburg has shrouded the southern cause in darkness and left him "in the depths of . . . gloom." He told General Kirby Smith frankly, "We are now in the darkest hour of our political existence." Deprived of rational grounds for hope, Davis fell back on his religious faith and adopted a kind of fatalism based on the belief that Providence controlled events. "It is not for man to command success," he wrote. Rather "he should strive to deserve it, and leave the rest to Him who governs all things, though to our short vision the Justice may not be visible." [39]

The disasters at Vicksburg and Gettysburg wrought a significant change in Confederate ideology. Recognizing the profound impact which these defeats had on the sinking spirit of the people, Davis abandoned the effort to give southerners positive goals for which to fight and fell back on the coercive effect of threats and dire predictions. Instead of picturing the bright future of the southern nation, he dwelt exclusively after this point on the dark night of oppression which he claimed would come if the South lost the war. Against the growing desire for peace and reunion Davis posed his description of an enemy so depraved and vicious that no tolerable peace was possible. Davis also threw aside the caution and circumspection which had shaped all his earlier statements about slavery and resorted to the racial scare tactics which southern leaders had often used to enforce internal unity. Henceforth his message was that the cruel Yankees aimed to subjugate the South utterly and make Negroes the masters of white men.

This transformation of southern ideology was in effect an admission

39. Jefferson Davis to R. W. Johnson, July 14, 1863, and Davis to E. Kirby Smith, July 14, 1863, in Rowland (ed.), *Jefferson Davis*, V, 548, 554.

of the desperate condition of the South. Through his public speeches Davis tacitly showed that there was no possibility of inspiring the people to united resistance except through a reliance on fear. The president of the Confederacy plainly was concerned that his countrymen would give up the struggle at the first opportunity which preserved a modicum of honor. To a demoralized public he argued essentially that there was no way out. In such circumstances Confederate ideology had practically ceased to exist as an ideology. No organized body of doctrine, principles, and goals remained, only the prod of fear.

In the dreary weeks immediately following the fall of Vicksburg and the retreat from Gettysburg, Davis unveiled a variety of threats and grim predictions and gave them the strongest phrasing which he could devise. To a senator from Arkansas, who was understandably discouraged about the course of the war in his area, Davis sent assurances that troops would defend that state and then asked, "What could be hoped for from our brutal enemy, what expected but such degradation as to a freeman would be worse than torture at the stake?" Davis also alluded to the prospect of a postwar revolution in the South's racial arrangements by saying, "Can any one not fit to be a slave, and ready to become one, think of passing under the yoke?" On August 1, 1863, the president issued a special proclamation to the soldiers of the southern armies which revealed his desperation. In this document Davis clearly was trying to contain the flood of desertion and demoralization that threatened to destroy the Confederate army. He appealed to all who were absent to return to their posts and promised them an amnesty, but he saved his strongest rhetoric for a description of the enemy's "malignant rage":

> [Defeat would mean] nothing less than the extermination of yourselves, your wives, and children. They seek to destroy what they cannot plunder. They purpose . . . that your homes shall be partitioned. . . . They design to incite servile insurrection and light the fires of incendiarism wherever they can reach your homes, and they debauch the inferior race . . .

by promising indulgence of the vilest passions as the price of treachery.

Fellow citizens, no alternative is left you but victory or subjugation, slavery, and the utter ruin of yourselves, your families, and your country.[40]

Davis was not alone in his resort to the tactics of fear. State leaders saw plentiful evidence around them of the deteriorating condition of morale, and, not surprisingly, they took up the same arguments which Davis used. In one of his last state papers, John Pettus, the outgoing governor of Mississippi, referred to "the known determination of the Lincoln Government to reduce this people to a condition far worse than European serfdom" and declared that "independence or death, or that which is worse than death, are the alternatives presented to this people." His successor, Charles Clark, relied more heavily on the power of racism to suppress interest in reconstruction. The enemy Clark said "will offer you a reconstructed Constitution, providing for the confiscation of your property, the immediate emancipation of your slaves, and the elevation of the black race to a position of equality—aye, of superiority, that will make them your masters and rulers." Governor Vance of North Carolina believed that the North would treat southerners as "a master who promises them *only life*." The legislature of Louisiana condemned the "ruthless barbarity" of the United States, and the Confederate Congress warned the southern people that "nothing short of your utter subjugation, the destruction of your State governments, the overthrow of your social and political fabric, your personal and public degradation and ruin, will satisfy the demands of the North."[41]

Frequently the press voiced similar sentiments, as did the Charleston *Mercury* late in July when it announced that northerners were "civilized savages . . . plunderers, liars, fanatics." The Richmond *Examiner* on July 12, 1863, demanded retaliation for alleged barbarities committed by the United States army and sixteen days later

40. Jefferson Davis to R. W. Johnson, July 14, 1863, in Rowland (ed.), *Jefferson Davis*, V, 549–50; Richardson (comp.), *Messages and Papers of the Confederacy*, I, 329.

41. *Official Records*, Ser. IV, Vol. II, 927, 960–62; Zebulon Vance to D. L. Swain, January 2, 1864, in Richard E. Yates, *The Confederacy and Zeb Vance* (Tuscaloosa, Ala.: Confederate Publishing Company, Inc., 1958), 97; *Official Records*, Ser. IV, Vol. III, 94 and 130.

stressed that peace by negotiation was impossible because Lincoln's government was intent on domination. The Richmond *Whig* also joined in the denunciation of the foe and warned in September, 1863, that if the Confederacy lost, all southerners would be "outlaws and felons" with no rights. Stressing the threat to white supremacy, a newspaper in Georgia's hill country warned that defeat would mean degradation and "social equality with our slaves."[42]

In the fall of 1863, Jefferson Davis decided to make an inspection tour like that of the previous year. Undoubtedly he hoped once again that his presence might lift depression and bolster morale. Leaving Richmond on October 6, Davis' train passed through Augusta and Atlanta on the way to Bragg's army in Tennessee. After addressing the soldiers, he continued on to Selma, Alabama, where he spoke to a welcoming crowd from his hotel balcony. Trying to provide encouragement, Davis described the military situation as promising but called for every man to do his duty and warned that "only by force of arms" could the South make the North see reason. Discounting the prospect of foreign intervention, Davis nevertheless predicted that if all did their part "next spring would see the invader driven from our borders."[43] The president also passed through Mobile, Macon, and Savannah, and occasionally made brief speeches which exhorted everyone to aid the army and held out hopes of success. Before returning to Richmond, he made his final stop in Charleston, South Carolina, where the superficial courtesy of his reception masked many seething animosities.

As was the case in Charleston, Davis' short visits could not remove the problems in Confederate morale. Usually the crowds greeted Davis enthusiastically, and his presence had a brief cheering effect in the areas which he visited. In the country as a whole, however, problems of demoralization and disaffection continued to grow. During the summer of 1863 the Richmond administration learned that

42. Charleston *Mercury*, July 22, 1863, p. 1; *Daily Richmond Examiner*, July 12, 1863, p. 2, July 28, 1863, p. 2; Richmond *Daily Whig*, September 9, 1863, p. 2; Rome (Ga.) *Weekly Courier*, September 18, 1863,*p. 1*.

43. *Daily Richmond Examiner*, October 20, 1863.

a secret peace society, also called the Washington Constitutional Union, existed in northern Alabama and in the Army of Tennessee. In fact this organization, whose object was to end the war, had started in 1862, and it had members in Georgia, Mississippi, East Tennessee, and possibly Florida as well. Resistance to it by the government was not sufficient to prevent the election of several of its members to state offices and even to the congress in 1863. Unknown to the authorities, another secret organization, the Order of Heroes of America, was gathering strength in North Carolina, southwest Virginia, and eastern Tennessee. The Heroes of America had an elaborate organization with secret signs and signals, and its purpose, not uncovered by the Confederacy until 1864, was to stimulate desertion, report information about Confederate troops, and in other ways aid the Union.[44]

These secret peace organizations were a serious matter, but probably of more significance were the signs of discontent which were out in the open. William W. Holden, editor of the Raleigh, North Carolina, *Standard*, effectively publicized his opposition to the administration and spread discontent about the war. In the summer of 1863, Holden started to organize his large following into a political movement, and the chief of the Bureau of War, R. G. H. Kean, noted anxiously in his diary that Holden's followers "are throwing off all disguises and have begun to hold 'Union' meetings in some of the western counties." On September 20, 1863, Kean wrote that "the trouble in North Carolina grows apace. The Reconstruction is openly advocated in many counties. In Alabama the same spirit begins to show itself. Mississippi beyond the Big Black is conquered." Despair prevailed so completely in Mississippi that prominent men such as Judge W. L. Sharkey, a former provisional governor, and other old Whigs took the oath of allegiance to the United States late in July, 1863.[45]

---

44. Younger (ed.), *Diary of R. G. H. Kean*, 73; Georgia Lee Tatum, *Disloyalty in the Confederacy* (Chapel Hill: University of North Carolina Press, 1934), 28, 60–61, 28.

45. Younger (ed.), *Diary of R. G. H. Kean*, 103–104; Tatum, *Disloyalty in the Confederacy*, 100–101.

Even without the numerous reports of disaffection which arrived at the War Department, Jefferson Davis could follow the deterioration of morale by scanning the Richmond papers. The *Examiner* frequently urged the death penalty as the only remedy for desertion and worked steadily in the fall of 1863 to counter hopes that a northern peace party would rise up and deliver the Confederacy. The *Examiner* also reported and condemned the fact that cotton planters near Vicksburg had abandoned the cause and were trading with the enemy. Most disturbing of all was the introduction in southern legislatures of propositions for reconstruction. Noticing that these proposals had appeared "in several of our State legislatures," the *Examiner* commented sternly and frankly:

> These deserve an unqualified condemnation. They are generally made in artful language; they are very innocent on their face; they are always accompanied by certain protestations that the interest of the South is not to be sacrificed; that the object is an "honourable" peace, and that the negotiation is to be an essay of Christian charity. There is no possible truth in such protestations. They are the convenient covers of traitorous designs or of cowardly acquiescence in the failure of our struggle.[46]

The North was correct, the editor concluded, in viewing these as "covert propositions of re-construction."

Thus by the end of 1863 the prospects of the southern nation had darkened greatly, and Confederate ideology had become little more than the invocation of threats that the future would be intolerable without victory. Seeking to revive the citizens' will to fight, Jefferson Davis had mixed cheering appraisals of the army's strength with predictions that the war would end early in 1864. Beneath these hopeful words he tried to place a foundation of fear through harsh denunciations of the foe and visions of racial upheaval. Aided by such tactics, the Confederacy held together in 1863 and struggled into another year of war. Yet Davis surely knew that if the danger of disintegration had been real in 1863, it would be far greater in 1864.

46. *Daily Richmond Examiner*, September 4, 11, and 30, 1863, October 20, 1863, October 17, 1863, p. 2, October 1, 1863, p. 2.

7

Fighting
Against
Disintegration

Viewed from the present, the events of 1864 often appear as part of an inexorable progression toward Appomattox. In fact, however, 1864 was a crucial year in which both the North and the South had a chance to attain their goals. After the important battles of 1863, it was clear, of course, that the northern armies enjoyed superior resources and that the South would remain primarily on the defensive. But Union commanders had not been able to achieve a breakthrough or win the kind of victories which would bring the end of the bloody conflict within sight. Despite the relative weakness of the Confederacy, northern support for the war was waning, and home-front morale crumbled in the face of heavy Union losses and a disappointing lack of progress. The South could win the Civil War simply by not losing, by resisting until northern war weariness forced the United States to give up the struggle.

The decline of northern support for the war represented both an opportunity for the Confederacy and the test of its war aims. The southern people and their leaders had to decide how to use their opportunity. On the one hand, it seemed possible that the South could obtain rather favorable peace terms from a northern administration struggling under military and political difficulties. On the other hand, there was also a chance—a longer one—that the southern government could gain its independence by convincing the North that it could not win.

Jefferson Davis never hesitated over this choice. Always resolved to gain independence, he gambled for the larger stakes and attempted to carry all the southern people with him, including those who were inclined to compromise for peace. The peculiar stubbornness and determination of this man virtually banished the idea of compromise from respectable discussion and placed southern morale in a position of central importance.

The Confederacy's prospect of winning complete independence depended on its ability to present firm opposition to the enemy. Unity and a display of unshaken determination to continue the war were prerequisites to all the South's hopes. But as Davis should have known, by 1864 the will of the people was weak. Economic hardships, class resentments, and war weariness depressed southerners' spirits, and unwillingness or simple inability to sacrifice further manifested itself in growing opposition to the central government. Rather than increasing, Confederate unity was breaking down, and thus Davis, who was still bent on independence, had to spend much of his time fighting against disintegration.

As 1864 began, Davis endeavored to explain to the people the importance of unity and to encourage them to maximize the South's chances by presenting a stout resistance to the United States. In his address to the newly assembled Second Congress on May 2, Davis warned that "our enemies have mistaken our desire for peace . . . for evidence of exhaustion." Then, in frank language, he sketched out the Confederacy's situation: "Every avenue of negotiations is closed against us . . . our enemy is making renewed and strenuous efforts for our destruction. . . . The sole resource for us . . . is to combine and apply every available element of power for [the] defense and preservation [of our liberties]." After delivering this sober appeal, he added the familiar hopeful prediction: "If our arms are crowned with the success [for] which we have so much reason to hope, we may well expect that this war cannot be prolonged beyond the current year."[1]

This speech indicated Davis' general political strategy for 1864, a strategy aimed at victory and dependent on outlasting the enemy.

1. Dunbar Rowland (ed.), *Jefferson Davis: Constitutionalist; His Letters, Papers, and Speeches* (10 vols.; Jackson, Miss.: Little & Ives, Co., 1923), VI, 241–42.

Since the Confederacy's hopes hinged on sagging northern morale as much as on the southern armies, Davis did not limit himself to reinforcing the southern will to fight. Dissension within the United States, particularly in the northwest, had interested him and many other southerners for a long time. Some members of the Confederate Congress had even believed that the northwest was ready to break away from the Union and had toyed with the idea of proposing an alliance. Thus it was not surprising that early in 1864 he considered ways to encourage peace forces in the United States.[2]

The Confederate government had reason to believe that dissident elements in the North possessed considerable power. In the 1862 elections northern Democrats had made substantial gains against Lincoln's party, and the peace wing of the Democracy waxed in strength during 1863. Moreover, when Clement Vallandigham, leader of the Ohio peace Democrats, traveled through the South in 1863 after his expulsion from the United States, he met with southern leaders and conveyed his views to the government. One of those who talked with him, Clement C. Clay, Jr., concluded that Vallandigham was "for peace, even at the expense of disunion, and the independence of the Confederacy." Then on March 14, 1864, J. W. Tucker, a South Carolinian who was active in the border state of Missouri, arrived in Richmond and wrote Davis about a secret political organization in the northwest. Tucker represented himself as being actively engaged in this organization and described its aims as the protection of states' rights, recognition of and friendly relations with the Confederacy, and the formation of a northwest republic composed of the states of Michigan, Minnesota, Wisconsin, Iowa, Illinois, Indiana, and Ohio. Declaring that his comrades favored war on the United States if necessary, Tucker asserted that the group had 490,000 members and had already destroyed some United States

2. T. L. Burnett to Colonel Robt. McKee, January 22, 1863, Ely M. Bruce to W. N. Haldeman, February 17, 1863, and Bruce to McKee, April 14, 1863, in McKee Collection, Alabama Department of Archives and History, Montgomery; Rome (Ga.) *Weekly Courier*, January 9, 1863. I wish to thank Larry E. Nelson, who has made a careful study of the relationship of the Confederacy to the Federal elections of 1864, for many valuable discussions and suggestions concerning this chapter.

ships and factories. On behalf of his organization, he asked the Confederate government for aid.[3]

Basing hopes on such secret organizations and on the open discontent of many northern Democrats, the Davis administration moved ahead with a plan to stimulate peace agitation in the United States. A. H. H. Stuart, a friend of Judah Benjamin, received an offer to head a mission in Canada. Through secret agents, Stuart later revealed, he was "to foster and give direct aid to a peace sentiment which it was understood was then active along the Border States, and particularly to give aid to a peace organization known as the 'Knights of the Golden Circle,' which flourished in the Northwestern States."[4] Jefferson Davis' memoirs are silent on the details of this Canadian mission, but they candidly admit that its purpose was to "influence popular sentiment in the hostile section. The aspect of the peace party was quite encouraging, and it seemed that the real issue to be decided in the Presidential election of that year, was the continuance or cessation of the war." Davis expected his commissioners to communicate with peace-minded northerners and "to make judicious use of any political opportunity that might be presented." Another part of their mission was to engineer the release of Confederate prisoners from camps in the northwest and thus augment Confederate strength while diverting Federal troops from battlefields in the South. After A. H. H. Stuart declined the task, the government settled on Clement Clay of Alabama and Jacob Thompson of Mississippi.[5]

These plans gave Davis hope that by the fall of 1864 Confederate independence would be much nearer, but during the winter and spring disturbing developments in North Carolina absorbed his attention. At precisely the time when unity was needed, war weari-

3. C. C. Clay, Jr., to W. L. Yancey, June 30, 1863, in Yancey Papers, Alabama State Department of Archives and History; Rowland (ed.), *Jefferson Davis*, VI, 204–206.
4. Quoted in Robert Douthat Meade, *Judah P. Benjamin: Confederate Statesman* (New York: Oxford University Press, 1943), 300.
5. Jefferson Davis, *The Rise and Fall of the Confederate Government* (2 vols.; London: Longmans, Green and Co., 1881), II, 611; Rowland (ed.), *Jefferson Davis*, VI, 226–27 and 236–38.

ness and growing demoralization threatened to take the Old North State out of the Confederacy. William W. Holden's peace movement had been gaining momentum since the summer of 1863. Like many other North Carolinians, Holden foresaw grave troubles for the Confederate States and felt that if southerners would make terms on the basis of the existing United States Constitution they could avoid the emancipation and confiscation which might follow defeat. The Raleigh editor developed additional sympathy for his movement by playing on the feeling that the Richmond government had slighted North Carolina's contributions and ignored its needs. Calling for an "honorable" peace, he suggested that the South should fight on while peace men in both sections pressured their governments to negotiate a settlement.[6]

Holden's appeal struck a responsive chord among the people, and peace meetings sprang up in many parts of North Carolina. According to his memoirs, one hundred meetings took place within the space of eight weeks. Thoroughly alarmed, Davis wrote to Governor Vance, who arranged for some prominent and loyal North Carolinians to remonstrate with the *Standard*'s editor. Their counsels did not avail, however, for Holden continued to call for peace negotiations. Although he claimed that peace advocates sought "negotiations with a view to separation," Holden threatened more ominously that North Carolina would stand by the government of the Confederate States only "as long as it is to the interest of North Carolina to do so, and no longer." The Raleigh editor believed that four-fifths of the people wanted reconstruction, and he answered his critics by saying that he was only following public opinion, not creating it. Indeed, both Governor Vance and Jonathan Worth, another leading North Carolina politician, agreed that a majority of the people supported Holden. In the fall of 1863, state elections brought victory to several avowed peace candidates.[7]

Zebulon Vance had come to office with Holden's political aid, but

6. Edgar Estes Folk, "W. W. Holden, Political Journalist, Editor of *North Carolina Standard*, 1843–1865." (Ph. D. dissertation, George Peabody College for Teachers, 1934), 576, 577, 567.

7. *Ibid.*, 573–74, 578–79, 588, and 577.

the governor reluctantly decided to break with his former mentor over the peace issue. Vance was certain that Holden's followers intended to call a state convention in May, 1864, for the purpose of taking North Carolina back into the Union, and privately he believed that North Carolinians would welcome such a step. To David L. Swain, the president of the University of North Carolina and an intimate friend, Vance wrote that the price of independence was more bloodshed and misery. Such sacrifice, he observed, "requires a deep hold on the popular heart, *and our people will not pay this price* I am satisfied for their independence. I am convinced of it." Nevertheless, because he felt that secession in the midst of war would be an eternal mark of shame for North Carolina, Vance resolved that he would do everything in his power to resist the peace movement, though he doubted that he could succeed.[8]

Searching for ways to counter Holden's influence, Vance wrote Davis on December 30, 1863. Discontent had advanced so far in North Carolina, the governor reported, "that it will be perhaps impossible to remove it, except by making some effort at negotiation with the enemy." Vance argued that if the United States rejected fair terms, southerners would draw together behind their government and that such an offer would demonstrate to "the humblest of our citizens . . . that the government is tender of their lives and happiness, and would not prolong their sufferings unnecessarily one moment."[9] This suggestion showed that Vance hoped to outmaneuver Holden by drawing his sting, by dealing sympathetically with the people's desire for peace while deflecting their action into another channel.

Davis' reply, written on January 8, 1864, revealed a gulf between the president and the governor in their approach to peace and to southern peace sentiment. Pointing out that the United States had rejected all previous overtures, Davis deplored the idea of renewing Confederate offers to negotiate. "This struggle," he wrote, "must con-

---

8. *Ibid.*, 614, and Zebulon Vance to David L. Swain, January 2, 1864, quoted in Richard E. Yates, *The Confederacy and Zeb Vance* (Tuscaloosa, Ala.: Confederate Publishing Company, Inc., 1958), 96.

9. Rowland (ed.), *Jefferson Davis*, VI, 141.

tinue until the enemy is beaten out of his vain confidence in our subjugation. Then and not till then will it be possible to treat of peace."
Before that time arrived, any offer of terms would "be received as
proof that we are ready for submission" and would encourage the foe.
Anticipating developments in North Carolina that would give "aid
and comfort to the enemy," the Confederate president cautioned
Vance against dealing too gingerly with "traitors." He urged the governor to defy rather than conciliate the leaders of the peace movement and argued that a resolute stand would eliminate the need to
use force later.[10]

Davis quickly buttressed his opposition to the peace movement
with strong action. On February 3, 1864, he sent a frank message to
the congress in which he called for a renewal of the suspension of the
writ of *habeas corpus*. Disloyal meetings and secret peace societies,
he reported, made suspension imperative. Despite the unpopularity of such stern measures, the congress recognized the danger and
passed the suspension of the writ without delay. By February 24,
1864, the Raleigh *Standard* had suspended publication rather than
run the risk of seizure by the government.[11]

It was much easier, however, for Davis to be stern and unyielding
in Richmond than it was for Vance to follow the same course in North
Carolina. Fighting for reelection, Governor Vance had to take account of the great popularity of Holden, who had entered the campaign against him. Although Holden's paper was shut down, his views
still enjoyed a wide circulation. While the former editor argued that
another year of war would be disastrous and called for a convention
of states, his followers organized mass meetings and a petition campaign to secure this aim. Moved by the growing public feeling, at
least two North Carolina legislators introduced peace resolutions before the General Assembly.[12]

    10. *Ibid.*, 143–46, 193–97, and 216–17.
    11. *Ibid.*, 164–69, and Folk "W. W. Holden," 622–23.
    12. Folk, "W. W. Holden," 616; Edwin G. Reade to William A. Graham, February 4,
1864, in Graham Papers, North Carolina Department of Archives and History, Raleigh;
Josiah Turner, Jr., to his wife, May 7, 1864, in Josiah Turner Papers, University of North
Carolina.

In this setting, Davis' advice was of little use to the politically adroit governor, who knew that he had to incline toward the peace forces in order to have a chance of success. Accordingly, Vance and his supporters worked to identify the governor with peace and Holden with war. They stressed the fact that Vance had suggested negotiations to Davis and claimed that the governor had inspired the peace efforts of Governor Brown of Georgia. In the words of one historian, the election campaign in North Carolina "tended to make all voters friends of peace." Vance branded Holden as "the *war* candidate" because the editor's plan to take North Carolina out of the Confederacy would involve the state in civil war with her neighbors. Speaking throughout the state, the governor argued that secession from the Confederacy would bring "a new war, a bloodier conflict than that you now deplore." When the state legislature met in May, Vance urged the lawmakers to define fair terms for peace and call on the state's congressmen to press for peace with independence after the next Confederate victory. This strategy proved effective, and Governor Vance, aided by overwhelming newspaper support and impressive talents at platform speaking, won reelection in July by a margin of 58,070 votes to 14,491.[13]

These results gratified Davis, but before the crisis had subsided in North Carolina, additional trouble had arisen in Georgia. The suspension of *habeas corpus*, which had been a necessary tool against Holden, sparked vehement protest from some quarters. Prominent men in Georgia combined this resentment with the yearning for peace to create a powerful movement which threatened to undercut Davis' strategy for 1864. The motives of Vice President Stephens and Governor Brown, who led the movement, are difficult to fathom completely, but personal animosity toward Davis played a role, and, in Stephens' case, a lingering fondness for the Union also seemed to be a factor. Both men certainly disapproved of existing policies and sought a better way to end the war. The lack of a two-party system in which alternative strategies could be openly proposed and debated

13. Folk, "W. W. Holden," 631–34; *Daily Richmond Enquirer*, March 5, 1864, p. 2; Folk, "W. W. Holden," 639–40, 645.

magnified the importance of their challenge to Davis' program.[14]

Months before the suspension of the writ of *habeas corpus*, Stephens and Brown were planning their assault on the Richmond administration, an assault designed to culminate during a special session of the legislature in March, 1864. Brown, after carefully rehearsing his role with the vice president, opened the legislative session by asserting that the congress, in "attempting" to suspend the writ, had authorized Jefferson Davis to make "*illegal and unconstitutional arrests.*" Turning to the question of peace, the governor said that only negotiations could end the fighting, and he demanded repeated offers of peace after each important Confederate victory. Linton Stephens, the vice president's half brother and closest confidant, followed up these defiant words by introducing resolutions which condemned the suspension of *habeas corpus* as "a dangerous assault upon . . . the liberty of the people." A separate set of resolutions echoed Brown's proposal of peace negotiations and called ominously for the people to act "through their state organizations and popular assemblies" to end the war. A few days later Alexander Stephens accepted a special invitation to address the legislature and threw his restless energies into a long tirade against the suspension of the writ of *habeas corpus* and other essential war measures.[15]

This concerted attack on the central government and the war by two of the South's highest officials again raised the specter of Confederate disunity. But for the vigorous opposition of some of Georgia's other officials, Brown and Stephens might have set off a disastrous process of political fission in the unstable Confederacy. Senator Herschel Johnson, one of those who was dismayed by the challenge to central authority, bluntly told Stephens, "You are wrong in view

14. Charleston *Mercury*, March 30, 1864, p.1; see Eric L. McKitrick, "Party Politics and the Union and Confederate War Efforts," in William Nisbet Chambers and Walter Dean Burnham (eds.), *The American Party Systems* (New York: Oxford University Press, 1967).

15. Louise Biles Hill, *Joseph E. Brown and the Confederacy* (Chapel Hill: University of North Carolina Press, 1939), 206–212; *The War of the Rebellion: A Compilation of the Official Records of the Union and Confederate Armies* (130 vols.; Washington: Government Printing Office, 1880–1901), Ser. IV, Vol. III, 234, hereinafter cited as *Offiicial Records*; James Z. Rabun, "Alexander H. Stephens and Jefferson Davis," *American Historical Review*, LVIII (1953), 307–310.

of your official position; you are wrong because the whole movement originated in a mad purpose to make war on Davis and Congress;— You are wrong because the movement is joyous to the enemy, and they are already using it in their press." Legislators who shared Johnson's thinking managed to adopt a resolution expressing confidence in the president as a counterweight to Linton Stephens' resolutions on *habeas corpus*. Before the peace resolutions passed, friends of the Confederate government added an amendment which pledged Georgia's energies to the war until independence was achieved. These were partial victories, but the United States had witnessed the spectacle of a second southern state considering separate negotiations, despite the fact that questions of war and peace were the responsibility of the Confederate government. Moreover, the agitation effectively nullified the suspension of the writ of *habeas corpus* in Georgia and encouraged lawmakers in Mississippi, Alabama, and North Carolina to adopt similar resolutions.[16] The challenge from Stephens and Brown left gaping holes in the facade of Confederate unity and resolution.

The peace movements in Georgia and North Carolina were only the most salient indications of an alarming state of morale throughout the Confederacy. Evidence mounted on every side that Davis could not secure the unity with which he sought to impress the North. Desertion from the armies continued at a high and increasing rate, despite repeated offers by Confederate officials of amnesty for all who returned to their posts. In areas near enemy lines trade with the United States occurred on a regular basis. Ironically this clandestine and demoralizing traffic spread partly because the hard-pressed Confederate government had itself entered into trade with the enemy in order to obtain necessary supplies.[17] Furthermore, military defeats stimulated the widespread lack of confidence in the ability of the government to protect its citizens. In March, 1864, for example, a

16. Hill, *Joseph E. Brown*, 213, 215, 219.
17. Ella Lonn, *Desertion During the Civil War* (New York: Century Co., 1928), 25–27, Chap. 3; Rowland (ed.), *Jefferson Davis*, VI, 278, 316–17; *Official Records*, Ser. IV, Vol. III, 645–48; R. R. Heath to James Seddon, September 24, 1864, in Letters Received, Confederate Secretary of War, in Record Group 109, National Archives, Microcopy M 437, Roll 130, pp. 611–21.

remarkable letter arrived at the War Department from a group of Virginians who lived along the shores of the Rappahannock. These people begged the government not to fish the river, because such activity "will inevitably draw the enemy . . . and expose the people . . . to be robbed and plundered of the little that is left them." Rather than run that risk, they preferred that the government abandon its effort to obtain food for the armies. Many southerners had reached the point of exasperation exhibited by one man, who told a government impressment agent that "he thought we (meaning the seceded States) had best compromise on the best terms we could and get back into the old Union . . . he thought the sooner this damned Government fell to pieces the better it would be for us."[18]

Class resentments also continued to weaken the southern war effort because class favoritism persisted. Either with or without the sanction of law, unpatriotic but wealthy citizens often found ways to avoid service. A rich Georgian informed the War Department that he knew over a hundred men who had bought exemptions and that the practice took place daily. Such favoritism was a predictable by-product of the southern social system, with its muted but real emphasis on hierarchy and the superiority of the upper class. Although special treatment for wealthy individuals often harmed the war effort the government's granting of considerations to "gentlemen" was a basic social pattern. A clerk in the War Department discovered to his amazement that in September, 1864, when the army was desperately short of horses and mules, the government was lending them to prominent citizens who had suffered relatively few of the calamities of war. About the same time, General Lee urged the War Department to look into charges that able-bodied men who should go to the field instead received details to serve in government bureaus. The harassed general also complained that rich young men sought election as magistrates and minor officials in order to avoid military service.[19]

The existence of these situations damaged morale among poorer

18. Citizens of King George County, Virginia, to James Seddon, received March 25, 1864, in Letters Received, Confederate Secretary of War, in RG 109, NA Microcopy M 437, Roll 140, pp. 910–12; *Official Records*, Ser. IV, Vol. III, 413–14.

19. J. B. Jones, *A Rebel War Clerk's Diary*, ed. Howard Swiggett (2 vols.; New York: Old Hickory Bookshop, 1935), II, 257, 279, 281.

Confederates. Mary Boykin Chesnut heard that "all the troops" from the mountains of North and South Carolina were disaffected and felt that "this is a rich man's war . . . they want no part in it, and they would gladly desert in a body." As 1864 advanced the Richmond administration received a steady stream of reports documenting the spread of demoralization. Judge Robert S. Hudson of Mississippi reported in March that "Mississippi is in a most deplorable condition, and is rapidly tending to the most deplorable disgrace. Very many of the middle class, a large number of the more intelligent, and nearly all of the lower class of her people are drifting to the Yankees." In neighboring Alabama the commandant of conscripts wrote that "a large portion of this State is in such a condition that the constant presence of an armed force is absolutely necessary to secure even respect." By May, Confederate authorities learned that the Peace Society had attracted a large membership in several counties of Alabama. Locally prominent citizens, such as the commandant of reserves, a Methodist minister, two justices of the peace, and two members of the state legislature belonged to this organization, which had also penetrated the army. Just before the fall elections the Jackson *Mississippian* came out for an "honorable peace," and Davis' old ally, James Phelan, warned that "the infernal hydra of reconstruction is again stirring its envenomed heads in our State." At about the same time the government discovered that the Heroes of America, another peace organization, was active in southwestern Virginia, North Carolina, and Tennessee. All these situations manifested what Judge Hudson called "a disposition among the people to rise up in opposition to the powers that be, declare for reconstruction, or anything else but the things that are."[20]

These growing signs of southern disunity presented a grave threat to Davis' hopes for independence and military effectiveness, but the Confederacy's chief executive clung firmly to his goals. Increasingly

20. Mary Boykin Chesnut, *A Diary from Dixie*, ed. Ben Ames Williams (Sentry ed.; Boston: Houghton Mifflin Company, 1949), 454; *Official Records*, Ser. I, Vol. XXXII, Pt. III, 625–27, Ser, IV, Vol. III, 251–53, 393–98, and Ser. I, Vol. XXXIX, Pt. II, 588–89; John K. Bettersworth, *Confederate Mississippi* (Baton Rouge: Louisiana State University Press, 1943), 210; *Official Records*, Ser, IV, Vol. III, 707–710, 802–816, and Ser. I, Vol. XLV, Pt. I, 1246–48.

isolated, he became a leader on the defensive, a president who could maintain the existence of his programs without being able to elicit the enthusiasm needed to make them work. Ironically, Davis' support in the latter stages of the war often came from his strongest critics. The editors of the Richmond *Examiner* and the Charleston *Mercury* shared his desire for independence, though they hardly approved of any other part of his program, and cold logic compelled them to oppose negotiations and support military needs. These unwilling allies, plus congressmen from overrun or threatened districts, constituted Davis' major source of popular backing in the difficult months of 1864. Among ordinary Confederates, he found it increasingly difficult to find support or a determined spirit of nationalism. Even some prominent members of the congress, believing that the Confederacy was sure to be overwhelmed, proposed in secret session that the South seek peace on the basis of reunion and the retention of slavery.[21] Their plan was blocked, but its appearance, in May, 1864, highlighted the desire for peace and the growing interest in compromise.

To attain the unity essential to his strategy for independence, the Confederacy's chief executive relied upon firm measures. His insistence on the need for a vigorous central government grew stronger in the closing months of the war as he struggled to overcome weakness in the armies and demoralization at home. Despite protests, he defended the suspension of the writ of *habeas corpus* and asked for its renewal after authorization expired in August, 1864. Martial law was one of the powers which the administration could use to carry out its policy against "yielding to the disaffected classes." The War Department also signaled that policy by denying a request from Governor Vance to suspend conscription in mountain counties of North Carolina where the residents stood at the edge of disloyalty.[22]

Forcing its conscription machinery to generate more men, the

21. Reminiscences of J. A. Orr, Mississippi Department of Archives and History, Jackson. The congressmen included Orr, Senator J. W. C. Watson of Mississippi, Senator William A. Graham of North Carolina, Herschel Johnson of Georgia, James L. Orr of South Carolina, William W. Boyce of South Carolina, and others. Their resolution was tabled in the House and defeated, 15–7, in the Senate.
22. James D. Richardson (comp.), *A Compliation of the Messages and Papers of the*

Davis government reached deep into society in the fall of 1864. J. B. Jones, who worked in the War Department, saw the practical results of the administration's revocation of details. Farmers who "a week ago thought themselves safe from the toils and dangers of war" streamed into Richmond, where "they murmured" but found that "there was no escape." So effective were the conscription guards in the city that people referred to them as "dog-catchers." The chief of the Bureau of War reported similarly in his diary: "The conscription is now being pressed mercilessly. It is agonizing to see and hear the cases daily brought into the War Office, appeal after appeal and *all* disallowed. Women come there and weep, wring their hands, scold, entreat, beg, and almost drive me mad."[23]

To increase the Confederacy's supply of vital materials, the Davis administration took the important step of expanding its powers over foreign trade. Late in 1863, the government compelled ship owners to carry one-third to one-half of their cargoes for the Confederacy. After the congress placed the exportation of cotton and other valuable items under the president's regulation, the government claimed one-half the space on all outgoing ships, except those owned completely by the states.[24] This action, though beneficial to the national cause, sparked a new round of vehement protests about states' rights.

In fact, 1864 brought a second peak of states' rights opposition, which seemed more broadly based and defiant than at any previous period in the Confederacy. This resurgence had its origin in the poverty and suffering that gripped the South rather than in differences over constitutional theory. By 1864 both the Richmond administra-

Confederacy, Including the Diplomatic Correspondence, 1861–1865 (2 vols.; Nashville: United States Publishing Company, 1906), I, 452–53; *Official Records*, Ser. I, Vol. LIII, 324–329.

23. Jones, *A Rebel War Clerk's Diary*, II, 308, 317; Edward Younger (ed.), *Inside the Confederate Government: The Diary of Robert Garlick Hill Kean* (New York: Oxford University Press, 1957), 174, hereinafter cited as *Diary of R. G. H. Kean*.

24. *Official Records*, Ser. IV, Vol. III, 10–11, 28–29, 42–43, 113–14, 78–82, 303–304, 380–81, 439, 442, 928–29, and 948–53. See also Louise B. Hill, "State Socialism in the Confederate States of America," in J. D. Eggleston (ed.), *Southern Sketches*, Number 9, First Series (Charlottesville: Historical Publishing Company, 1936), 29–31.

tion and the states had left narrow ideas of limited government behind. Neither had found a solution, however, to the deteriorating conditions of life, though the states went to great lengths to try. In this simple desire to relieve their hard-pressed citizens, state leaders often found themselves opposing the programs of the central government. Increasing numbers of southerners had given all that they could to the cause, yet the Davis administration demanded still more. Only the states could protect such people from further destitution or in some cases starvation. Responding to growing demoralization and tangible needs, state leaders attempted to shield their citizens from further sacrifice, and when they came into conflict with Confederate programs, they raised the familiar cry of states' rights as justification.

The controversy over shipping regulations provided a clear example of this situation. Undeniably the Confederate government needed the war material that it could import under these regulations, but few states owned their own ships, and they needed the imports also. As the Atlanta *Daily Intelligencer* pointed out, Davis' regulations were hurting Georgia, Mississippi, Alabama, and North Carolina. Governors Vance and Brown, especially, operated extensive import-export programs to relieve the poor in their states. Using chartered ships, they imported food, clothing, blankets, and cotton and wool cards and distributed the cargoes to the needy. Davis' regulations struck at the heart of these programs, and the two state executives refused to stand idly by and see their efforts destroyed. They demanded that all ships carrying state cargoes be exempted from the regulations and pressured the congress to overturn the administration's policy. When Davis proved adamant, Brown and Vance took their grievance to a meeting of governors in October, 1864, and obtained a resolution demanding that the congress change the law. Strenuously but unsuccessfully the resolution asserted that the Confederate regulations violated states' rights.[25]

25. Atlanta *Daily Intelligencer*, July 1, 1864; Rowland (ed.), *Jefferson Davis*, VI, 297–98, 336, 400–401, and Richardson (comp.), *Messages and Papers of the Confederacy*, I, 466–70, 505–513.

Another Confederate policy that damaged the welfare of citizens in the states was the distilling of whiskey from grain. With hunger widespread, many southerners were enraged that scarce foodstuffs were being used for liquor instead of bread. Yet the War Department contracted to buy whiskey for the army and helped obtain grain for the distillers. Early in 1864 Governor Vance protested against the operation of a Confederate distillery in North Carolina and invoked a state anti-distilling law against it. The Richmond administration stood firm and eventually declared that all state laws against distilling were unconstitutional if applied to the central government. But the consumption of large amounts of scarce grain rankled among the common people and evoked further challenges on this issue from Virginia and South Carolina.[26]

During 1864 South Carolina's governor, M. L. Bonham, tried by another means to relieve hard-pressed southern farmers. Throughout the war leaders of the Palmetto state had shown a keen concern for the safety of Charleston. Yet in June, 1864, Governor Bonham pleaded with Secretary of War Seddon to rescind an order directing three regiments of state troops from mountain areas to the port city. The white population of the mountain districts, Bonham said, had been stripped of laborers and defenders. "If these troops . . . are now called out," the governor warned, "there will be great suffering next year, and . . . possible starvation." Bonham declared that many parts of his state were already short of food and unable to supply themselves without outside assistance. On other occasions Bonham also protested against irregular or unjust impressments.[27]

North Carolina's Governor Vance similarly interfered with Confederate military activities in April, 1864, and sought a suspension of enrollment of young boys and older men in order to benefit agriculture. He wrote to Seddon "that the partial abstraction even of these men from their crops at any time between this and August would be followed by the most distressing consequences." To buttress this appeal, Vance then resorted to constitutional arguments and contended

26. *Official Records*, Ser. IV, Vol III, 23–24, 875–80.
27. *Ibid.*, Ser. I, Vol. XXXV, Pt. II, 519 and Ser. IV, Vol. II, 863–64.

that if the enrollment continued North Carolina would be deprived of all military capacity contrary to the "genius of our new Government." He insisted that Confederate agents stop their work until the legislature met.[28]

Vance worked hard to alleviate shortages and suffering among North Carolinians, and, unfortunately for the national war effort, he was particularly well situated to accomplish his aim. More than one-third of the factories making wool and cotton cloth east of the Mississippi were in North Carolina. Steadily and efficiently, Vance appropriated the entire production of these plants for North Carolina's soldiers and home population. He even used conscripts detailed from Confederate service to help manufacture cloth which was sold cheaply to the civilian population. With the aid of leather and wool drawn from other states, Vance accumulated a vast surplus of uniforms, shoes, and blankets for North Carolina's soldiers. Once this hoard was in place, it was politically difficult to give any part of it away while suffering still existed in the state. At the end of the war, even though the state warehouses were bulging, he refused to release his stores to Lee's hungry and tattered soldiers.[29]

As other governors labored to relieve their constituents, some ironic situations developed. The career of Alabama's Thomas Watts, which took a sharp turn when he became governor, illustrated the primacy of local problems over abstract constitutional theories. Watts, a former Whig, had served as attorney general in Davis' cabinet from April, 1862, to October, 1863. During his tenure in Richmond, he drafted several opinions notable for their strong defense of the powers of the central government. Reversing a position taken by his predecessor, Judah Benjamin, Watts held that governors had no right to make appointments or fill vacancies in state troops tendered to the Confederacy, because the president directed all troops in national service. In another opinion he assured the president that the conscription act was constitutional, since the central government

28. *Ibid.*, Ser. IV, Vol. III, 307.
29. *Ibid.*, 38, 671–72, 690–92, 746; Yates, *Confederacy and Zeb Vance*, 84; Frank L. Owsley, *State Rights in the Confederacy* (Chicago: University of Chicago Press, 1925), 126.

had unrestricted power to provide for the nation's defense.[30] Yet a sudden transformation of the attorney general occurred when he left Richmond to become governor of Alabama, for within a few months Watts was expounding states' rights theories with a vigor and defiance worthy of Joe Brown.

After issuing a mild warning against illegal impressments in January, 1864, Watts adopted the sharper tone of a states' rights advocate. Objecting strenuously to the enrollment of state reserve troops in Confederate organizations, Watts charged that the Confederate officials were doing "much injury—actual injury—to the planting interest of the State" by "taking men over forty-five years old and boys under eighteen from their farms at this season of the year and placing them in camps to do nothing, and let their crops be destroyed." Watts declared that he would not permit the troops to be taken from his control and angrily warned, "The States have some rights left." By November, 1864, the governor had developed his spirit of resistance to the point of belligerency. Since 1862 the War Department had insisted that exemptions applied only to those in the specified categories at the date of passage of the exemption act, and Watts certainly understood this policy. Nevertheless, he aggressively defended state officers who had been elected after the passage of the last exemption act and sought to shield them from the draft. At one point Watts even threatened to "resist . . . with all the forces of the State."[31] Placed in the governor's chair and confronted with the needs of his state, this defender of the national government quickly discarded his constitutional theories in favor of the tendentious but useful rhetoric of states' rights.

Joe Brown also challenged the Confederacy's enrolling officers and charged that they were "dragging from their homes hundreds who leave helpless families with no prospect of support." Both Brown and Vance discovered that they could protect many of their constituents from conscription by certifying that virtually all state office-

30. Rembert W. Patrick, *Jefferson Davis and His Cabinet* (Baton Rouge: Louisiana State University Press, 1944), 306.

31. *Official Records*, Ser. IV, Vol. III, 37, 463–64, 820, 848.

holders were essential to the government. Not only did this device keep some sorely needed men at home, but it also represented a fine opportunity to distribute patronage and win gratitude. Testifying to a similar situation in the other states, the head of the Conscription Bureau complained that his agency encountered most of its difficulties with governors, judges, and politicians. "From one end of the Confederacy to the other," Superintendent Preston commented, "every constituted authority . . . is engaged in opposing the enrolling officer in the execution of his duties."[32]

In the closing stages of the war, a related cause of controversy between the Confederacy and the states was an understandable lack of confidence in the military capabilities of the Confederate government. State executives felt a responsibility to defend their citizens, and if the central government could not protect the population, the governors stood ready to make other arrangements and cite states' rights theory as justification. An embarrassing situation of this nature arose in September, 1864. President Davis' home state, Mississippi, defied the Confederate government and the conscription law in order to have troops at hand. On September 20 Governor Charles Clark bluntly notified Confederate officials that "the State of Mississippi has to defend herself in [the] future," and that he intended to use the powers of the state to call out volunteers from all age groups for six months. Eventually a court test resolved the issue in favor of the central government, but not before Governor Clark had dared the Confederacy to use force against him. The form of this controversy involved states' rights, but its cause was different. Even the Confederate officer who dealt with Clark believed that the governor was moved not by "a factious spirit of opposition" but by a genuine, "overweening solicitude for the defense of the State (which has greatly suffered)."[33] As the Confederacy collapsed, other state leaders held back forces to defend their own territory rather than send them vainly to the front.

These controversies tried Jefferson Davis' patience, and he complained of the "persistent interference of some of the State Authori-

32. *Ibid.*, 385–86, 384, 344–49, 181, 307, 425–28, 224–25.
33. *Ibid.*, 710, 740, 902–903.

ties" who treated the Confederacy "as if it were the public enemy [rather] than the Government which they themselves had established for the common defense." Stubbornly his administration insisted upon the supremacy of Confederate law and served notice that until the establishment of a supreme court it would not regard any adverse rulings on conscription by state courts as definitive. Until the very end Davis believed that a national army and central direction were essential. Even after the surrender at Appomattox he denied a request from soldiers who wanted to return to their homes and argued that the Confederacy must not reduce its forces to a collection of independent state armies.[34]

The Confederate president also remained unmoved on his ultimate goal: independence. Despite the indications that a growing number of southerners favored the idea of striking a bargain with Lincoln and returning to the Union, Davis strove to present a firm, unyielding position to the foe. In July, 1864, he agreed to meet with two northerners, Colonel James F. Jacquess, a self-appointed peacemaker, and James R. Gilmore, a journalist. Knowing that these two men would publish his views to the world, Davis seized the opportunity to state the Confederacy's goal in unmistakable terms. After making his customary explanations that the South desired peace and sought only to be left alone, he said: "We are not fighting for slavery. We are fighting for Independence, and that, or extermination, we *will* have." Davis also told his visitors that there were "essential differences" between the North and the South which would "make them two nations" however the war ended. As Jacquess and Gilmore left the room they heard Davis reemphasize his determination to achieve independence: "Say to Mr. Lincoln from me, that I shall at any time be pleased to receive proposals for peace on the basis of our Independence. It will be useless to approach me with any other."[35]

The South's leader could have made no clearer statement, either

34. Jefferson Davis to Samuel J. Person, December 15, 1864, in Rowland (ed.), *Jefferson Davis*, VI, 418–21; *Official Records*, Ser. IV, Vol. III, 956–66; Jefferson Davis to Lt. Colonel C. H. Lynch and others, April 18, 1865, in Rowland (ed.), *Jefferson Davis*, VI, 548–49.

35. Quoted in Robert F. Durden, *The Gray and the Black: The Confederate Debate on Emancipation* (Baton Rouge: Louisiana State University Press, 1972), 70–71.

to the United States government or to his own citizens, of his purpose. Just as he had upon reaching Montgomery in 1861, Davis rejected any idea of compromise or reunion. The bitter experiences of war, combined with his tendency to pursue goals with single-minded dedication, had made him into a stubborn southern nationalist. A few graphic, conversational remarks which he made about this time underlined the president's resolve. In March a clerk in the War Department reported that he had overheard Davis say that twelve- and fourteen-year-old boys would "have their trial" before the war was over and that Confederates could eat rats if necessary.[36]

Such determination to continue the bloodshed would have been criminal if the southern armies had been without hope, but in the spring and summer of 1864 a succession of bloody, indecisive battles shocked the North and gave new life to southern hopes that the Confederacy might outlast its adversary and win independence. In the spring General Ulysses S. Grant renewed his attempts to break through the Confederate armies surrounding Richmond. In the Battle of the Wilderness, near Fredericksburg, Union forces lost over 26,000 men, but Grant pushed on to Cold Harbor, where he committed what some historians have called "a ghastly mistake." Hurling three corps against Lee's intrenched troops, the Union commander lost 12,000 men in a single attack, and the carnage "produced a shudder in the North [and] intensified the peace movement and the opposition to Lincoln." These costly battles ended Lee's hopes of gathering enough strength to conquer the Union armies, but Grant paid a fearful price and lost a number of men equal to Lee's entire force. To J. B. Jones and other Confederates, the chances of peace at that time seemed "bright and brightening."[37] Although Sherman had begun his advance into Georgia, southerners hoped and assumed that Joseph E. Johnston could block his progress. As long as the war remained at a stalemate, the northern public grew more frustrated and depressed, and the agitation for peace increased.

36. Jones, *A Rebel War Clerk's Diary*, II, 175.
37. J. G. Randall and David Donald, *The Civil War and Reconstruction* (2nd ed.; Boston: D. C. Heath and Company, 1961), 419–21, 423; Jones, *A Rebel War Clerk's Diary,*, II, 268.

The Confederacy—its people, its leaders, and the press—watched northern politics with intense concentration and tried to discern the direction of events. Nearly exhausted themselves, southerners sensed that the war could not go on much longer and hoped that internal dissensions in the United States might prove the Confederacy's deliverance. Admitting that "rumors of Peace float around us, and men dream of Peace at night," the Richmond *Examiner* admonished its readers in July to remember, "Hard fighting has proven the best recipe." That same month the *Examiner* reported signs that civil war was about to break out in New York, Kentucky, and Ohio. Similarly, the Charleston *Mercury* declared in June that the northern peace party was "a party of despair" and that southern strength and victories would nourish it. The Rhetts' organ also predicted that if the war went badly, northern Democrats would soon raise the cry of "the best we can get" and begin to negotiate. According to the *Mercury*, the northern Democracy was moving toward peace.[38]

In fact, there was a peace faction in the Democratic party which succeeded partially in writing its views into the platform. The Confederacy's agents in Canada even managed to aid the Democrats somewhat by maneuvering Lincoln into the unpopular statement that abolition was a condition of peace. But the Democracy's nominee, General George McClellan, threw his party's attitude toward peace into doubt when he stressed in his letter of acceptance that he was determined to restore the Union. To compound this potential roadblock to southern independence, a clear and immediate danger was shaping up in Georgia. It was essential to Davis' hopes of wearing down northern morale that the Confederacy stop Sherman's army and hold Atlanta, but General Johnston continued to fall back toward the city. At length, exasperated by Johnston's silence about his plans and his refusal to indicate that he could hold Atlanta, Davis replaced him with the one-legged General John Hood. The Confederacy's grand strategy had reached a crucial juncture, for as Mary Boy-

38. *Daily Richmond Examiner*, July 26, 1864, p. 2, and July 23, 1864, p. 2; Charleston *Mercury*, June 6, 1864, p. 1, June 22, 1864, p. 1, August 17, 1864, p. 1, and September 5, 1864.

kin Chesnut wrote, "Our all depends on that Army at Atlanta. If that fails us, the game is up."[39]

Hood, however, could not stop Sherman's troops, and the Federal army occupied Atlanta on September 2. In both sections people recognized the significance of this crucial event. A tremor of joy ran through the North and revived the sagging prospects of the Republican party, while dark gloom fell over thousands of southern homes. On receiving the news, Mrs. Chesnut wrote, "There is no hope." Another diarist, J. B. Jones, admitted on September 5 that , "The loss of Atlanta is a stunning blow," and ten days later he made a statement which mirrored the depression of thousands of Confederates: "Our fondly-cherished visions of peace have vanished like a mirage of the desert."[40]

Yet, although Davis' strategy had received what proved to be a fatal blow, the northern elections had not been held, and the Confederate president shook off his momentary depression in order to urge a renewed effort in the two months remaining. The press joined in this movement, and shortly after admitting the significance of Sherman's prize, many papers reversed themselves. The Richmond *Examiner*, for example, predicted that the South could still win a peace through staunch resistance and bravely called the fall of Atlanta "a trifling affair . . . puffed . . . out of all proportion." On September 20 the Charleston *Mercury* identified the Virginia front as the key to the war and proclaimed that if Lee's army held firm, the South would be independent.[41]

On the same day, J. B. Jones noted in his diary that a rumor had reached Richmond to the effect that General Sherman had invited Vice-President Stephens, Governor Brown, and Senator Herschel Johnson to meet with him and discuss Georgia's return to the Union. Immediately Davis left for Georgia to prevent any negotiations, try to rouse the people, and confer with his generals. In a series of speeches he held out the hope that by energetic action southerners could drive Sherman's army out of Georgia and even destroy it. Admitting that

39. Randall and Donald, *The Civil War and Reconstruction*, 475; Chesnut, *Diary*, 425.
40. Chesnut, *Diary*, 434; Jones, *A Rebel War Clerk's Diary*, II, 277, 283.
41. *Daily Richmond Examiner*, September 5 and 6, 1864, and September 12, 1864, p. 2; Charleston *Mercury*, September 20, 1864.

the situation was grave, Davis confronted an audience in Macon with the stark fact that "two-thirds of our men are absent—some sick, some wounded, but most of them absent without leave." The president promised clemency for those who returned and asserted that "if one-half of the men now absent without leave will return to duty, we can defeat the enemy."[42]

Moving into Alabama, he urged every man to "go to the front" and declared: "Victory in the field is the surest element of strength to a peace party. Let us win battles and we shall have overtures soon enough." Davis then headed back into Georgia and South Carolina, where he vehemently condemned the idea of accepting reconstruction, even with slavery maintained, and opposed the idea of a convention. Lincoln, he argued, offered southerners nothing but the opportunity to acknowledge their crimes, emancipate their slaves, turn over their leaders, and enjoy the privilege of "voting together with your negroes." At Columbia, South Carolina, he still held out hope of influencing the northern elections: "Within the next thirty days much is to be done. . . . Let fresh victories crown our arms, and the peace party, if there be such at the North, can elect its candidate."[43]

No great victory was forthcoming, however, and Abraham Lincoln won reelection to another four-year term. Many newspapers tried to put the best face on this development, as did the Richmond *Examiner*, which suggested that Lincoln's victory would unite the South because it was "the only circumstance that could effectually and eternally crush out from the Southern mind and heart the latent sentiment in favor of reconstruction, which has existed from the beginning." But mere words lacked the power to banish reality, and despondency spread throughout the Confederacy. Jefferson Davis reacted to the wreck of his greatest hopes by succumbing to the nervous ailments which often afflicted him in times of stress. Vice-President

42. Jones, *A Rebel War Clerk's Diary*, II, 287; Rowland (ed.), *Jefferson Davis*, VI, 341 and 343. Newspapers roundly criticized Davis for making these remarks, although their pages had often revealed similar information.
43. Rowland (ed.), *Jefferson Davis*, VI, 347, 352, 358, 355–56.

Alexander Stephens traded recriminations with Davis over the question of who had done the most to encourage northern peace forces before the Federal elections. Thousands of private citizens in the South began to prepare themselves in their own ways for the end.[44]

Inevitably, as Sherman's army marched through Georgia toward the sea and southerners considered their situation, the crumbling facade of southern unity disintegrated further. Trouble again began to brew in Georgia, where Linton Stephens introduced resolutions calling for a convention of all the states. Loyal correspondents warned Davis that "Reconstruction and separate State action is boldly talked," and that "a Convention in the present frame of the public mind, means reconstruction."[45] In Richmond R. G. H. Kean, chief of the Bureau of War, heard that planters were selling their slaves rapidly and sensed that his countrymen anticipated the total collapse of the government. In South Carolina Congressman William Boyce declared that the Confederate states had become a military despotism and advocated a convention of the states to end it. Discontented and despondent citizens supported Boyce's proposal, and, according to Mrs. Chesnut, the growing movement "worked like a dry rot in the Army."[46]

With the fortunes of the Confederacy at their lowest point, members of the congress demanded changes in the administration. First Louis Wigfall of Texas tried, with meager results, to get three states to call a convention and remove all military power from Davis' hands. The Virginia delegation, including Speaker of the House Thomas Bocock, then took the lead late in January, 1865, and sought the res-

44. *Daily Richmond Examiner*, November 4, 1864, p. 2; Jones, *A Rebel War Clerk's Diary*, II, 355; Hudson Strode, *Jefferson Davis* (3 vols.; New York: Harcourt, Brace & Company, 1955–1964), III, 122–23; *Official Records*, Ser. IV, Vol. III, 840 and 934–40.

45. Rowland (ed.), *Jefferson Davis*, VI, 402–406; Samuel Clayton to Jefferson Davis, January 10, 1865, in Official Records, Ser. IV, Vol. III, 1010–1011; James A. Nisbet to James Seddon, January 10, 1865, in Letters Received, Confederate Secretary of War, in RG 109, NA, Microcopy M 437, Roll 150, pp. 215–16; Warren Akin to his wife, January 10, 1865 in letters of Confederate congressmen in possession of Bell I. Wiley.

46. Younger (ed.), *Diary of R. G. H. Kean*, 186; A. T. Caperton to Judah Benjamin, October 17, 1864, in C. S. A.. (Pickett) Papers, Library of Congress; Charleton *Mercury*, October 13, 1864; Chesnut, *Diary*, 448.

ignation of the entire cabinet. After several days Secretary of War Seddon, who felt this censure with special keenness because he was a Virginian, insisted on resigning, but Davis used Seddon's departure as the occasion for a long statement on the independence of the executive branch and the president's control over the tenure of cabinet officers. The congress also demanded that Robert E. Lee take on new duties as general-in-chief, and some even urged that the general be named dictator. Eventually Davis yielded to the pressure, appointed Lee to the command of all the armies, and even swallowed his pride by bowing to the clamor for the reinstatement of General Joseph E. Johnston, in whom the president had no confidence. None of these concessions, however, could disguise the fact that the president's relations with the congress had reached rock bottom. Davis himself felt that the senate had tried "to destroy the confidence of the people in me," and he complained to Secretary of the Navy Stephen Mallory about the "trials to which the Congress has of late subjected the Executive."[47]

Although the fortunes of the southern nation were sinking fast in January, 1865, Davis had one more opportunity to define the Confederacy's goals, and again he proved adamant for independence. Francis Preston Blair, Sr., arrived in Richmond and initiated unofficial talks which paved the way for the Hampton Roads conference. Sure of his own mind, Davis was convinced that he knew what was in President Lincoln's mind also. In an exchange of letters prior to the conference at Hampton Roads, both men found a way to reveal plainly the distance between their positions. Davis expressed his willingness to appoint a commission for the purpose of restoring peace "to the two countries," and Lincoln offered to receive any agent sent "with a view of securing peace to the people of our common country." But the desire for an end to the war was so great that Davis could not

47. David W. Lewis to Jefferson Davis, December 30, 1864, in Keith Read Papers, University of Georgia; Thomas S. Bocock to Jefferson Davis, January 21, 1865, in the Papers of Burton Harrison and Family, Library of Congress; Jefferson Davis to James Seddon, February 1, 1865, in Rowland (ed.), *Jefferson Davis*, VI, 458–61; *Daily Richmond Examiner*, January 9, 1865, p. 2; Richardson (comp.), *Messages and Papers of the Confederacy*, I, 570; Rowland (ed.), *Jefferson Davis*, VI, 491–92, 524–25, 586–87.

ignore it altogether. Therefore he appointed three commissioners to meet with Lincoln and persisted until Alexander Stephens, the chief prophet of peace, agreed to be among them.[48]

Vice-President Stephens hoped that the United States would agree to an armistice and join the South in an effort to drive French influence from Mexico, but Lincoln and Secretary of State William Seward dashed such optimistic and unrealistic suggestions. Lincoln was willing to discuss many secondary issues, but he insisted upon reunion, no cessation of hostilities without the disbanding of all Confederate forces, and, with less clarity, the acceptance of emancipation.[49] These were terms which the Confederate government could not accept, and Stephens knew it. Davis had maneuvered his chief domestic critic into the position of confirming the president's judgment about the possibilities for a negotiated settlement.

The Hampton Roads conference was not, however, merely an empty ritual which clarified the differences between Davis and his vice president. Lincoln made certain overtures to the South which, though they fell short of Alexander Stephens' visions, did present some real inducements for the South to abandon the conflict and voluntarily reenter the Union. The Federal president was deeply concerned about the possibility of a lingering guerrilla war, and for months he had been broadcasting his promise to look with favor upon all applications for pardon. His strongest bait, however, concerned the disposition of the slavery question. During the northern election campaign Seward had declared that emancipation was a war measure, and Lincoln repeated this notion at Hampton Roads. According to the United States president, the courts would decide after the war whether some, all, or none of the slaves had gained their freedom. Seward even suggested that the South could reenter the Union and defeat the Thirteenth Amendment. Without commenting on Seward's statement, Lincoln advised Stephens to encourage Georgians to ratify the amendment prospectively, so that it would take

48. Richardson (comp.), *Messages and Papers of the Confederacy*, I, 521; James Z. Rabun, "Alexander H. Stephens and Jefferson Davis," p. 318.

49. Randall and Donald, *The Civil War and Reconstruction*, 524–25.

effect in five years. Moreover, Lincoln promised to show liberality on questions of confiscation and seek a $400 million indemnity for southern slaveholders. Ludwell Johnson, who has examined this matter very closely, concludes that the great emancipator was trying to build "a new conservative coalition which would include Southerners."[50]

Johnson relied primarily on Alexander Stephens' account of the Hampton Roads conference as described in his history of the war, written almost five years after the event, but contemporary evidence confirms that discussions of this nature did take place. R. G. H. Kean, who received his information from John Campbell, his superior in the War Department and one of the Confederate commissioners, recorded in his diary that Lincoln had said that the slavery question was one for the courts. North Carolina's Senator William A. Graham also learned from Judge Campbell that "the dissent of ten States could still reject" the Thirteenth Amendment. On February 2, 1865, the Charleston *Mercury* reported rumors that the United States had proposed reunion with the preservation of slavery, except for runaways who had come into Union lines. In addition, there was to be no slavery permitted in the territories.[51]

Jefferson Davis did his best to quash any possibility that the Confederacy would respond to such a lure. Dissatisfied with the brief, noncommittal character of the commissioners' report, he summoned Assistant Secretary of War Campbell to his office and urged him "to add that Lincoln and Seward insisted on abolition and submission." When Campbell replied that the report, which did not go so far, accurately expressed the result of the conference, Davis indicated that he wanted "to add the other to influence the people." Next Davis asked all three commissioners to change their text, but they refused. Campbell, at least, felt that the Confederate government should re-

---

50. Jones, *A Rebel War Clerk's Diary*, II, 352; Ludwell Johnson, "Lincoln's Solution to the Problem of Peace Terms, 1864–1865," *Journal of Southern History*, XXXIV (1968), 576–86.

51. Younger (ed.), *Diary of R. G. H. Kean*, 196–97; William A. Graham to David L. Swain, February 12, 1865, in Swain Papers, University of North Carolina; Charleston *Mercury*, February 2, 1865, p. 1.

new contact with the United States and make a definite offer of terms. Having failed to obtain a strong statement from his commissioners, the Confederate president drafted one himself and submitted it to the congress with the relevant documents. In his letter of transmittal, Davis declared without qualification that the United States had refused to consider other terms "than those which the conqueror may grant," or allow peace on any other basis "than our unconditional submission to their rule, coupled with the acceptance of" the Thirteenth Amendment. That evening he made the same assertion in an impromptu speech at the African Church in Richmond.[52]

Thus Davis steered his sinking government into the last days of the war with unaltered purpose. A daughter of his old friend Clement Clay reported, "He looks badly—old, grey, and *wrinkled*. I never saw a more troubled countinance [*sic*] in my life." Yet he still tried to impart to the people some of his own determination. On March 31, 1865, in an address to the congress he called upon the people's "undying, unconquerable resolve to be free" and raised the specter of racial revolution by predicting that if defeated, southerners would have to live "in a country garrisoned by their own negroes." On April 4 the government had to abandon Richmond, but Davis defiantly pledged that "again and again we will return, until the baffled and exhausted enemy shall abandon in despair his endless and impossible task of making slaves of a people resolved to be free." Eighteen days later, in Charlotte, North Carolina, the cabinet unanimously recommended the surrender of Joseph Johnston's army, the last major Confederate force east of the Mississippi, and Davis reluctantly consented.[53]

From that point, the president of the Confederacy was in flight from the United States army. Unable to discard the dream which he had cherished so long, Davis occasionally indulged in fanciful speculations about how he could have turned disaster into victory, but he

---

52. Younger (ed.), *Diary of R. G. H. Kean*, 202; Richardson (comp.), *Messages and Papers of the Confederacy*, I, 519; *Daily Richmond Enquirer*, February 9, 1865.

53. Celeste (?) Clay to her sisters, January 17, 1865, in Clement C. Clay Papers, 1861–1865, in Record Group 109, National Archives.

had not lost all sense of reality, as some have suggested. He admitted to his wife that miracles were no longer possible, and he urged her to divide her baggage to facilitate rapid flight.[54] Attempting to make his way to the Trans-Mississippi Department where he hoped to continue resistance, the Confederate president finally was captured near Irwinsville, Georgia, on May 10.[55]

Thus the trying and tumultuous life of the Confederacy ended for Jefferson Davis. But before it did, one last revealing episode had taken place. Pursuing his passion for independence to its logical end, Davis made the boldest proposal of his career as president. He advocated and threw the influence of his administration behind a plan to arm southern slaves and place them in the Confederate armies, with emancipation and residence in the South as a reward for faithful service. This proposal sparked an acrimonious debate which raged through the last months of the southern nation. Although conditions had become rather chaotic in the Confederacy by that time, the debate on emancipation revealed much about slavery's relationship to Confederate purpose and the perception of that purpose by different classes.

54. Richardson (ed.), *Messages and Papers of the Confederacy*, I, 549; Rowland (ed.), *Jefferson Davis*, VI, 531, 563–85, 559–60.
55. Thinking perhaps of the favorable terms that General Sherman offered General Johnston before President Johnson intervened, Davis hoped to carry on the fight "until we could get some kind of treaty to secure the political rights of the States." See Davis' handwritten notations on a copy of an article published by his former secretary, Burton Harrison, in *Century Magazine* (November, 1883), in the Papers of Burton Harrison and Family, Box 8, Manuscript Division, Library of Congress.

8

Slavery
and
Confederate Purpose

From 1861 to the present, Americans have seen a close connection between slavery and the purpose of the Confederacy. Probably most people have based this perception upon prewar events, for throughout the long sectional conflict southern leaders openly revealed their fear of northern abolitionism and their determination to defend the South's peculiar institution. Jefferson Davis himself warned that those who advocated the exclusion of slavery from the territories actually sought the destruction of slavery in the states, and in 1858 he angrily denounced "the war that is made against our institutions."[1]

After secession, other events reinforced the linkage between slavery and Confederate purpose. The framers of a new southern constitution gave a far more prominent position to slavery than it had in the fundamental law of the United States by referring to the institution by name and guaranteeing both protection of slavery in the territories and unrestricted transportation of slaves throughout the new southern nation. Certain southern newspapers, such as the Charleston *Mercury*, glorified slavery and prophesied a bright future for the Confederacy as an expanding slaveholding republic. With frank contempt for Jefferson's rhetoric of equality, the editors of the *Mercury* demanded the reopening of the African slave trade and the exclusion of all nonslaveholding states from the new government. Crowning

1. Jackson (Miss.) *Mississippian and State Gazette* October 21, 1857, p. 1; Percy Lee Rainwater, *Mississippi: Storm Center of Secession, 1856–1861* (Baton Rouge: Otto Claitor, 1938), 26; Dunbar Rowland (ed.), *Jefferson Davis: Constitutionalist; His Letters, Papers, and Speeches* (10 vols.; Jackson, Miss.: Little & Ives, Co., 1923), III, 173.

this structure of proslavery evidence was the speech delivered by Vice-President Alexander Stephens at the Savannah Athenaeum on March 21, 1861. Stephens declared that slavery was the Confederate "cornerstone" and thus provided quasiofficial proof that the southern nation rested upon the principle of human bondage.[2]

As in many human situations, however, the actual relationship between slavery and Confederate purpose was rather complex. Different social classes and regions within the South had different motives for leaving the Union. Although the desire to protect slavery predominated among the causes of secession, especially for the leadership class, other factors exerted a significant influence in society as a whole. A majority of southerners clearly shared Jefferson Davis' reluctance to secede, and nothing short of the outbreak of war proved powerful enough to induce the people of Virginia, North Carolina, Tennessee, and Arkansas to cast their lots with the Confederacy. Sporadic protests in other southern states demonstrated that non-slaveholders often harbored misgivings about the war and went into battle for reasons other than the protection of slavery. Some, no doubt, feared that Lincoln's followers wanted to elevate the status of the Negro above that of the white farmer, but others fought simply because they considered themselves southerners or had no choice but to defend their homes.

Signs of this complex blend of motives emerged in some Confederate newspapers during the first days of the war. The *Daily Richmond Examiner*, for example, declared on March 14, 1861, that the Union had crumbled because North and South had evolved into two nations, and its rival, the *Richmond Weekly Whig*, dismissed slavery as merely one of the "incidents of the controversy" over centralization. By the summer of 1862 even the Charleston *Mercury* had adopted the argument that political centralization was "the prime cause of the dissolution of the Union."[3] To encompass the diversity

2. Charles Robert Lee, Jr., *The Confederate Constitutions* (Chapel Hill: University of North Carolina Press, 1963), 194–95, 111–17; Charleston *Mercury*, February 13, 1861, p.1, February 23, 1861, p. 4, July 11, 1861, p. 1, April 11, 1862, p. 1; Augusta *Constitutionalist*, March 30, 1861.
3. *Daily Richmond Examiner*, March 14, 1861, p. 2; *Richmond Weekly Whig*, May 11, 1861, p. 4; Charleston *Mercury*, July 29, 1862, p. 1.

of motives among his fellow citizens, Jefferson Davis carefully pitched his justification of the new nation upon the level of constitutional principles and stressed the right of southerners to self-government. According to his statements, the goal of the Confederacy was independence rather than the perpetuation of slavery, and during his first year as president, Davis' only public reference to slavery attempted to place the issue within a context of constitutional rights.

Wartime developments tested the South's ambivalence about its national purpose. Although some men believed simply that they were fighting for slavery, the president of the Confederacy customarily stressed other goals and insisted upon strong legislation which alienated a large number of slaveholders. Eventually Davis' total dedication to independence raised an explicit challenge to the priority of defending slavery. When the need for additional manpower in the southern armies became critical, he proposed arming and emancipating the slaves as the only means to avoid northern domination. Predictably, this idea raised a storm of protest, and in the last months of the Confederacy an acrimonious debate raged over the issue of Confederate emancipation. Confused as this debate was, since it occurred amid the tumult and disorganization of a dying nation, it revealed much about slavery's place in the divided southern mind and the attitudes of certain classes in the Confederacy.

During the forty years before the Civil War, spokesmen for the proslavery argument had labored to create uniformity in the minds of southerners on the question of slavery. Inner doubt and external disapproval were the targets of their attack, and after an isolated beginning in South Carolina in the 1820s, these advocates of slavery attracted a growing number of intellectual and political leaders to their crusade. Attacking the old, apologetic defense that slavery was a necessary evil which southerners had inherited, the proslavery theorists vigorously publicized their conviction that slavery was a positive good, a moral, social, and political desideratum.[4]

Led by such men as Dr. Thomas Cooper of South Carolina, Thomas

4. William Sumner Jenkins, *Pro-Slavery Thought in the Old South* (Chapel Hill: University of North Carolina Press, 1935).

Dew and George Fitzhugh of Virginia, and Josiah Nott of Alabama, the proslavery movement developed considerable intellectual momentum and extended and refined its arguments as the years advanced. Its thinkers contributed to a conservative, organic conception of society and produced two separate theories about the benefits of slavery. The dominant school of propagandists and politicians emphasized the biological difference between the races and proclaimed the absolute equality of white men in the presence of the inferior Negro. Josiah Nott skillfully adapted this theory to the latest intellectual currents by capitalizing on scientific discoveries about the antiquity and persistence of racial differences. George Fitzhugh, however, took another tack and insisted that slavery was a perfect social system, appropriate for all communities, even those composed exclusively of white people. Thus in a variety of ways, influential southerners attempted to build support for their peculiar institution.[5]

Despite the fundamental importance of slavery to the economic and social system, this new philosophy had to overcome religious and political values which were deeply rooted in southern culture. Antebellum southerners regarded their land as a Christian community, and many of them knew that the New Testament's injunction to "do unto others as you would have them do unto you" posed a challenge to plantation life. During the early years of the nineteenth century, the leading evangelical denominations had nurtured moral opposition to the slave regime. Moreover, southern patriots of the Revolutionary era had felt the inspiration of liberal idealism and given eloquent expression to man's desire for freedom. Thomas Jefferson's Declaration of Independence and his tentative opposition to slavery were part of a political legacy which subsequent leaders could not wholly deny. As Charles G. Sellers, Jr., has pointed out, there were men of eminent respectability who could not stomach the claims of proslavery advocates. When Senator John C. Calhoun declared in

5. William Stanton, *The Leopard's Spots: Scientific Attitude Toward Race in America, 1815–1859* (Chicago: University of Chicago Press, 1960), 65, 158; George M. Fredrickson, *The Black Image in the White Mind: The Debate on Afro-American Character and Destiny, 1817–1914* (New York: Harper & Row, 1971), 58–62.

the mid-1830s that slavery was "a good—a great good," one of Jefferson's former law students, Senator William C. Rives of Virginia, rose to denounce this "obsolete and revolting" idea and to affirm that slavery was "a misfortune and an evil in all circumstances."[6]

In time, however, and with the aid of the sectional crisis, proslavery theorists overpowered their critics and gained the dominant position in public discourse. By 1860 the churches had come around to a united defense of slavery, although religious leaders did not accept all the proslavery argument and continued to defend scriptural teachings that the human race was one, against Josiah Nott's anthropology. Southern politicians also professed, at least in public, a virtually unanimous belief in the good of slavery. Yet proslavery thought in 1860 was a relatively new intellectual phenomenon, and it constantly produced dissonant vibrations with southern tradition as well as world opinion. Southerners could neither obliterate their history nor isolate themselves from world events, and thus they remained somewhat uncomfortable with their new social ideology.

Some makers of public opinion in the Confederacy admitted the existence of this unsettled state of mind. The editor of the Richmond *Examiner* wrote publicly in July, 1861, that "there is . . . lurking in the Southern community a deep-seated feeling of aversion to slavery." The source of this feeling, the *Examiner* believed, was partly demographic—since some southerners had northern backgrounds —and partly religious. "Teachings which were not desisted from, even at the South, until a few years ago," the *Examiner* explained, had indoctrinated the popular mind with a moral resistance to slavery. Concurring in this assessment, the Richmond *Enquirer* admitted:

> If the crisis had come thirty years ago, it would have found our churches and our public men in a condition of dreary doubt as to the justice and beneficence of those institutions, which form the basis of our community. The cant of the "Nineteenth Century," with its impossible "equality" between those races which are not equal by nature, had invaded the Christian Churches, as well as tainted the principles of statesmen; and it

6. Charles Grier Sellers, Jr., "The Travail of Slavery," in Charles G. Sellers, Jr., (ed.), *The Southerner as American* (Chapel Hill: Univeristy of North Carolina Press, 1960), 40–71.

needed the long strife of parties, and patient investigation of principles to bring the religious world up to the point at which it could recognize and sanction our cause.[7]

In some quarters the liberal religious impulse remained strong enough to produce a reformist attitude toward slavery, and many devout southerners believed that God's purpose in the war was to ameliorate the condition of the bondsman. In June, 1861, a resident of Georgia wrote to his local newspaper on the question, "How to Treat Our Slaves." Although he affirmed the rightness of slavery, this correspondent argued that "we are not fighting for the opportunity of making the condition of our servants harder" but to "revive the patriarchal character of the institution" and better the condition of the slaves. Many of the clergy shared this determination to make the reform of slavery a primary goal of the war. The Episcopal bishop of Georgia, Stephen Elliott, predicted a continuation of the bloodshed "until we ourselves shall learn to value the institution [more highly] . . . and to treat it as a sacred trust from God." As a result of the work of clerical leaders and concerned laymen, particularly Calvin Wiley of North Carolina and James Lyon of Mississippi, a movement took shape to reform slavery by guaranteeing the bondsmen's right to religious training, family ties, and personal security against violent whites. Working simultaneously in the several states of the Confederacy, proponents of reform brought bills to revise the legal structure of slavery into their state legislatures, and these proposals were gaining support when the end of the war came.[8]

While president, Jefferson Davis had contact with an Episcopal bishop who was working for better religious instruction among the slaves, and since Davis joined the Episcopal Church in 1862, it is likely that he took this movement seriously. In fact, the Confederate president was one of many leading southerners whose lives furnished evidence of concern about the morality of slaveholding. Both Davis

7. *Daily Richmond Examiner*, July 19, 1861, p. 2; *Semi-Weekly Richmond Enquirer*, July 14, 1863, p. 1.

8. Rome (Ga.) *Weekly Courier*, June 28, 1861, December 12, 1862, p. 1; Bell Irvin Wiley, *Southern Negroes, 1861–1865* (New Haven: Yale University Press, 1938), 166–70.

and his elder brother, Joseph, employed highly unusual methods of managing their slaves. On Briarfield and Hurricane, the Davis plantations in Mississippi, bondsmen administered a system of limited self-government which included the disciplining of all slaves who were accused of misconduct. A jury of slaves sitting under a black judge determined the appropriate penalty for unruly workmen, and sheriffs and constables who were part of the slave community inflicted the punishment. The Davis brothers intervened in this process only to lighten a sentence.[9]

Bondsmen on the two Mississippi plantations also had their own gardens, and any slave who could make money for himself was allowed to pursue his own occupation and to compensate his master by paying the equivalent of an unskilled laborer's wages. Several of Jefferson Davis' slaves prospered under this system, especially Ben T. Montgomery and his sons, who bought Briarfield from the Federal government in 1866. None of the slaves on the Davis plantations had to answer to names taken from leading figures in ancient history, as was the custom on some plantations, and some bondsmen earned their master's trust and held positions of great responsibility. James Pemberton, who served Davis during the early days of his military career, managed Briarfield for years in the absence of his owner, and after Pemberton died in 1852 white overseers never could achieve the same degree of productivity and efficiency.[10]

One of Davis' first acts as president was to veto a bill which did not close every loophole to a revival of the African slave trade. No doubt many Confederates breathed a sigh of relief when Davis took this action, for it put a distasteful subject out of reach and officially separated the new Confederate government from the extreme wing of agitators who would defy world opinion as well as traditional southern values. As the Anderson, South Carolina, *Intelligencer* remarked, "a large majority at the South" regarded the reopening of the slave

9. Bishop William Meade to Jefferson Davis, January 21, 1862, in Rowland (ed.), *Jefferson Davis*, V, 186–88; Varina Howell Davis, *Jefferson Davis, Ex-President of the Confederate States of America: A Memoir* (2 vols.; New York: Belford Company, 1890) I, 174–78, 203, 284, 479, hereinafter cited as *A Memoir*.

10. Varina Howell Davis, *A Memoir*, I, 174–78, 203, 284, 479.

trade "as impolitic and unwise, to say nothing of the enormity of the offence." The public's opposition to the slave trade was one of many indications that southerners had not completely adopted the proslavery position. The Richmond *Examiner* noted that most leading Virginians had been willing to admit indirectly that slavery was "morally wrong," and the paper sadly concluded that "the Southern mind is far, as yet, from justifying its own institutions."[11]

There is abundant evidence that prominent southerners had misgivings or were deeply disturbed about slavery. Mary Boykin Chesnut, the wife of a former senator from South Carolina who owned many slaves, was keenly aware of the injustice and immorality which were basic to the slave regime. Confiding her thoughts to her diary in March, 1861, she lamented the fact that bondsmen often were punished "when their masters and mistresses are brutes, not when they do wrong," and as a wife she knew that on too many plantations the women lived "surrounded by prostitutes." "God forgive us," she exclaimed, "but ours is a monstrous system, a wrong and an iniquity!" On another occasion she summed up her feelings with the words, "I hate slavery." Mrs. Chesnut's feelings were not unusual, nor were they the kind of thoughts which respected southerners kept only to themselves. In 1864 the Chesnut's minister voiced sentiments which were a characteristic part of traditional southern attitudes before the proslavery argument appeared. After explaining that he was not for slavery but instead was fighting for political freedom for the South, this preacher asserted that "every day shows that slavery is doomed," and Mrs. Chesnut added, "For that he thanked God." A devout Georgian held the similar view that "Providence by this cruel war is intruding to make us willing to relinquish slavery by feeling its burdens and cares."[12]

11. James D. Richardson (comp.), *A Compilation of the Messages and Papers of the Confederacy, Including the Diplomatic Correspondence, 1861–1865* (2 vols.; Nashville: United States Publishing Company, 1906), I, 59; Anderson (S.C.) *Intelligencer*, February 21, 1861, p. 4, and April 4, 1861, p. 4; *Daily Richmond Examiner*, June 29, 1861, p. 2.

12. Mary Boykin Chesnut, *A Diary from Dixie*, ed. Ben Ames Williams (Sentry ed.; Boston: Houghton Mifflin Company, 1949), 21, 122, 434–35; Robert Myers (ed.), *The Children of Pride* (New Haven: Yale University Press, 1972), 1116, 1122.

234   After Secession

If forty years of proslavery agitation had not banished the misgivings of slaveholders, how then did they justify their social arrangements? A number of distinguished historians have argued that
southerners could not reconcile their primary institution with their
traditional religious and political values, and that the resulting inner
doubts about slavery produced mental conflict of great significance.
According to Charles G. Sellers, Jr., "Southerners of the generation
before the Civil War suffered the most painful loss of social morale
and identity that any large group of Americans have ever experienced." Taking this argument one step further, Ralph Morrow has
written that slaveholders could not tolerate the constant criticism
which was premised on values they themselves shared. Eventually
they became irrational and "suggestible" and sought an "exit" from
their dilemma through "a trial by arms." Thus in the view of these
scholars, guilt over slavery drove southerners into the tragic conflict between North and South and led to the creation of the Confederacy.[13]

Both historical evidence and psychological theories indicate, however, that this view is a misstatement of the situation. Conflicts
between an individual's values, which psychologists have labeled
cognitive dissonance, do indeed create discomfort and stimulate a
vigorous search for ways to reduce the dissonance. In many cases
neither an individual nor a society is able to eliminate this problem
entirely, but at length people arrive at some viewpoint which re-
duces the conflict to its lowest possible level. Once one has developed
a rationalization which harmonizes the clash between his contradic-
tory values, any movement away from that position will increase the
mental pain and therefore will be avoided.[14]

Southerners experienced the unavoidable tension between their
dependence on slavery and their devotion to democratic values and
liberal religious beliefs, and therefore they searched for some way to

13. Sellers, "The Travail of Slavery," 51–52; Ralph E. Morrow, "The Proslavery Argument Revisited," *Mississippi Valley Historical Review*, XLVIII (1961), 79–94; see especially
p. 94.
14. Leon Festinger, *A Theory of Cognitive Dissonance* (Evanston: Row, Peterson, and
Co., 1957), Chaps. 1–3.

relieve the stress. The proslavery theories of George Fitzhugh represented one attempt to remove this contradiction by repudiating democracy and extolling a hierarchical slave society as the perfect political system for all communities and epochs. But political equality among whites was deeply ingrained, and since no candidate for public office in the South could ever espouse Fitzhugh's extravagant ideas, it was not surprising that his theories became an intellectual curiosity which he himself abandoned. Religious values also were too strong to be reversed, although clergymen gave ground before the proslavery movement and ceased their attacks on slavery. Southerners found that they could not reject their liberal values, yet at the same time the power of racism and economic interest deterred them from abandoning slavery.[15] Thus they were trapped within the boundaries of their incompatible beliefs.

To reduce this unsettling conflict, they developed a private attitude which stopped far short of the public claims of proslavery theorists and resembled instead the traditional southern apology for slavery as an inherited burden. The key to the slaveholder's mentality was the fact that, no matter how disturbing the maintenance of slavery was, any scheme of emancipation loosed fears which were far more unpleasant. Therefore, the majority justified their connection with slavery by concluding that there was no acceptable alternative. Just as southern patriots at the founding of the republic had regarded the peculiar institution as a necessary evil, so those southerners who entered the Civil War felt that their generation could do nothing to alter the structure of society. Extending the old defense that the colonists had entailed slavery on their descendants, most Confederates assured their consciences that they were doing everything which honorable men could do with an intractable problem.

This attitude appeared clearly in Jefferson Davis' private letters and even occasionally in his public speeches before the Civil War. Although he was familiar with the latest developments of proslavery

15. Fredrickson, *Black Image in the White Mind*, 65–68. A reactionary wing of the planter class discarded liberal values and espoused privilege and aristocracy, but these men were a minority even of their class.

theory and scientific racism, Davis never used these concepts in his private communication. Proslavery theories constituted his ammunition for public debate, but among his friends he referred to slavery as an immense, practical fact which was beyond his power to influence. In the midst of a fierce debate in the Senate in 1860, he wrote to his close friend Franklin Pierce and sadly asked, "Do we ever speak of any thing but that over which we have no control, slavery of the negro?" Ten years earlier he had defined the southern dilemma, as he saw it, with admirable clarity: "Is it well to denounce an evil for which there is no cure? Why not . . . declaim against disease, pain, or poverty, as wrong. There are many evils in the condition of man which we would be glad to remedy; but, not being able, we permit them to exist as less than those which would follow an interference with them."[16]

Mary Boykin Chesnut shared Davis' feeling of helplessness, despite her hatred of slavery. Although she felt that "two thirds of my religion consists in trying to be good to Negroes," the fear of slave uprisings often paralyzed her good intentions. When Mrs. Chesnut and her sister learned that two slaves had strangled an elderly woman on a nearby plantation, they were so frightened and upset that they talked through the night rather than run the risk of sleep. On better days these women went about their business, but Mrs. Chesnut believed that one's humanitarian concern for the Negroes carried "no reward but the threat of John Brown hanging like a drawn sword over your head."[17]

Although Mrs. Chesnut was not always as frightened, racism was a constant damper on her moral revulsion to slavery. To her the black man was "a creature whose mind is as dark and unenlightened as his skin," and she described her servants as "dirty, slatternly, idle, ill-smelling by nature." When a slave woman on the Chesnut plantation beat her own daughter for being careless with an infant, Mrs. Chesnut took the commotion as evidence that "it takes these half-Africans but a moment to go back to their naked savage animal na-

16. Jefferson Davis to Franklin Pierce, January 30, 1860, in Rowland (ed.), *Jefferson Davis*, IV, 185, also I, 286.
17. Chesnut, *Diary*, 139–40, 163.

ture." On the whole, she believed that "the best way to take Negroes to your heart is to get as far away from them as possible. . . . People can't love things dirty, ugly, and repulsive." Obviously these powerful emotions sapped the energies that Mrs. Chesnut could have directed against the peculiar institution. Those whose moral sense was not as keen as Mrs. Chesnut's easily reached the conclusion that there was no alternative to slavery. Eliza F. Andrews expressed this feeling well when she described her father: "He was a large slaveholder himself, and honestly believed, like most of his class, that a condition of mild servitude secured by strict regulations against abuses, was the best solution of the 'negro problem' bequeathed us by our ancestors. We were in the position of the man who had the bull by the horns and couldn't let loose if he wanted to, for fear of being gored." [18]

Since southerners—even those who hated slavery—believed that Negroes were inferior, repulsive, and dangerous, they bitterly resented criticisms by reformers who did not live in the South. They felt that northern abolitionists had no true conception of the slaveowner's dilemma and were guilty of hypocrisy and dangerously irresponsible behavior. Southerners knew that the people of New England had sold their slaves to the South and that northerners had not scrupled at the extermination of thousands of Indians. During his years in the United States Senate, Jefferson Davis frequently had challenged northerners to admit their own racism and had asked his critics whether the North would welcome the freedman. Throughout the war southern newspapers carried accounts documenting northern prejudice and mistreatment of the Negro. The Charleston *Mercury*, for example, reported the disastrous results of Lincoln's attempt to colonize blacks on Isle à Vache, near Haiti, the rioting against Negroes in New York, and many instances in which Union soldiers abused and injured escaped slaves. [19]

Mary Boykin Chesnut reached the heights of her eloquence when

18. *Ibid.*, 144, 163, 433, 199–200; Eliza Frances Andrews, *The War-Time Journal of a Georgia Girl, 1864–1865*, ed. Spencer Bidwell King, Jr. (Macon, Ga.: Ardivan Press, 1960), 279–80.

19. Chesnut, *Diary*, 138; *Congressional Globe*, 36th Cong., 1st Sess., 601; Charleston *Mercury*, January 5, 1864, March 1, 1864, and April 16, 1864.

she denounced northern reformers for overlooking the injustice in their own society and attacking a social order whose burdens they did not bear. Moral superiority was pleasant, Mrs. Chesnut knew, for reformers such as Stowe, Greeley, Thoreau, Emerson, and Sumner:

> They lived in nice New England homes, clean, sweetsmelling, shut up in libraries, writing books which ease their hearts of their bitterness against us. . . . Think of these holy New Englanders forced to have a Negro village walk through their houses whenever they see fit. . . . [Southern women] have a swarm of blacks about them like children under their care, not as Mrs. Stowe's fancy painted them, and they hate slavery worse than Mrs. Stowe does. Bookmaking which leads you to a round of visits among crowned heads is an easier way to be a saint than martyrdom down here, doing unpleasant duty among the Negroes with no reward. . . . The Mrs. Stowes have the plaudits of crowned heads; we take our chances, doing our duty as best we may among the wooly [sic] heads.[20]

The son of the Georgia minister Charles Colcock Jones similarly believed that the North's attitude of moral superiority was the grossest hypocrisy. "We have our sins and our shortcomings, and they are many," Charles C. Jones, Jr., admitted, "but without the arrogance of the self-righteous Pharisee we may honestly thank God that we are not as they are." From this strong conviction it was only a short step to the belief that God was on the side of the Confederacy. Writing to his son in September, 1862, the elder Jones exclaimed, "Wonderful is it how they [northerners] leave out in their calculations right and justice and God, who rules over the nations. . . . Up to this hour we can say the Lord has been on our side."[21]

Thus Confederates had the conviction that although slavery was not the most desirable social arrangement, it was the best which anyone could manage under the circumstances. Southerners had not made the transition from their traditional values to a complete acceptance of the proslavery argument, but they had used parts of that argument to bolster their personal justifications of slaveholding. When confronted by their opponents, they almost unanimously asserted

20. Chesnut, *Diary*, 163.
21. Myers (ed.), *Children of Pride*, 695, 969.

that they were not guilty of moral wrong and accused the North of hypocrisy. This set of feelings and ideas provided Confederates with a framework for dealing with the existence of slavery. Although they could not achieve complete peace of mind, they were able to control and minimize their mental conflict.

Like all rationalizations, however, these ideas were appropriate for a given set of circumstances, and as these circumstances changed, southerners' ideas about slavery also had to alter. Steadily and inexorably, the Civil War created massive pressures to revise the status quo in regard to slavery, and Confederates responded with differing degrees of flexibility. Some, like Jefferson Davis and the Chesnuts, adjusted to new developments rapidly and moved far beyond conventional points of view. This portion of the planter class did the first innovative thinking about southern racial arrangements in generations, while other southerners refused to adjust and clung stubbornly to the past. The gap between these two groups produced the Confederate debate on emancipation and revealed how many people felt in the end about the relationship of slavery to Confederate purpose.

The demands of war continually increased the need to exploit all sources of Confederate manpower. Fighting at a numerical disadvantage with the North, white southerners realized rather early that effective use had to be made of the slave population. From the beginning of the war, the central government impressed or hired slave labor for use on fortifications and entrenchments. Eventually the government pressed blacks into service in hospitals, factories, and many noncombatant positions in the army. But as Union troops advanced into the South and as desertion from the Confederate armies continued to grow, it became increasingly apparent that the limited employment of black labor would not suffice. The logic of a total war effort demanded use of the black population as soldiers.

In his brilliant analysis of race relations in the history of Brazil and the United States, Carl Degler singled out the North American attitude toward arming slaves as a distinguishing feature of racism in the United States. "The most striking" difference between the southern and the Brazilian slave systems, Degler wrote, was the southerners' resistance to arming slaves. In regard to this question, "the two systems could not have been more divergent." Throughout Brazilian history the Portuguese and their successors sent slaves into combat and in fact relied upon them as an indispensable element in the defense of a vast, largely unpopulated, and frequently invaded land. The North American colonists, on the other hand, denied the possession of firearms to Negroes even before the legal formulation of slavery. Yet on a few occasions southerners had armed their slaves. South Carolina authorized the enlistment of slaves in the early eighteenth century when that colony was extremely vulnerable to attack. During the revolution against Britain there was repeated discussion of arming slaves and freeing those who survived, and after the Continental army met with several major setbacks, the proposal finally obtained approval.[22]

Thus, it would be incorrect to assume that the arming of slaves was a forbidden thought to southerners. During the Confederacy there was no lack of suggestions that the government employ black soldiers. A substantial number of people, both prominent and obscure, dared to make such proposals. As early as July, 1861, one W. S. Turner of Helena, Arkansas, petitioned the War Department on behalf of himself and others for authority to organize regiments of slaves. Turner believed that Negroes would fight eagerly against the Yankees, and although Confederate officials denied his request, they noted in the process that "if the necessity were apparent there is high authority for the employment of such forces. Washington himself recommended the enlistment of two negro regiments in Georgia, and the [Continental] Congress sanctioned the measure."[23]

Later, when the prospects of the Confederacy were less bright than they had been in the first summer of the war, more southerners turned to the idea of black troops. On the Chesnut plantation the

22. Carl N. Degler, *Neither Black Nor White: Slavery and Race Relations in Brazil and the United States* (New York: Macmillan, 1971), 75–82.
23. W. S. Turner to Leroy Pope Walker, July 17, 1861, and A. T. Bledsoe to W. S. Turner, August 2, 1861, in *The War of the Rebellion: A Compilation of the Official Records of the Union and Confederate Armies* (130 vols.; Washington: Government Printing Office, 1880–1901), Ser. IV, Vol. I, 482, 529, hereinafter cited as *Official Records*.

overseer suggested arming and freeing the slaves at the end of 1861, and in March, 1862, Mr. Chesnut's slaves offered to join the fight if he would arm them. James Chesnut could not take such action as an individual, but the concept gained favor in his family. After Federal troops captured New Orleans in April, 1862, Congressman Duncan Kenner of Louisiana sought an interview with Jefferson Davis and urged upon the president the conclusion that the Confederacy could not obtain foreign recognition and independence unless it abolished slavery. Davis discouraged this idea, although in the following winter of 1862–1863 Mary Boykin Chesnut, who was friendly with the president, believed that "General Lee and Mr. Davis and our soldiers everywhere want the Negroes to be put in the Army."[24]

In July, 1863, after the serious defeats at Gettysburg and Vicksburg, Congressman E. S. Dargan of Alabama implored the administration to abolish slavery in order to obtain foreign recognition. Dargan declared that the country would strongly prefer emancipation to defeat. About the same time other Alabamians, according to the clerk of the Confederate Senate, became "thoroughly aroused to the issues before them," and men who previously had refused to furnish slave laborers for the army offered them freely and were "proposing to use them as soldiers." On August 29, 1863, the Alabama General Assembly passed a joint resolution calling upon the government to use "in some effective way a certain percentage of the male slave population" as a response to the arming of Negroes by the Federal government. The legislature's resolutions implied that the slaves should be used in industry, but B. H. Micou, an Alabamian whose brother had practiced law with Judah Benjamin, wrote to the secretary of state and advocated recruiting Negro soldiers to remedy the desperate situation.[25]

The successful use of black troops by the Union army intensified

24. Chesnut, *Diary*, 169, 203–204, 292; Robert Douthat Meade, *Judah P. Benjamin: Confederate Statesman* (New York: Oxford University Press, 1943), 264.

25. E. S. Dargan to James Seddon, July 24, 1863, in *Official Records*, Ser. IV, Vol. II, 664–65; Edward Younger (ed.), *Inside the Confederate Government: The Diary of Robert Garlick Hill Kean* (New York: Oxford University Press, 1957), 96, hereinafter cited as *Diary of R. G. H. Kean*; *Official Records*, Ser. IV, Vol. II, 767; Meade, *Judah Benjamin*, 289.

the pressure on southerners to bring slaves into the war effort. In significant and disturbing numbers the boldest slaves were leaving their plantations and going into Union lines, where they joined other blacks who had already come under Federal control.[26] As if to emphasize this loss, several slaves escaped from the Confederate White House and went north to aid the abolitionists. Yet while Lincoln rejoiced at the contributions of Negroes to the Union war effort, the Confederacy's soldiers received no reinforcements. It seemed that the South was wasting one of its valuable resources while the North found a way to exploit it.

Thus the idea of using slaves as soldiers continued to arise, and in January, 1864, Major General Patrick Cleburne of the Army of Tennessee made the most comprehensive argument yet advanced within the South for arming and freeing the slaves. In a written proposal to his military superiors, Cleburne sketched out the South's deepening crisis and emphasized Davis' statement that "no effort must be spared to add largely to our effective force as promptly as possible." He then asserted that "every patriot will freely . . . give up the negro slave rather than be a slave himself" and called attention to the beneficial effect which emancipation would have on foreign relations. Thirteen of Cleburne's fellow officers joined him in this proposal, but a council of his superiors refused to sanction the idea. General Joseph E. Johnston declined to forward the document to Richmond on the grounds that it was more political than military in nature.[27]

One of Cleburne's critics, however, did send the proposal on to the Confederate administration. There it stopped, for the president, who had learned to appreciate the power which his opponents had to damage morale, feared the effects of any controversy during the first part of 1864. With national elections approaching in the United States, Davis gave first priority to bolstering Confederate unity and determination in order to encourage northern peace elements. Re-

26. W. E. B. Du Bois, *Black Reconstruction in America, 1860–1880* (New York: Harcourt, Brace and Company, 1935), Chap. 4.
27. *Official Records*, Ser. I, Vol. LII, Pt. II, 586–92. See also Robert F. Durden, *The Gray and the Black: The Confederate Debate on Emancipation* (Baton Rouge: Louisiana State University Press, 1972), Chap. 2.

plying to the officer who had sent the document, Davis expressed his strong desire "to avoid all publicity" and to keep the idea "out of the public journals." Davis also instructed Secretary of War Seddon to explain the importance of secrecy to General Johnston, and Seddon's letter reveals the depth of Davis' fear that such an issue might divide the Confederacy at the moment when it most needed to be unified. According to the secretary, Davis felt "that the dissemination, or even promulgation of such opinions under the present circumstances of the Confederacy . . . can be productive only of discouragement, distraction, and dissention. . . . Such views can only jeopard among the States and people unity and harmony when for successful cooperation and the achievement of Independence both are essential."[28]

Davis' hopes for 1864, however, collapsed with the fall of Atlanta and the reelection of Abraham Lincoln, and as the situation of the Confederacy grew more desperate, suggestions for arming the slaves reappeared. Citizens such as one man who signed himself "A Native Georgian" wrote to the War Department and insisted that the South place slaves in the ranks. This correspondent advocated emancipating all who fought, although he hoped to colonize them after the war and retain slavery among the Negroes who stayed at home. Even the state governors, who often had caused Jefferson Davis much irritation, recommended "a change of policy" at their meeting in October, 1864. Despite the vagueness of their suggestion that the government "appropriate" slaves "to the public service as may be required," the governors had given momentum to a trend of public opinion.[29]

Finally Davis felt that the time for action had arrived, and on November 7, 1864, he made a proposal that startled many. Addressing the Confederate Congress, he recommended that the government purchase and train forty thousand Negro laborers, who would be offered the promise of emancipation and future residence within

28. *Official Records*, Ser. I, Vol. LII, Pt. II, 596; James Seddon to J. E. Johnston, January 24, 1864, in Letters Sent, Confederate Secretary of War, in Record Group 109, National Archives, Microcopy M 522, Roll 9, pp. 21–22.
29. "A Native Georgian" to James Seddon, September 29, 1864, in *Official Records*, Ser. IV, Vol. III, 693–94; Rowland (ed.), *Jefferson Davis*, VI, 400–401.

their states as a reward for faithful service. Then, proceeding by indirection, he expressed the opinion that Negro soldiers were not yet necessary, though "should the alternative ever be presented of subjugation or of the employment of the slave as a soldier, there seems no reason to doubt what should then be our decision."[30] At last the idea of arming the slaves had surfaced from private discussions into public debate.

The idea of arming and emancipating southern slaves came as a shock to many Confederates and quickly provoked a storm of protest. Yet to a portion of the upper class this notion probably was no surprise. Davis himself had lived for years with the assumption that slavery was not a permanent institution in North America. In the 1850s he had committed to paper a personal theory which predicted that as population density increased, "wasteful" slave labor would give way to more efficient white workers and that the black population would gradually migrate southward to tropical regions. Soon after the secession of Mississippi he had said to his wife, "In any case, I think our slave property will be lost eventually." Apparently he reasoned that, even if no other causes intervened, the South would have to abandon slavery in time because it could not support "the immense standing army" that would be required to keep the slaves in bondage.[31] Thus, despite the claims of proslavery theorists, Davis had known that the slaves wanted their freedom and that the costs of keeping them in shackles were rising inexorably. The South could not preserve its world forever.

Similarly, within days of the capture of Fort Sumter, Mary Boykin Chesnut told her maid, "Let the war end either way and you will be free. We will have to free you before we get out of this thing." Since Mrs. Chesnut believed that "slavery has to go, of course," she immediately saw the logic of bringing the black population into the war effort. With amazement she commented in May, 1862, that South Carolina planters shrank from the idea of putting slaves, their "sacred

30. Richardson (comp.), *Messages and Papers of the Confederacy*, I, 492–96.
31. "Notes on the proposition to restrict . . . slavery . . .," in Davis Papers, Library of Congress; Varina Howell Davis, *A Memoir*, II, 11–12.

property," to work on fortifications. "How long," she asked, "before they will lay violent hands on Negroes and put them in the army?" Months before Jefferson Davis made his proposal Mrs. Chesnut had started lobbying among her friends for the enlistment of slaves.[32]

Although Davis had referred in his address on November 7, 1864, to the use of slaves as a possibility, he had unmistakably announced his belief that blacks who served in the army should obtain their freedom and the right to return to their homes after the war. Such a position required considerable explanation to southerners who believed that whites and blacks could not live together on terms of freedom. Davis himself had voiced the standard southern dogma in 1848 when he declared, "Our slaves are a distinct race, physically differing so much from ourselves that no one can look to their emancipation without connecting with it the idea of removal, separation of the races."[33] Consequently the Richmond administration proceeded to disseminate a vision of postwar racial arrangements which would preserve white supremacy.

Judah Benjamin, the president's closest adviser, shared the thinking of the administration in December, 1864, with Fred A. Porcher, a Charleston newspaper owner who supported the use of Negro soldiers. The central government could purchase and emancipate the slaves that it needed, but Benjamin pointed out that the states would have to determine the status of families of these men. Expressing confidence that the state legislatures would pass laws providing for their "ultimate emancipation after an intermediate stage of serfage or peonage," Benjamin made clear his conception of the extent of black freedom:

> We might then be able, while vindicating our faith in the doctrine that the negro is an inferior race and unfitted for social or political equality with the white man, yet so modify and ameliorate the existing condition of that inferior race by providing for it certain rights of property, a cer-

32. Chesnut, *Diary*, 43, 73, 222, 394.
33. *Appendix* to *Congressional Globe*, 30th Cong., 1st Sess., 911. Northerners also rejected the idea of a biracial society. See C. Vann Woodward, "Our Racist History," *New York Review of Books*, XII (February 27, 1969), 5–11.

tain degree of personal liberty, and legal protection for the marital and parental relations, as to relieve our institutions from much that is not only unjust and impolitic in itself, but calculated to draw down on us the odium and reprobation of civilized man.[34]

Thus Benjamin suggested that the Confederacy abandon neither racism nor white supremacy and that state legislation after the war should maintain the essential aspects of southern race relations. In the context of the vast conflict and the Confederacy's desperate need for men, Davis' actual proposal was the minimum sacrifice that he believed to be required for independence. The question that remained was whether other Confederates could view the issue in the same light.

The Richmond administration quickly mobilized all its energies to promote this measure. Secretary Seddon, the one key cabinet member who had resisted the tendency of events, swung into line with the president's position, at least publicly. Welcome support came from Governor William Smith of Virginia, who recommended the arming of slaves to his legislature on December 7, 1864. With forceful logic Smith made the key argument upon which supporters of the administration relied: that no loyal Confederate could object to using slaves when the consequence of not using them would be defeat, emancipation, and the virtual enslavement of white southerners by their conquerors. Robert E. Lee added a vital element of patriotic legitimacy to these arguments when he made public his desire to put slaves into the army at once and grant them immediate freedom. With Lee's firm declaration, the government's chance of winning approval for its plan dramatically improved, but at the end of February, 1865, Jefferson Davis was still arranging newspaper backing and prodding the congress to act.[35]

Formidable opposition to the plan had developed quickly in almost all sectors of southern society, but particularly in the planter class.

34. Judah Benjamin to Fred A. Porcher, December 21, 1864, in *Official Records*, Ser. IV, Vol. III, 959–60.

35. *Official Records*, Ser. IV, Vol. III, 756–71, 915–16; Robert E. Lee to E. Barksdale, February 18, 1865, quoted in Durden, *The Gray and the Black*, 206–207; Jefferson Davis to John Forsyth, February 21, 1865, in Rowland (ed.), *Jefferson Davis*, VI, 482.

From the early days of the war the behavior of this class had been perplexing. Although the conflict directly concerned their property interests, planters regularly refused to commit any of their slave property to the war effort. Confederate generals reported that slave-owners declined to allow their bondsmen to work on fortifications and complained that the slaves received harsh treatment or learned bad habits during Confederate service. In 1862 the secretary of war had to appeal to the governor of Alabama to encourage planters to furnish slaves for the construction of an important railroad. Governor John Gill Shorter did his best to cooperate and eventually obtained a state law covering impressment of slaves. But "my enforcing it," he noted ruefully several months later, "was the strongest element which carried the state so largely against me" at the polls. During 1863 the central government went to great lengths to cooperate with slaveowners, but in November of that year Seddon recommended enactment of a national law on the impressment of slaves, since voluntary hire had not worked. Even after the government obtained the right to use force, access to slave labor was often unsatisfactory. One Confederate congressman remarked, "They give up their sons, husbands, brothers and friends, and often without murmuring, to the army; but let one of their negroes be taken, and what a houl [*sic*] you will hear."[36]

In 1864 the planters' resistance to the idea of arming and emancipating slaves was strong and tenacious. They made their opinions known in the congress, and in October the chief of the Bureau of War observed that Davis' plan "finds little favor except with that portion who represent imaginary constituencies. The representation of the planters are averse to it strongly." J. B. Jones reported in De-

36. Harrison A. Trexler, "The Opposition of Planters to the Employment of Slaves as Laborers by the Confederacy," *Mississippi Valley Historical Review*, XXVII (1940), 211–24; John Gill Shorter to Major General D. H. Maury, August 14, 1863, in Governor's Letter Books, Alabama State Department of Archives and History, Montgomery; George Randolph to J. G. Shorter, October 2, 1862, in *Official Records*, Ser. IV, Vol. II, 106; Rowland (ed.), *Jefferson Davis*, V, 427, 431, 437, 432; James Seddon to Jefferson Davis, November 26, 1863, in *Official Records*, Ser. IV, Vol. II, 990–1018; Warren Akin to Nathan Land, October 31, 1964, in letters of Confederate Congressmen in possession of Bell I. Wiley.

cember that "the rich men are generally indignant at the President and Gov. Smith for proposing to bring a portion of the negroes into the army. They have not yet awakened to a consciousness that there is danger of losing *all*." In February, 1865, Jones felt that a public meeting in Richmond caused "great excitement among the slave-owners," but many continued to oppose the recruitment of slaves.[37]

The press, which usually had close connections with the planter class, also raised strong opposition to Davis' project. Even before the president spoke, the Charleston *Mercury* vented its outrage at the suggestion of the governors that the Confederacy "appropriate" as many slaves as required to the public service. The *Mercury* insisted that the states had exclusive control over slavery and deplored the fact that "before a Confederacy which was established to put at rest forever all such agitation is four years old, we find the proposition gravely submitted that the Confederate Government should emancipate slaves in the States." Similarly, on the morning after Davis broached his suggestion the *Daily Richmond Examiner* announced its opposition to the president and its dedication to slavery: "The existence of a negro soldier is totally inconsistent with our political aim and with our social as well as political system. . . . If a negro is fit to be a soldier he is not fit to be a slave. . . . To our own hearts it would be confession, not only of weakness, but of absolute inability to secure the object for which we undertook the war." Two days later the editor of the *Examiner* bluntly warned Davis and the Confederate authorities "to mind their own business." In this torrent of outrage the Charleston *Mercury* did not forget the attitudes of nonslaveholders. To guard against the possibility that some of the small farmers might support the plan, the *Mercury* warned that the "poor man" would be "reduced to the level of a nigger, and a nigger . . . raised to his level."[38]

But the administration's efforts to promote its proposal and a grow-

---

37. Younger (ed.), *Diary of R. G. H. Kean*, 177; J. B. Jones, *A Rebel War Clerk's Diary*, ed. Howard Swiggett (2 vols.; New York: Old Hickory Bookshop, 1935), II, 353, 416–17.
38. Charleston *Mercury*, November 3, 1864; *Daily Richmond Examiner*, November 8, 1864, p. 2, November 10, 1864, p. 2; Charleston *Mercury*, January 26, 1865, p. 1.

ing recognition of the seriousness of the Confederacy's situation eventually produced some progress. Mrs. Chesnut heard someone say with regret, "If we had only freed the Negroes at first, and put them in the Army." On December 20, 1864, the Richmond *Examiner* gave implicit approval to the arming of slaves when it advocated impressing 100,000 bondsmen and letting Lee use them in *"any* way he may think needful." After Confederate General John Hood met defeat in Tennessee and Sherman occupied Savannah, R. G. H. Kean noticed an increase of support for the enlistment of Negroes. "Men are beginning to say," he wrote, "that when the question is between slavery and independence, slavery must go, and this is logical because when independence is lost slavery is at the same blow destroyed." In January, 1865, Kean's subordinate in the War Department, J. B. Jones, also agreed that the bill to arm slaves was gaining friends.[39]

The superintendent of Virginia Military Institute, convinced by the "tone of public sentiment" that "the call of General Lee for negro troops will be responded to," wrote the secretary of war in February, 1865, and offered the facilities of his institution for training black soldiers. Some planters also expressed their readiness to arm and free their slaves in order to swell the ranks of the army. Other citizens informed the War Department that they were willing to serve as commanders of Negro regiments. One officer from New Orleans offered to lead Negro troops and predicted that the excess officers in shorthanded regiments from Mississippi and Louisiana would be glad to accept similar positions. At the head of new black troops, he predicted, "their despondency would be turned into joy and they would enter with renewed zeal and alacrity into the discharge of their new duties."[40]

One of the most important sources of support for Jefferson Davis' proposal was the army. In October, 1864, the Richmond *Enquirer*

39. Chesnut, *Diary*, 456; *Daily Richmond Examiner*, December 20, 1864, p. 2; Younger (ed.), *Diary of R. G. H. Kean*, 182; Jones, *A Rebel War Clerk's Diary*, II, 372.

40. J. T. L. Preston to John Breckinridge, February 17, 1865, in *Official Records*, Ser. IV, Vol. III, 1093; Durden, *The Gray and the Black*, 80–81, 272–73; Edward Pollard to Jefferson Davis, January 13, 1865, in Letters Received, Confederate Secretary of War, in Record Group 109, National Archives, Microcopy M 437, Roll 150, pp. 353–56.

had invited its readers to express their opinions on the question of conscripting Negroes, and several men replied from the field. On November 14, for example, the *Enquirer* published three letters from soldiers, two of which gave strong approval to the use of Negro troops. Secretary of State Judah Benjamin and General Lee also encouraged the army to make its voice heard in February, 1865, after opponents of the plan frequently asserted that the enlistment of blacks would disband the army due to the soldiers' aversion to Negroes. Within a week Major General John B. Gordon responded with the news that the officers and men of his corps of the Army of Northern Virginia were "decidedly in favor of the voluntary enlistment of the negroes as soldiers." The Richmond *Whig* reported on February 21 that all but one company of the Thirtieth Virginia Infantry had voted by overwhelming margins that Negroes should have a chance to defend the country. According to the Richmond *Sentinel*, a flood of letters was arriving from the army, and "with a singular unanimity, *all* are in favor of it." Apparently the men who still remained in the Confederate ranks early in 1865 were stubborn individuals, and after all their sacrifices they were determined to have independence. A resolution from the Fifty-sixth Virginia Regiment, drawn largely from slaveholding areas, showed how the desire for independence sometimes overcame slaveholders' principles:

> Resolved, That slavery is the normal condition of the negro . . . that involuntary servitude is as indispensable to the moral and physical advancement, prosperity and happiness of the African race as is liberty to the whites; but if the public exigencies require that any number of our male slaves be enlisted in the military service in order to the successful resistance to our enemies, and to the maintenance of the integrity of our Government, we are willing to make concessions to their false and unenlightened notions of the blessings of liberty.[41]

It would be fascinating to know how nonslaveholders stood on the question of arming and freeing the slaves. Years of proslavery propa-

41. *Daily Richmond Enquirer*, November 14, 1864, p. 1; Judah Benjamin to Robert E. Lee, February 11, 1865, in *Official Records*, Ser. I, Vol. XLVI, Pt. II, 1229; J. B. Gordon to W. H. Taylor, February 18, 1865, in *Official Records*, Ser. I, Vol. LI, Pt. II, 1063; Richmond *Whig*, February 21, 1865, p. 1; Richmond *Sentinel*, February 13, 1865, Richmond *Whig*, February 23, 1865.

ganda had attempted to teach them that the status of white farmers depended absolutely on slavery and that any threat to the institution was a threat to their social position. And some yeomen viewed the situation in this light. In November, 1864, for example, Judge Robert Hudson wrote Jefferson Davis from a county in Mississippi which had few slaves and reported that the president's proposal had met with "great and general opposition." One young soldier complained to his father that the army already had "too many" Negroes who as servants drew "better rations than the white man," and a hill-country newspaper in South Carolina (which later changed its position) angrily warned the congress to "not go to promising freedom to niggers." But there is also evidence that feeling among nonslaveholders ran the other way and that class resentments against the rich predominated over racial fears. James Chesnut noticed that "many people were lighthearted at the ruin of the great slave owners." One yeoman rejoiced that the planters could "tyrannize now over only a small parcel of women and children, those only who are their very own family." In Richmond, in December, 1864, J. B. Jones wrote that resentment over the exemptions, furloughs, and details granted to rich slaveowners was stimulating the development of "a rapidly growing *Emancipation Party*."[42] Certainly the only source of strong support for Davis' proposal was the army, and nonslaveholders formed the majority of soldiers. Overall, however, there is too little evidence to reach any conclusion about the attitude of the nonslaveholders. They distinguished themselves by their relative silence in the heated emancipation debate. The rich, slaveholding planters led the chorus of opposition which delayed Davis' plan so long.

Finally, however, conditions were right for making the enlistment of Negro troops a reality. By March, 1865, according to J. B. Jones, letters were "pouring into the [War] department from men of military skill and character asking authority to raise companies, battalions, and regiments of negro troops." On March 6, 1865, the Virginia

---

42. Robert Hudson to Jefferson Davis, November 25, 1864, in *Official Records*, Ser. I, Vol. XLV, Pt. I, 1246–48; Thom Richards to his father, January 11, 1865, in Letters Received, Confederate Secretary of War, in RG 109, NA, Microcopy M 437, Roll 150, pp. 651–57; Edgefield (S.C.) *Advertiser*, December 14, 1864, February 22, 1865; Chesnut, *Diary*, 497; Jones, *A Rebel War Clerk's Diary*, II, 349, 347.

legislature approved legislation making it legal for black soldiers to carry arms and ammunition. Two days earlier it had authorized the Confederacy to call one quarter of the state's male slaves into the army, and, more importantly, had instructed Virginia's congressmen to vote for a Confederate law to that effect. This instruction proved to be vital, for when the bill, which passed the House by the narrow margin of 40 to 37, came to a vote in the Senate, Virginia's two senators provided the margin for passage by a vote of 9 to 8.[43]

Although Jefferson Davis was delighted to have this law at last, he was disappointed that the measure made no provision for the emancipation of Negro soldiers. Therefore, after he signed the bill into law, the president proceeded to "bootleg" the promise of freedom into the enlistment process. According to the regulations on enlistment which the War Department issued, no slave could enter military service unless he gave his consent and his master provided "a written instrument conferring, as far as he may, the rights of a freedman." The Confederacy also enjoined its officers to give "humane attention" to the welfare of their new troops and "to protect them from injustice and oppression." These regulations "excited much criticism," according to R. G. H. Kean, but this reaction did not dissuade Davis from his efforts to make emancipation the reward of service. Pressing the states to complete the grant of freedom, he praised Governor Smith of Virginia for his "promise to seek legislation to secure unmistakable freedom to the slave who shall enter the Army, with a right to return to his old home," after discharge.[44]

Davis had hopes, even at this late date, of recruiting a large number of black men for the Confederate armies, but most planters re-

43. Jones, *A Rebel War Clerk's Diary*, II, 451; *Official Records*, Ser. I, Vol. XLVI, Pt. III, 1315 and Ser. I, Vol. LI, Pt. II, 1068; *Journal of the Congress of the Confederate States of America, 1861–1865* (7 vols.; Washington: Government Printing Office, 1905), VII, 612–13 and IV, 671. Statistical analysis of the voting in congress on this issue has yielded no clear insights, for a variety of reasons. See Thomas B. Alexander and Richard E. Beringer, *The Anatomy of the Confederate Congress: A Study of the Influences of Member Characteristics on Legislative Voting Behavior, 1861–1865* (Nashville: Vanderbilt University Press, 1972), 248, 250–51, 253–57, 259, 261.

44. *Official Records*, Ser. IV, Vol. III, 1161–62; Younger (ed.), *Diary of R. G. H. Kean*, 204; *Official Records*, Ser. I, Vol. XLVI, Pt. III, 1366–67.

sisted his attempts to the last. J. B. Jones wrote that slaveowners were opposed to Negro troops even after a few companies paraded in Richmond, and Davis himself admitted at the beginning of April that he was "laboring without much progress" to make the law effective.[45] What was the explanation for such adamant and enduring opposition? Certainly one contributing factor was the exhaustion and war-weariness which gripped most southerners in the first months of 1865. The position of the Confederacy was so manifestly precarious that Davis' bid to infuse new strength into the Confederate armies probably seemed a desperate and futile measure. After enduring a great amount of suffering, many southerners shrank from new sacrifices which in all likelihood would only prolong a losing cause.

Another reason for the persistent opposition was that many politically observant planters cherished real hopes of keeping their slaves after defeat. For months Lincoln had been hinting that something less than full emancipation might result from the war. During the presidential campaign in the fall of 1864 Lincoln's secretary of state, William Seward, had proclaimed that the Emancipation Proclamation was only a war measure whose action would cease with the cessation of hostilities. Probably many southerners interpreted this, as did J. B. Jones, as a promise "that slavery will not be disturbed in any State that returns to the Union." Clement Clay took note of Lincoln's wavering on the question of the status of the slaves, and Senator William A. Graham of North Carolina was "convinced" in January, 1865, that the United States would "guarantee slavery as it now exists, and probably make other concessions" in order to restore the Union. After the Hampton Roads conference rumors spread about Lincoln's view that the courts would decide how far the effect of the Emancipation Proclamation reached. Even General Sherman, commander of the Federal army which was marching through the heart of the Confederacy, was quoted in the Richmond *Examiner* and other papers as saying, "Slavery will exist in the South after the conclusion of peace, let the war terminate as it may,—and further, that he (Sher-

45. Jones, *A Rebel War Clerk's Diary*, II, 457; Jefferson Davis to Robert E. Lee, April 1, 1865, in *Official Records*, Ser. I, Vol. XLVI, Pt. III, 1370.

man) expects to own a thousand slaves himself one of these days." [46]
Obviously no slaveholder who doubted the Confederacy's ability to
win the war was willing to surrender for Jefferson Davis what Abraham Lincoln would allow him to keep.

But for a great many of the most powerful southerners the idea of
arming and freeing the slaves was repugnant because the protection
of slavery had been and still remained the central core of Confederate purpose. Before the Richmond newspapers yielded with ill grace
to the plea of necessity, they eloquently expressed the feeling that
slavery was the South's primary concern. The Richmond *Examiner*
rewarded Robert E. Lee for his support of Davis' proposal by publicly questioning his credentials as "a good southerner." Undoubtedly the *Examiner* summed up what many slaveholders felt when it
blasted President Davis for wanting to "surrender . . . the essential
and distinctive principle of Southern civilization." Slavery was the
basis of the planter class's wealth, power, and position in society. The
South's leading men had built their world upon slavery and the idea
of voluntarily destroying that world, even in the ultimate crisis, was
almost unthinkable to them. Such feelings moved Senator R. M. T.
Hunter to deliver a long speech against the bill to arm the slaves immediately before he cast his vote in favor of it, as instructed by the
Virginia legislature. [47]

Jefferson Davis, on the other hand, had made clear from the first
days of the war that his paramount goal was the attainment of independence. Although it had grieved him to participate in the destruction of the Union, once the rift had occurred he banished all thoughts
of voluntary reconstruction. Then despite powerful opposition he
fought for such measures as conscription, central direction of the
army, and the suspension of *habeas corpus* because they were essential for victory. In 1864 he refused to consider the idea of seeking

46. Jones, *A Rebel War Clerk's Diary*, II, 282; Clement Clay to Judah Benjamin, September 12, 1864, in *Official Records*, Ser. IV, Vol. III, 636–40; Durden, *The Gray and the
Black*, 173; Younger (ed.), *Diary of R. G. H. Kean*, 194–98; Charleston *Mercury*, February
2, 1865, p. 1; *Daily Richmond Examiner*, December 31, 1864, p. 2.
47. *Daily Richmond Examiner*, February 25, 1865, p. 1, January 14, 1865, p. 2, March
8, 1865, p. 1, and March 9, 1865, p. 1.

a settlement and staked everything on Confederate independence. In private he told his wife that he was willing to sacrifice his life to establish the southern nation, and he was just as willing to sacrifice slavery.[48]

Historians may argue indefinitely and inconclusively about what decision the Confederacy made in its debate on emancipation.[49] Perhaps it is incorrect to speak of a decision on the part of an entity as complex as a nation, especially one enveloped in the turmoil and confusion of defeat. In 1864 and 1865 a few individuals like Jefferson Davis proved capable of adapting to change and subordinating slavery to some other goal, but the attitude of most influential southerners toward emancipation was quite clear. Planters in every state raised a bitter, prolonged, and tenacious resistance to the idea of arming and freeing their bondsmen, and even the grudging nature of the acceptance which some finally gave to the measure revealed a unifying conception of the purpose of the Confederacy. Judged by their own statements, most slaveowning southerners went into the war to protect slavery and stubbornly maintained that goal. As they had fought the Republicans, so they fought Confederate impressment and then Confederate recruitment of slaves. From 1861 through 1865 their actions showed that their basic commitment was to slavery rather than independence and Confederate nationalism.

48. Jefferson Davis to Varina Howell Davis, June 13, 1862, in Rowland (ed.), *Jefferson Davis*, V, 277.

49. See Durden, *The Gray and the Black*, viii, and the review by Emory M. Thomas in *Journal of Southern History*, XXXIX (1973), 300–301.

9

An Assessment of Jefferson Davis as a Political Leader

Jefferson Davis took office as president of the Confederacy amid signs of popular acclaim, yet in a short period of time he became the focus of intense criticism which persisted throughout the war. So vocal were his opponents and so bitter was their hostility toward him, that disapproval of Davis' acts often became an independent force tearing down public morale. Although he always had his defenders, Davis was one of the more unpopular chief executives in American history. After the war, the fact that he had led the losing side helped greatly to seal judgments against him. The decline of his popularity while in office pointed to certain deficiencies in his personality and leadership, but it also stemmed in part from the reaction of a proud people to the prospect of defeat. It is important in assessing Davis to separate his failings from those of others and to weigh his defects against his strengths. Posterity's strong prejudice against a loser must be resisted by anyone who wishes to reach a fair conclusion.

The beginning of Davis' presidency certainly was bright. Few southerners were surprised when the Montgomery Convention selected him, for as Mary Boykin Chesnut remarked, "Everybody wanted Mr. Davis to be either General-in-Chief or President." On his way to Montgomery, crowds greeted Davis' train and called for him to appear. The *Daily Richmond Enquirer* described his journey as "one continuous ovation" and asserted that "never were a people more enraptured with their Chief Magistrate than ours are with President Davis." Within a few months the first hints of opposition in the congress appeared, but the press overwhelmingly continued to support the chief executive. When the appointed date for elections under the permanent constitution arrived in the fall of 1861, Davis had no opposition. Heartily endorsing his reelection, the Richmond *Examiner* declared that the president "commands the popular confidence."[1]

Yet, about this time the first generalized criticism of the Confederate president was appearing. From the start of the war, many southerners were overconfident and expected their armies to humiliate the Federal troops in one short campaign. Davis, however, was keenly aware of the inexperience and weakness of the Confederate army and had decided upon a cautious, defensive strategy. This policy provoked discontent after southern troops won a convincing victory at Manassas. Confederate newspapers clamored for an attack and raised the cry, "On to Washington." According to the Richmond *Examiner*, "*All the papers of any influence, throughout the South, unite in calling for an immediate forward movement.*"[2]

This heady impatience turned to anger and dismay early in 1862 when Davis' fears about the weakness of the South's military position proved to be accurate. Psychologically unprepared for military reverses and for the prospect of a long war, many southerners turned their frustrations on Davis and blamed him for what seemed inexplicable. Prominent newspapers led this outcry and analyzed supposed mistakes on the part of Davis which had led to enemy victories. The *Daily Richmond Examiner* deplored the removal of General John Floyd from command at Fort Donelson, expressed its displeasure with the cabinet, and declared on March 11, 1862, that the people's confidence in the government was shaken. The Charleston *Mercury* was even stronger in its denunciations. After publishing a long list of

1. Mary Boykin Chesnut, *A Diary from Dixie*, ed. Ben Ames Williams (Sentry ed.; Boston: Houghton Mifflin Company, 1949), 5; *Daily Richmond Enquirer*, May 30, 1861; *Daily Richmond Examiner*, August 6, 1861, p. 2 and September 16, 1861, p. 2.

2. Jefferson Davis to J. E. Johnston, September 8, 1861, in Dunbar Rowland (ed.), *Jefferson Davis: Constitutionalist; His Letters, Papers and Speeches* (10 vols.; Jackson, Miss.: Little & Ives Company, 1923), V, 129; quoted in the Charleston *Mercury*, October 1, 1861, p. 1 and October 8, 1861, p. 1.

alleged presidential blunders in their paper, the Rhetts insultingly urged Davis to "give up the notion of being a Washington, Jackson and Calhoun combined" and to "find his proper level, like Presidents Tyler and Polk." Throughout 1862, the *Mercury* sought to unmask the "incompetency" of the chief executive so that "able men" in the states and in the congress could assume real leadership. The Richmond *Enquirer*, one of the few journals which stood by Davis during 1862 deplored these "untimely dissensions" and called for an end to the "perpetual hounding" of the president.[3]

Such criticisms angered and depressed Jefferson Davis. He usually tried to respond patiently and constructively, but a group of congressmen who urged various changes in defense felt that wrath which was his more natural reaction. After examining their suggestions, the president sent a stinging reply which declared that the government had anticipated all their ideas plus many others "which the writer seems not to have thought of." Exasperated by the fact that he encountered opposition when unity was required, Davis "talked seriously of resigning" early in 1862. But if Davis bristled at the criticism which he received in 1862, he had to learn to live with far stronger judgments in the two and a half years which followed. As his wife noted, there was an upsurge of opposition in the press after the disasters of Gettysburg and Vicksburg. Journals like the Charleston *Mercury* blamed the South's reverses on Davis and on allegedly ill-advised appointments which he had made. Naturally popular disapproval of Davis' policies increased as troubles multiplied, and in August, 1864, Mary Boykin Chesnut exclaimed, "How they dump the obloquy on Jeff Davis."[4]

3. *Daily Richmond Examiner*, March 11, 1862, p. 2, March 12, 1862, p. 2, March 20, 1862, p. 2, May 1, 1862, p. 2; Charleston *Mercury*, February 27, 1862, p. 1, March 3, 1862, p. 1, March 4, 1862, p. 1; *Daily Richmond Enquirer*, October 10, 1862, p. 2 and October 24, 1862, p. 2.

4. Jefferson Davis to E. Barksdale and others, March 4, 1862, in Rowland (ed.), *Jefferson Davis*, V, 211; Thomas Bragg Diary, 1861–1862 (Southern Historical Collection, University of North Carolina), January 17, 1862; Edward Younger (ed.), *Inside the Confederate Government: The Diary of Robert Garlick Hill Kean* (New York: Oxford University Press, 1957), 89, hereinafter cited as *Diary of R. G. H. Kean*; Varina Howell Davis, *Jefferson Davis, Ex-President of the Confederate States of America: A Memoir* (2 vols.; New York: Belford Company, 1890), II, 412, hereinafter cited as *A Memoir*; Charleston *Mercury*, September 5 and 10, 1863; Chesnut, *Diary*, 424.

Sometimes the attacks of the press were in a personal vein, as on February 9, 1864, when the *Daily Richmond Examiner* charged that almost everyone agreed that Davis was "capable of employing the great powers of Government for the unworthy gratification of animosity." More often the newspapers found ample scope for their criticism in the actions and policies of the president. On December 21, 1864, for example, the *Examiner* declared that "every military misfortune of this country is palpably and confessedly due to the personal interference of Mr. Davis." A few weeks later this paper supported the summoning of a convention for the purpose of creating a general-in-chief with authority over Davis and of making other changes which would limit his influence. Voicing another frequently heard charge against the chief executive, the Charleston *Mercury* declared on May 14, 1864: "From the commencement of the war, the Confederate Government, in every sort of way, has endeavored to establish a despotic authority over the people of the Confederate States."[5]

Some of the criticism of Davis's actions appeared before he had been in office long enough to deserve much responsibility for events, and throughout the war a portion of the hostility toward the Confederate president was unjustified. The strong measures which he demanded to prosecute the war clearly were necessary, although they were unpalatable. Inevitably, too, part of the opposition to Davis arose from the need of a beleaguered society to vent its frustrations on some appropriate, available object. As Davis himself noted, "It is comfortable to hold some one responsible for one's discomfort." He was aware of the fickle quality of public opinion and shared his amusement over one incident with General Lee in September, 1862. After Lee's army had marched into Maryland, Davis informed his general that "the feverish anxiety to invade the North" had been replaced by "apprehension for the safety of the Capitol." Those "who so vociferously urged a forward movement . . . would now be most pleased to welcome the return of that Army."[6]

5. *Daily Richmond Examiner*, February 9, 1864, December 21, 1864, p. 2 and January 9, 1865; Charleston *Mercury*, May 14, 1864.
6. Rowland (ed.), *Jefferson Davis*, V, 580, 346.

One could not fault the industry of the chief executive or minimize the difficulties under which he labored. The highest office of
the Confederacy probably would have been a torment for any occu-
pant, and poor health and family grief increased the burden of Jefferson Davis. The facial neuralgia and nervous complaints which
had troubled him in the past continued to be a handicap during the
Civil War. In July, 1861, Mrs. Chesnut reported that Davis was in
"wretched health," and by September he again was sick. Another
spell of illness occurred in June, 1862, and throughout the spring of
1863 Davis' health was unreliable. The diary of J. B. Jones contains
numerous entries for this period such as, "The President is sick, and
has not been in the Executive office for three days," or "The President is in a very feeble and nervous condition." Another particularly
severe period of weakness struck Davis at the beginning of 1865,
when many citizens in Richmond actually thought that he was dead
or dying. To compound these difficulties, the president and his wife
experienced their share of personal grief during the short existence
of the Confederacy. In June, 1862, their infant son almost died, and
then on April 30, 1864, their older boy fell to his death from a balcony at the Confederate mansion. Mrs. Chesnut, who went to her
friends' home on the evening of the accident, wrote that after she
left "Mr. Davis' step still sounded in my ear as he walked that floor
the livelong night."[7]

It is undeniable that much of the hostility toward Davis arose from
deficiencies in his political leadership and personality. Even without
sickness and family tragedy, the personal limitations of the man would
have brought him considerable trouble. Many of his opponents tried
to describe his failings, but none succeeded better than his wife,
who gave an honest and damaging assessment of Davis' personality
despite the adulation which she usually displayed in recounting his
actions. From the moment when she learned that her husband had

7. Chesnut, *Diary*, 84, 130; Rowland (ed.), *Jefferson Davis*, V, 284; J. B. Jones, *A Rebel
War Clerk's Diary*, ed. Howard Swiggett (2 vols.; New York: Old Hickory Bookshop, 1935),
I, 269, 294, 270, 291, 293, 297, 306, 328, 339, 367, 355; *The War of the Rebellion: A Compi-
lation of the Official Records of the Union and Confederate Armies* (130 vols.; Washington:
Government Printing Office, 1880–1901), Ser. IV, Vol. III, 1000–1004, hereinafter cited as
Official Records; Varina Howell Davis, *A Memoir*, II, 311, 496–97; Chesnut, *Diary*, 405.

been elected president, Varina Howell Davis was fearful that he would fail as a political leader. "He did not know the arts of the politician," she said, "and would not practise them if understood." She also realized that Davis damaged his influence by refusing to entertain other leaders and seek their friendship. Many quarrels among politicians were smoothed by social intercourse, but her husband refused to cooperate in such activities:

> He was a nervous dyspeptic by habit, and if he was forced to eat under any excitement, was ill after it for days. He said he could do either one duty or the other—to give entertainments or administer the Government—and he fancied he was expected to perform the latter service in preference; and so we ceased to entertain, except at formal receptions or informal dinners and breakfasts given to as many as Mr. Davis's health permitted us to invite. In the evening he was too exhausted to receive informal visitors.

At the beginning of 1864, Mrs. Davis' influence apparently gained the upper hand, for the president and his family announced a series of receptions on Tuesday evenings, but these lasted only about a month.[8]

Probably such entertaining would have been beneficial, as Mrs. Davis thought, but she would have needed to give several parties a week to counter all the negative effects of her husband's character. The Confederate president was notoriously irritable and difficult to approach. Few people outside his family knew him well. Again Varina Howell Davis' memoir provides a frank look at his temperament:

> He was abnormally sensitive to disapprobation; even a child's disapproval discomposed him. He felt how much he was misunderstood, and the sense of mortification and injustice gave him a repellent manner. It was because of his supersensitive temperament and the acute suffering it caused him to be misunderstood, I had deprecated his assuming the civil administration.

Whatever his other talents, Davis was a high-strung man who tended to be snappish. Thomas Bragg, who liked Davis and regarded him as "able and honorable," admitted that the Confederate president was

8. Varina Howell Davis, *A Memoir*, II, 12, 161; *Daily Richmond Enquirer*, January 18, 1864, p. 2; Jones, *A Rebel War Clerk's Diary*, II, 128 and 152.

"somewhat irritable when opposed." Secretary of War James Seddon, who remained more than two years in an office which saw five different occupants, had the right to claim special talent at satisfying the chief executive, yet Seddon described him as "the most difficult man to get along with he had ever seen." There were frequent resignations from the cabinet, and a total of fourteen men served in the six cabinet-level positions during the war. Many of these departures could have been prevented had Davis shown more grace and cordiality.[9]

Compounding his short temper was an unattractive streak of self-righteousness. If Davis' wife admitted in print that her husband had a "supersensitive temperament" which gave him a "repellent manner" when misunderstood, one can imagine how others must have regarded him. One of the president's basic traits was the strict observance of internalized standards of honor. This quality gave Davis a certain rigid nobility, but it encouraged him to condemn others easily and to assume a superiority to those who did not seem to live up to his own requirements. He revealed this trait in a letter written to his wife on May 16, 1862. Commenting on the growth of opposition to his leadership, Davis pictured himself as a man of pure intentions beset by those whose motives were petty:

> As the clouds grow darker, and when, one after another, those who are trusted are detected in secret hostilities, I feel . . . that cramping fetters had fallen from my limbs. . . . They who engage in strife for personal or party aggrandisement, deserve contemptuous forgetfulness. To me who have no political wish beyond the success of our cause, no personal desire but to be relieved from further connection with office, opposition in any form can only disturb me insomuch as it may endanger the public welfare.[10]

The heroic tone of this letter betrays a man who dramatized his own virtues and could easily become supercilious.

---

9. Varina Howell Davis, *A Memoir*, II, 163; Bragg Diary, January 17, 1862; Younger (ed.), *Diary of R. G. H. Kean*, 153. The fourteen appointees do not include those who served on an interim basis.

10. Rowland (ed.), *Jefferson Davis*, V, 246.

Such personal characteristics inevitably led to frequent collisions with other imperious and prominent Confederate leaders. Often in such cases Davis was at fault. At the end of 1863 he alienated R. M. T. Hunter, who had left his post as secretary of state to become a senator from Virginia. Hunter called on the president at his home one day, but Davis entertained him "with abuse of Virginia instead of conversing on important business." On another occasion Davis lost his temper with the prolix spokesman for a delegation of North Carolinians who had come to discuss that state's defenses. In 1862 he broke with Alabama's Senator William L. Yancey over some minor appointments which Yancey had recommended. Clearly Davis had the constitutional right to appoint whomever he desired, but many political leaders would have followed the safer course of granting the wish of an important congressman.[11]

At times Davis seemed unable to pass up an opportunity to give offense. In March, 1862, for example, when he was vexed by requests from the congress for information about Confederate defenses, Davis coolly drafted replies to irritate the lawmakers. On another occasion he answered an inquiry about why Robert Toombs had not won promotion above his initial rank of brigadier general by exposing in detail the low impression which all of Toombs' superiors held of his military abilities. Concluding the letter, Davis expressed the hope that Toombs might become less resentful, but such a development was unlikely after the president had mercilessly collected and publicized these adverse judgments on a man of great political stature. In 1864 circumstances made it unnecessary for Davis to act on an army appointment which the senators from Louisiana had recommended, but after explaining the situation Davis went on to assert that he would have ruled against them. He duplicated this kind of needless irritation a few months later when he wrote the governors of six states that he would "refrain" from mentioning the unconstitutionality of several proclamations on the status of aliens because

11. Younger (ed.), *Diary of R. G. H. Kean*, 127; Bragg Diary, December 19, 1861; Jefferson Davis to W. L. Yancey and C. C. Clay, April 21, 1862, in Rowland (ed.), *Jefferson Davis*, V, 234.

he wanted to avoid "any question that could produce a conflict between the general and state governments." Obviously had Davis truly wished to avoid conflict, he would not have referred to the matter at all.[12]

Sorry as this record was, it represented a marked improvement over Davis' performance as secretary of war during the 1850s. At that time both the Mississippi politician and General Winfield Scott, the army's highest-ranking officer, had brought disrepute upon themselves by engaging in an interminable, spiteful, and petty quarrel over certain expenses claimed by Scott. Each man penned such long letters justifying his position that their angry correspondence literally could have filled a book. Perhaps with this unsavory incident in mind, Davis made a conscious effort to hold his tongue while serving in the Confederacy's highest office. While the new government was still in Montgomery Mrs. Davis reported that her husband was striving to answer all unsolicited advice "in softly modulated, dulcet accents." In May, 1862, the president himself wrote to his wife that, "I wish I could learn just to let people alone who snap at me." Occasionally he even solicited frank advice from prominent men. After Thomas Bragg left the cabinet, Davis wrote him and requested frequent and free recommendations on policy, and in January, 1865, the president sent for Virginia's W. C. Rives and drew him into an extensive discussion of what the government needed to do to meet the crisis of the Confederacy.[13]

From the beginning of the war Davis made a special effort to cooperate with the governors. After tactfully handling several collisions with John Letcher of Virginia, the president remarked that he had a "fixed determination not to have conflict with the Governors of the States." His correspondence with Governor H. T. Clark of North Carolina in 1862 displayed the technique of balancing implied criticisms with words of praise or apology. This attempt to stay on the

12. Bragg Diary, March 4, 1862; Jefferson Davis to D. W. Lewis, September 21, 1863, in Rowland (ed.), *Jefferson Davis*, VI, 43–44, also 264–65 and 338–40.

13. Rowland (ed.), *Jefferson Davis*, Vols. II and III, *passim*; Chesnut, *Diary*, 52; Rowland (ed.), *Jefferson Davis*, V, 246; Bragg Diary, August 8, 1862; Younger (ed.), *Diary of R. G. H. Kean*, 192.

good side of the highest official from North Carolina continued when Zebulon Vance won election as governor. On several occasions Davis warmly thanked Vance for acts of cooperation or offered to be of assistance, but the two men did not always understand each other, and their respective positions eventually placed them in an antagonistic relationship. Davis even tried to mollify Georgia's touchy chief executive, Joseph E. Brown. On May 20, 1863, for example, he assured the governor that, "I shall be glad at all times to receive an expression of your views upon matters of public policy," and in September of that year he asked Brown to come to Richmond for consultation about the military situation and the feelings of the people.[14] In the end, of course, all these efforts were unsuccessful.

Davis also made a few gestures of respect and deference to the congress in order to further good relations with the legislative branch. Although he had the power to proclaim the admission of prosouthern governments from Missouri and Kentucky to the Confederacy, he submitted all the relevant documents to the congress because it was meeting at the time that negotiations came to fruition. In February, 1862, he attempted to flatter the newly elected members of the first congress under the permanent constitution by expressing his intention to rely upon their able advice. In general, however, his relations with the congress were distant and cool, so much so that J. B. Jones recorded his surprise at seeing Davis "in earnest conversation with several members of Congress, standing in the street." The austere and formal chief executive did not often "descend from his office to this mode of conference."[15]

At times Davis seemed to be keenly aware of the importance of

14. Jefferson Davis to John Letcher, September 14, 1861, Davis to H. Clark, April 8, 1862 and August 2, 1862, and Davis to Zebulon Vance, November 1, 1862 and July 14, 1863, in Rowland (ed.), *Jefferson Davis*, V, 132, 229–30, 309, 362–63, 545–47; Davis to Joseph E. Brown, May 20, 1863, in Allen D. Candler (ed.), *The Confederate Records of the State of Georgia* (6 vols.; Atlanta: Chas. P. Byrd, 1910), III, 339; Davis to Brown, September 12, 1863, in *Official Records*, Ser. IV, Vol. II, 804–805.

15. James D. Richardson (comp.), *A Compilation of the Messages and Papers of the Confederacy, Including the Diplomatic Correspondence, 1861–1865* (2 vols.; Nashville: United States Publishing Company, 1906), I, 144–46; Rowland (ed.), *Jefferson Davis*, V, 206; Jones, *A Rebel War Clerk's Diary*, II, 330.

maintaining warm relations with other leaders and the people. He
gave some sage advice to General J. C. Pemberton, who often was as
inept in this area as the president himself. "In your situation," Davis
wrote, "much depends upon the support and good will of the people." To gain this support, Davis urged "conciliation" and "patience
in listening to suggestions." Again, in July, 1863, Davis offered valuable advice to General E. Kirby Smith, who was assuming almost independent direction of the distant Trans-Mississippi Department.
Davis suggested to Smith that "much discontent may be avoided by
giving such explanations to the Governors of the States as will prevent them from misconstruing your actions, and men are sometimes
made valuable coadjutors by conferring with them without surren-
dering any portion of . . . control."[16] No doubt Davis' friends wished
that he had been as adept in carrying out such advice as he was in
giving it.

In practice, however, neither Jefferson Davis nor many of the
other leaders with whom he had to deal had the personality which
could overlook a slight or sustain an atmosphere of harmony. The
consequence was an unending series of quarrels with various state
leaders and congressmen. One argument with Governor Vance became so acrimonious that Davis abruptly broke off communication
with the comment: "I must beg that a correspondence so unprofitable in its character . . . may here end, and that your future com-
munications be restricted to such matters as may require official action."[17] A large proportion of the letters which passed between Davis
and Governor Brown of Georgia were intended by both sides to have
all the charm of an artillery shell.

Nor were the president's relations with the congress more satisfactory. Early in 1863 he held some meetings with representatives
from Arkansas about the defense of that state, but the congressmen
were so dissatisfied that they charged him with "trifling" with them.
At the end of 1863 a movement developed in the congress to impose

16. Jefferson Davis to J. C. Pemberton, May 12, 1863, in Rowland (ed.), *Jefferson Davis*,
V, 485, also 552–54.
17. Jefferson Davis to Zebulon Vance, March 31, 1864, *ibid.*, VI, 218.

a two-year limitation on the tenure of cabinet officers, a step clearly designed to give force to the lawmakers' lack of confidence in certain appointees. This proposal did not succeed, but it helped spark a controversy between the senate and the chief executive over the appointments of the quartermaster general and other officers. Before the end of the Civil War, some congressmen attempted to force the resignation of the cabinet and reduce the influence of the president on military operations of the Confederacy.[18] Only the exigencies of war, which usually compelled congressmen to follow the president's lead, saved Davis from more serious opposition in the congress.

All these controversies damaged public morale, and some of Davis' appointments further sapped people's enthusiasm for the cause. Although Davis made friends with difficulty, he defended those he had with an excessive tenacity and proved too indulgent to their failings. Quickly the public and the press learned that Davis had certain "pets" who could do no wrong, at least nothing which merited their removal from office. General J. C. Pemberton was one of the president's favorites and, as a result, held a series of positions which should have been entrusted to someone else. After Governor Francis Pickens of South Carolina complained about the general's lack of competence, Davis assigned Pemberton to another responsible post in Alabama and Mississippi. Within a year letters from that region indicated that most of the people wanted Pemberton replaced, and an Alabama congressman, E. S. Dargan, warned that retaining the general in command would completely demoralize the two states. Unfortunately, however, Davis saw a parallel between the criticism of Pemberton and himself, and he even compared the undistinguished soldier to Lee.[19]

Many southerners also complained about Commissary-General Lucius Northrop, who failed to deal successfully with the difficult problem of supply, but Davis told a delegation of congressmen that

18. Rowland (ed.), *Jefferson Davis*, V, 457–60; Jones, *A Rebel War Clerk's Diary*, II, 116, 131; Younger (ed.), *Diary of R. G. H. Kean*, 126, 130, 133, 135, 136; *Daily Richmond Examiner*, January 19, 1864, p. 1.
19. Rowland (ed.), *Jefferson Davis*, V, 310–12, 590–92, 587–88; *Official Records*, Ser. IV, Vol. II, 713, 717.

Northrop was "one of the greatest geniuses in the South." Another commander who lost the public's trust was Braxton Bragg, but the president stubbornly defended Bragg and brought him to Richmond as chief military adviser in 1864 when dissension in the Army of Tennessee necessitated his removal. One comment by Mrs. Davis illuminates her husband's excessive loyalty to Bragg. In April, 1865, when she was fleeing from the Federal army, Mrs. Davis looked toward a possible future in the Trans-Mississippi Department and wrote: "Though I know you do not like my interference, let me entreat you not to send B. B. [Braxton Bragg] to command there, I am satisfied that the country will be ruined by its intestine feuds if you do so."[20]

Just as Davis favored certain officers, there were other military men with whom he could not get along. At an early date he lost confidence in General P. G. T. Beauregard, although this Louisiana soldier had many well-placed supporters and an outstanding grasp of strategic concepts. Davis' relations with General Joseph E. Johnston also deteriorated rapidly. Unfortunately for Davis, Johnston had a large public following, and even Mrs. Chesnut admitted that, "Joe Johnston, whether advancing or retreating, is magnetic; he does draw the good will of those by whom he is surrounded." Thus Johnston served as a focus for dissatisfaction with the way the government was prosecuting the war. Frequently those who believed that Davis was destroying the South felt confident that Johnston could save it. As late as January, 1865, Louis Wigfall, a prominent senator from Texas, declared, "Make Joe Johnston dictator and all will be well." But Davis believed that Johnston was "unfit for the conduct of a campaign" and long resisted reappointing him to command in 1865. At one point he even wrote that he would rather lose public confidence than reassign the general.[21]

This comment raises a question about Davis' awareness of the importance of internal morale. The spirit of the people was a vital factor for a nation at war and Davis could not afford to disregard it. He des-

20. Jones, *A Rebel War Clerk's Diary*, II, 131; Rowland (ed.), *Jefferson Davis*, VI, 539.
21. Chesnut, *Diary*, 317, 467; Rowland (ed.), *Jefferson Davis*, VI, 491–92.

perately needed to build public confidence instead of throwing it away. At times, however, he seemed to have a clear grasp of the necessity for popular support. In July, 1863, for example, he wrote to Robert E. Lee that "this war can only be successfully prosecuted while we have the cordial support of the people." Five months later he responded to some complimentary resolutions from the Mississippi legislature by declaring that "next to the blessing of God, the cordial support of the people is most potential for the maintenance of our independence." In his frequent correspondence with various officials about disaffected areas in the South, Davis also showed that he was aware of the decline of morale and the need to revive it. He never shared the wild notions of some enthusiastic Confederates such as T. R. R. Cobb, who believed that the patriotism of the people would stand any sacrifice and who advocated a strategy of reducing the army, allowing Federal forces to invade at will, and then "suffer[ing] & wait[ing] for the exhaustion of our enemies."[22]

The southern people would not have tolerated the events outlined by Cobb, for lack of commitment among its citizens was a crucial problem for the Confederacy. Davis was correct when he identified popular support as a paramount consideration, and therefore any assessment of him as Confederate president must rest to a great degree upon his sensitivity to problems of morale and his effectiveness in eliciting the enthusiasm and energies of the people. It is in this area that the judgment of Davis must be most harsh.

The Confederacy's chief executive proved insensitive to the problems of ordinary southerners, who suffered greatly from inflation, shortages, speculation, and impressment. Although hundreds of thousands of small farmers and their families faced unprecedented need, the central government ignored their problems and often made them worse by new policies which demanded further sacrifice. Moreover, Confederate laws and regulations often favored the wealthy, a fact

---

22. Rowland (ed.), *Jefferson Davis*, V, 580; Jefferson Davis to Charles Clark, December 28, 1863, in *Official Records*, Ser. IV, Vol. II, 1065; Thomas R. R. Cobb to G. W. Randolph, August 28, 1862, in Letters Received, Confederate Secretary of War, in Record Group 109, National Archives, Microcopy M 437, Roll 40, pp. 1057–61.

which nonslaveholding families recognized and resented. The Davis administration did not give these people enough economic security or social justice to allow them to go the last mile for a government which many had been reluctant to form in the first place. Since the Confederacy depended largely on its nonslaveholding class, their disaffection held grave consequences for the cause.

Why did Davis neglect this vital area? Mary Boykin Chesnut reported that his aides showed the president only about one in sixty letters from desperate women and children, but he did not lack information on the problem. Correspondence of this sort to the War Department was voluminous, and Davis read and endorsed many such letters, including reports from disaffected areas. Moreover, both the secretary of war and the governors of the states brought such matters directly to his attention and urged government action to alleviate the poverty and distress of the common people. From 1863 through the end of the war J. B. Jones carried on a campaign to prod the administration into providing food to the poor in Richmond and wrote several letters directly to Davis.[23]

Probably part of the explanation for the conduct of the president was an understandable reluctance to provoke opposition from those who thought that the Confederate government was already too powerful. Extreme concern for states' rights characterized many of the leaders of the slaveholding class, and they resisted any action which developed substantial power in the central government. Governor Brown's vicious assault on conscription and on the suspension of *habeas corpus* was only part of a continuing and vocal opposition. Amid cries of despotism and denunciations of "King Davis," the Confederate president naturally became cautious. From a political point of view, such criticism placed Davis in a painful dilemma. The opposition of influential and articulate elements of southern society made it dangerous to help the common people, on whom the success of the cause also depended. Davis held back from aiding the poor without satisfying his critics.

Another reason for Davis' failure to respond was the limitation

23. Chesnut, *Diary*, 327; Jones, *A Rebel War Clerk's Diary*, II, 56–57, 187, 271.

which his class perspective placed on his actions. In March, 1864, he addressed a group of returned Confederate prisoners and appealed to them to go back to the ranks after a brief visit at home. "You will find your families," Davis said, "suffering less than you have been led to suppose." On the surface this statement seemed to show the president's awareness of the difficulties which ordinary southerners faced, but in fact he probably did not appreciate the extent of destitution which gripped many farms. Davis personally was no epicure, and he was willing to make almost any sacrifice to achieve independence, but the war did not force him to do much belt tightening. In March, 1864, Mrs. Davis found that her family was not living within its income and considered giving up the carriage and horses. One month later both the president and his wife showed some indignation at the conduct of extortioners. Yet the Davis family was merely pinched rather than suffering, for on January 30, 1864, Mary Boykin Chesnut attended a luncheon given by Mrs. Davis and reported the following menu: "gumbo, ducks and olives, *suprême de volaille*, chickens in jelly, oysters, lettuce salad, chocolate cream, jelly cake, claret cup, etc."[24] Hunger and want were necessarily somewhat abstract and theoretical problems to the Davises.

Davis also allowed himself to be too absorbed in military affairs and details of administration. He spent most of his time struggling to strengthen the army or coordinate its operations. According to many critics, his devotion to these matters often resulted in the waste of valuable time on minor details. J. B. Jones reported that "the President attends to many little matters," and R. G. H. Kean complained that Davis wasted his efforts on "little trash which ought to be dispatched by clerks in the adjutant general's office." As Kean believed, Davis probably tried to be familiar with too many questions of secondary importance, although one should note that historians have commended Lincoln for a similar absorption in detail.[25] Perhaps success or failure determine the judgments on administrative style.

24. *Daily Richmond Enquirer*, March 17, 1864, p. 2; Chesnut, *Diary*, 395, 367; Jones, *A Rebel War Clerk's Diary*, II, 190.
25. Jones, *A Rebel War Clerk's Diary*, II, 320; Younger (ed.), *Diary of R. G. H. Kean*, 100; see James G. Randall, *Lincoln the President* (4 vols.; New York: Dodd, Mead & Company, 1945–1955), III, 5.

There also was a strange and unworkable pattern to Davis' approach to public business. Long periods of isolated administrative labor in Richmond alternated with whirlwind trips into the country to make contact with the people and revive popular morale. Each of his three trips into the deep South—in the autumns of 1862, 1863, and 1864—were of this nature. At these particular times he displayed an acute awareness of the need to strengthen the will of the people, but he devoted little preparation to this task and gave it no sustained attention. As a consequence of this fact and of the inadequate policies which resulted, the Confederacy lost the support of a large and increasing proportion of its population.

As Confederate president, Davis presided over a disastrous decline of southern morale which doomed his hopes of establishing a new nation. He needed to instill in his countrymen the fierce determination to achieve independence which he personally felt, but instead their enthusiasm turned into despair, and their unity degenerated into division. The Confederacy was collapsing from within long before Federal armies managed to apply irresistible pressure from without. Thus, the greatest failure of Jefferson Davis' leadership lay in the domestic arena, in his inability to create the internal unity and spirit essential for the growth of Confederate nationalism.

But this was not the only deficiency in Confederate nationalism. The South's problem was not solely the tenuous dedication of its nonslaveholding citizens, and its failure was not simply the shortcoming of its president. Davis had to deal with a ruling class which seemed incompetent to rule and unwilling to accept leadership. The planters themselves proved to be contentious and narrow, unimaginative and inflexible, and only weakly committed to southern nationalism. As a group they did much to obstruct the achievement of independence and frustrate Davis' efforts toward that goal.

Looking back over events in 1864, Governor Zebulon Vance of North Carolina wrote that secession "was a revolution of the politicians not the people."[26] The planters had taken the South out of the

26. Zebulon Vance to D. L. Swain, September 22, 1864, quoted in Richard E. Yates, *The Confederacy and Zeb Vance* (Tuscaloosa, Ala.: Confederate Publishing Company, Inc., 1958), 112.

Union in order to defend slavery. This narrow class interest had united them, and they had used their leading positions in society to initiate a revolution. But once the revolution had begun, they did not seem willing or able to complete it. No common conception of a government in their interests united them. Some saw that strong measures were necessary to win the war, and they supported Jefferson Davis, but many more lapsed into a double negativism and damned both the United States and their new government, struggling for its life.

Perhaps the decades of quarreling with the North had frozen southern leaders into a defensive posture and developed only their abilities to react against a government while the powers of creative statesmanship atrophied. Whatever the cause, the record of the Confederacy's political leaders was a sorry one. Early in 1861 T. R. R. Cobb proclaimed himself "sick at heart with the daily manifestations of selfishness, intrigue, low-cunning, and meanness among those who should have an eye single to the protection of their people and the preservation of their government."[27] The record of the influential planters did not improve as the war went on. Independence was presumably their goal, but in moments of crisis many seemed devoted only to the protection of privilege and slavery. They wanted to keep their way of life as it had been, unchanged through a colossal war and unaltered in a world that was being transformed. The times demanded more of them—more flexibility, more imagination, and more willingness to sacrifice. As a class they seemed caught in an image of the past and unable to adapt to the challenges of reality and change.

In 1861 a prominent Virginian described Jefferson Davis as "a very intelligent man . . . far above the average of the modern race of American Presidents."[28] This assessment may be too generous, but if the comparison is made to his class and to southern leaders of his generation, the conclusions are valid. As Confederate president,

27. T. R. R. Cobb to his wife, February 16, 1861, in T. R. R. Cobb Letters, University of Georgia.
28. W. C. Rives to his wife, May 18, 1861, in W. C. Rives Collection, Library of Congress.

Davis displayed a keen intelligence and a capacity for creative leadership which was far above the average. He perceived the need for central direction and for major innovations such as conscription far earlier than most southerners, and indeed earlier than his northern counterpart. In a time of rapid change he was flexible and able to adapt. Yet his dedication to the goal of independence never wavered. In the central area of slavery and race relations, Davis demonstrated a capacity to grow which far outstripped most of his fellow southerners. That growth, one must add, stopped far short of a concept of racial equality in America, but here Davis differed little from Abraham Lincoln, who also could not visualize full citizenship for black people or a genuinely multiracial society. Both men and both sections were limited by racism and trapped in the tragedy of a war which often evaded its central issue—the position of the black race in America. This failing was a failing of their generation.

Selected Bibliography

PRIMARY SOURCES

MANUSCRIPTS

Bragg, Thomas. Diary, 1861–1862. Southern Historical Collection, University of North Carolina, Chapel Hill.

Cannon, W. R. Papers. Miscellaneous Manuscript Collection, Library of Congress, Washington, D.C.

Chesnut-Miller-Manning Papers. South Carolina Historical Society, Charleston.

Clay, Clement C. Papers. Duke University, Durham, North Carolina.

Clay, Clement C. Papers, 1861–1865. National Archives, Washington, D.C.

Cobb, Howell. Papers. University of Georgia, Athens.

Cobb, T. R. R. Letters. University of Georgia, Athens.

C. S. A. (Pickett) Papers. Library of Congress, Washington, D.C.

Culver, Telamon. Collection. University of Georgia, Athens.

Davis, Jefferson. Papers. Duke University, Durham, North Carolina.

Davis, Jefferson. Papers. Fleming Collection, New York Public Library.

Davis, Jefferson. Papers. Library of Congress, Washington, D.C.

Davis, Jefferson. Papers. Samuel Richey Confederate Collection, Miami University, Oxford, Ohio.

Graham, W. A. Papers. North Carolina Department of Archives and History, Raleigh.

Harrison, Burton and Family. Papers. Library of Congress, Washington, D.C.

Hammond, J. H. Papers. Library of Congress, Washington, D.C.

Hunter, R. M. T. Papers. University of Virginia, Charlottesville.

Jemison, M. S. Papers. University of Alabama, University, Alabama.

Johnson, H. V. Papers. Duke University, Durham, North Carolina.

Johnston, A. S., and W. P. Johnston. Papers. Mrs. Mason Barret Collection, Tulane University, New Orleans, Louisiana.

McKee Collection. Alabama State Department of Archives and History, Montgomery.

Miles, W. P. Letters. University of North Carolina, Chapel Hill.

Orr, J. A. Reminiscences. Mississippi Department of Archives and History, Jackson.

Read, Keith. Papers. University of Georgia, Athens.

Rhett, R. B. Papers. University of South Carolina, Columbia.

Rives, W. C. Collection. Library of Congress, Washington, D.C.

Shorter, John Gill. Letterbook. Alabama State Department of Archives and History, Montgomery.

Toombs, Robert. Papers. University of Georgia, Athens.

Turner, Josiah. Papers. University of North Carolina, Chapel Hill.

Watts, T. H. Letterbook. Alabama State Department of Archives and History, Montgomery.

Yancey, W. L. Papers. Alabama State Department of Archives and History, Montgomery.

NEWSPAPERS

Anderson (S.C.) *Intelligencer*, 1861–1862

Asheville (N.C.) *News*, 1862

Atlanta Daily *Intelligencer*, 1861–1865

Charleston *Mercury*, 1861–1865

Charlotte (N.C.) *Whig*, 1861–1862.

Charlottesville (Va.) *Daily Chronicle*, 1864–1865 (incomplete)

Edgefield (S.C.) *Advertiser*, 1861–1865 (Owned by the South Caroliniana Library and reproduced from the original file of Mrs. J. L. Mims of Edgefield.)

Fredericksburg (Va.) *Democratic Recorder*, 1862 (incomplete)

Huntsville (Ala.) *Confederate*, 1862–1864

Richmond *Enquirer*, 1861–1865

Richmond *Examiner*, 1861–1865

Richmond *Whig*, 1861–1865

Rome (Ga.) *Weekly Courier*, 1861–1863

Spartanburg (S.C.) *Carolina Spartan*, 1861–1864

GOVERNMENT DOCUMENTS

Published

Acts of the General Assembly of the State of Georgia Passed in Milledgeville at the Annual Session in November and December, 1862; also Extra Session of 1863. Milledgeville, Ga.: Boughton, Nisbet, Barnes & Moore, 1863.

Acts of the General Assembly of the State of Georgia Passed in Milledge-ville at the Annual Session in November and December, 1863; also Extra Session of 1864. Milledgeville, Ga.: Boughton, Nisbet, Barnes & Moore, 1864.

Congressional Globe, 1846–1861.

Georgia. House. *Journal*, 1863. Milledgeville, Ga.: Boughton, Nisbet, Barnes & Moore, 1863.

Georgia. Senate. *Journal*, 1863. Milledgeville, Ga.: Boughton, Nisbet, Barnes & Moore, 1863.

Journal of the Congress of the Confederate States of America, 1861–1865. 7 vols. Washington: Government Printing Office, 1904–1905.

Public Laws of the State of North Carolina Passed by the General Assembly at Its Session of 1862–1863. Raleigh: W. W. Holden, 1863.

Senate Executive Documents. 30th Congress, 1st Session. Volume 7, Number 52.

Unpublished

Library of Congress

Confederate States of America. War Department. Communication from the Secretary of War (transmitting a report by the Assistant Quartermaster in charge of the tax-in-kind, Larkin Smith), January 19, 1864.

———. Instructions to be observed by officers and agents receiving the tax-in-kind, March 29, 1864.

National Archives

Compiled Service Records of Confederate General and Staff Officers, & Nonregimental Enlisted Men. Record Group 109. Microcopy 331.

Confederate States of America. Treasury Department. Letters Received by the Confederate Secretary of the Treasury, 1861–1865. Record Group 109. Microcopy M 499.

Confederate States of America. War Department. Agricultural Detail Book. Virginia, 1864–1865. Record Group 109. Chapter I, Volume 236.

———. Agricultural Exemption Book. Virginia, 1864. Record Group 109. Chapter I, Volume 235.

———. Classification Ledger of Details, 1864–1865. Record Group 109. Chapter I, Volume 255.

———. Classification Ledger of Exemptions, 1864–1865. Record Group 109. Chapter I, Volume 254.

———. Exemptions for Pay, 1863. Record Group 109. Chapter I, Volume 262.

————. General Orders of the Confederate Adjutant and Inspector General's Office, 1861–1865. Record Group 109. Microcopy T 782.

————. Letters Received, Confederate Quartermaster General, 1861–1865. Record Group 109. Microcopy M 469.

————. Letters Received, Confederate Secretary of War, 1861–1865. Record Group 109. Microcopy M 437.

————. Letters Sent, Confederate Secretary of War, 1861–1865. Record Group 109. Microcopy M 522.

————. Letters Sent by the Confederate Secretary of War to the President, 1861–1865. Record Group 109. Microcopy M 523.

————. List of Details and Exemptions in Virginia to August, 1864. Record Group 109. Chapter I, Volume 235½.

————. Lists of Quartermasters and Commissaries, 1861–1865. Record Group 109. Entry 46.

————. Quartermaster Department. Letters and Telegrams Sent, 1861–1865. Record Group 109. Microcopy T 131.

————. Record of the Appointment of Quartermasters, 1861–1863. Record Group 109. Chapter V, Volume 231.

————. Record of Enlisted Men Detailed, January-November, 1864. Record Group 109. Chapter IV, Volume 107.

————. Record of Exemptions in Virginia, 1862–1863. Record Group 109. Chapter I, Volume 251.

————. Station Book of Quartermasters. Record Group 109. Chapter V, Volume 228.

United States. Commission of Claims. Records of the Commissioners of Claims, 1871–1880.

North Carolina Department of Archives and History, Raleigh.

Cumberland County. Minutes. Court of Pleas and Quarter Sessions, 1863–1865.

Duplin County. Minute Docket. Court of Pleas and Quarter Sessions, 1861–1865.

Johnston County. Minute Docket. Court of Pleas and Quarter Sessions, 1863–1865.

Sampson County. Clerk of Superior Court. Minutes. County Court, 1861–1865.

Wake County. Record of the Court of Wardens of the Poor, 1846–1872.

Wayne County. Clerk of Superior Court. Minutes. Court of Pleas and Quarter Sessions, 1863–1865.

BOOKS

Andrews, Eliza Frances. *The War-Time Journal of a Georgia Girl, 1864– 1865.* Edited by Spencer Bidwell King, Jr. Macon: Ardivan Press, 1960.

Bettersworth, John K. *Mississippi in the Confederacy: As They Saw It.* Jackson, Miss.: Mississippi Department of Archives and History, 1961.

Burnham, W. Dean. *Presidential Ballots, 1836–1892.* Baltimore: Johns Hopkins University Press, 1955.

Candler, Allen D., ed. *The Confederate Records of the State of Georgia.* 6 vols. Atlanta: Chas. P. Byrd, 1910.

Chesnut, Mary Boykin. *A Diary from Dixie.* Edited by Ben Ames Williams. Sentry edition. Boston: Houghton Mifflin Company, 1949.

Davis, Jefferson. *The Rise and Fall of the Confederate Government.* 2 vols. London: Longmans, Green and Co., 1881.

Davis, Varina Howell. *Jefferson Davis, Ex-President of the Confederate States of America: A Memoir.* 2 vols. New York: Belford Company, 1890.

De Leon, Thomas Cooper. *Four Years in Rebel Capitals.* Mobile: Gossip Printing Company, 1890.

Dumond, Dwight L., ed. *Southern Editorials on Secession.* New York: Century Company, 1931.

Jones, J. B. *A Rebel War Clerk's Diary.* Edited by Howard Swiggett. 2 vols. New York: Old Hickory Bookshop, 1935.

Matthews, James M., ed. *Statutes at Large of the Confederate States of America.* Richmond: R. M. Smith, 1862–1864.

Matthews, James M., ed. *The Statutes at Large of the Provisional Government of the Confederate States of America.* Richmond: R. M. Smith, 1864.

Myers, Robert Manson, ed. *The Children of Pride.* New Haven: Yale University Press, 1972.

Ramsdell, Charles W., ed. *Laws and Joint Resolutions of the Last Session of the Confederate Congress.* Durham: Duke University Press, 1941.

Richardson, James D., comp. *A Compilation of the Messages and Papers of the Confederacy, Including the Diplomatic Correspondence, 1861–1865.* 2 vols. Nashville: United States Publishing Company, 1906.

Rowland, Dunbar, ed. *Jefferson Davis: Constitutionalist; His Letters, Papers, and Speeches.* 10 vols. Jackson, Miss.: Little & Ives Company, 1923.

U.S. War Department. *The War of the Rebellion: A Compilation of the Official Records of the Union and Confederate Armies.* 130 vols. Washington: Government Printing Office, 1880–1901.

Younger, Edward, ed. *Inside the Confederate Government: The Diary of Robert Garlick Hill Kean.* New York: Oxford University Press, 1957.

Secondary Sources

BOOKS

Alexander, Thomas B., and Richard E. Beringer, *The Anatomy of the Confederate Congress: A Study of the Influences of Member Characteristics on Voting Behavior, 1861–1865*. Nashville: Vanderbilt University Press, 1972.

Amlund, Curtis Arthur. *Federalism in the Southern Confederacy*. Washington: Public Affairs Press, 1966.

Andrews, J. Cutler. *The South Reports the Civil War*. Princeton: Princeton University Press, 1970.

Barney, William L. *The Secessionist Impulse: Alabama and Mississippi in 1860*. Princeton: Princeton University Press, 1974.

Black, Robert C., III. *The Railroads of the Confederacy*. Chapel Hill: University of North Carolina Press, 1952.

Bettersworth, John K. *Confederate Mississippi*. Baton Rouge: Louisiana State University Press, 1943.

Boulding, Kenneth E. *The Image*. Ann Arbor: University of Michigan Press, 1956.

Bragg, Jefferson Davis. *Louisiana in the Confederacy*. Baton Rouge: Louisiana State University Press, 1941.

Brewer, James A. *The Confederate Negro: Virginia's Craftsmen and Military Laborers, 1861–1865*. Durham: Duke University Press, 1969.

Bryan, T. Conn. *Confederate Georgia*. Athens: University of Georgia Press, 1953.

Commager, Henry Steele. *The Defeat of the Confederacy*. Anvil Original edition. Princeton: D. Van Nostrand Company, Inc., 1964.

Connelly, Thomas L., and Archer Jones. *The Politics of Command: Factions and Ideas in Confederate Strategy*. Baton Rouge: Louisiana State University Press, 1973.

Coulter, E. Merton. *The Confederate States of America, 1861–1865*. Baton Rouge: Louisiana State University Press, 1950.

Coser, Lewis. *The Functions of Social Conflict*. Glencoe, Ill.: Free Press, 1956.

Craven, Avery O. *The Growth of Southern Nationalism, 1848–1861*. Baton Rouge: Louisiana State University Press, 1953. Volume VI of 10 vols., in Wendell Holmes Stephenson and E. Merton Coulter (eds.), *A History of the South*.

Dodd, William E. *Jefferson Davis*. Philadelphia: George W. Jacobs & Company, 1907.

Degler, Carl N. *Neither Black Nor White: Slavery and Race Relations in Brazil and the United States*. New York: Macmillan Company, 1971.

Dorman, Lewy. *Party Politics in Alabama From 1850 Through 1860*. Wetumpka, Ala.: Alabama State Department of Archives and History, 1935.

Du Bois, W. E. B. *Black Reconstruction in America, 1860–1880*. New York: Harcourt, Brace and Company, 1935.

Dumond, Dwight L. *The Secession Movement, 1860–1861*. New York: Macmillan Company, 1931.

Durden, Robert F. *The Gray and the Black: The Confederate Debate on Emancipation*. Baton Rouge: Louisiana State University Press, 1972.

Eaton, Clement. *A History of the Southern Confederacy*. New York: Macmillan Company, 1923.

Eckenrode, H. J. *Jefferson Davis: President of the South*. New York: Macmillan Company, 1923.

Ettinger, Amos A. *The Mission to Spain and Pierre Soulé, 1853–1855*. New Haven: Yale University Press, 1932.

Faulk, Odie B. *Too Far North . . . Too Far South*. Los Angeles: Westernlore Press, 1967.

Festinger, Leon. *A Theory of Cognitive Dissonance*. Evanston: Row, Peterson, and Co., 1957.

Filler, Louis. *The Crusade Against Slavery, 1830–1860*. New York: Harper & Row, 1960.

Fleming, Walter L. *Civil War and Reconstruction in Alabama*. New York: Columbia University Press, 1905.

Fredrickson, George M. *The Black Image in the White Mind: The Debate on Afro-American Character and Destiny, 1817–1914*. New York: Harper & Row, 1971.

Fuess, Claude M. *The Life of Caleb Cushing*. 2 vols. New York: Harcourt, Brace, and Company, 1923.

Garber, Paul Neff. *The Gadsden Treaty*. Philadelphia: University of Pennsylvania Press, 1923.

Goff, Richard D. *Confederate Supply*. Durham: Duke University Press, 1969.

Gray, Wood. *The Hidden Civil War: The Story of the Copperheads*. New York: Viking Press, 1942.

Hamilton, Holman. *Prologue to Conflict: The Crisis and Compromise of 1850*. Lexington: University of Kentucky Press, 1964.

Harris, William C. *Leroy Pope Walker: Confederate Secretary of War*. Tuscaloosa, Ala.: Confederate Publishing Company, Inc., 1961.

Hartz, Louis. *The Liberal Tradition in America*. New York: Harcourt, Brace, and Company, 1955.

Hearon, Cleo. *Mississippi and the Compromise of 1850*. Chicago: n.p., 1913.

Hill, Louise Biles. *Joseph E. Brown and the Confederacy*. Chapel Hill: University of North Carolina Press, 1939.

Hodgson, Sister M. Michael Catherine. *Caleb Cushing: Attorney General of the United States, 1853–1857*. Washington: Catholic University of America Press, 1955.

Hoole, William Stanley. *Alabama Tories: The First Alabama Cavalry, U.S.A., 1862–1865*. Tuscaloosa, Ala.: Confederate Publishing Company, Inc., 1960.

Howard, Perry H. *Political Tendencies in Louisiana*. Rev. ed.; Baton Rouge: Louisiana State University Press, 1971.

Jenkins, William Sumner. *Pro-Slavery Thought in the Old South*. Chapel Hill: University of North Carolina Press, 1935.

Jones, Archer. *Confederate Strategy from Shiloh to Vicksburg*. Baton Rouge: Louisiana State University Press, 1961.

Kerby, Robert L. *Kirby Smith's Confederacy: The Trans-Mississippi South, 1863–1865*. New York: Columbia University Press, 1972.

Kinchen, Oscar A. *Confederate Operations in Canada and the North*. North Quincy, Mass.: Christopher Publishing House, 1970.

Klein, Philip Shriver. *President James Buchanan: A Biography*. University Park, Pa.: Pennsylvania State University Press, 1962.

Klement, Frank L. *The Copperheads in the Middle West*. Chicago: University of Chicago Press, 1960.

Klingberg, Frank W. *The Southern Claims Commission*. Berkeley: University of California Press, 1955.

Lee, Charles Robert, Jr. *The Confederate Constitutions*. Chapel Hill: University of North Carolina Press, 1963.

Lipset, Seymour Martin. *Political Man: The Social Bases of Politics*. Anchor Books edition. Garden City, N.Y.: Doubleday & Company, 1963.

Livermore, Thomas L. *Numbers and Losses in the Civil War in America: 1861–1865*. Bloomington: Indiana University Press, 1957.

Lonn, Ella. *Desertion During the Civil War*. New York: Century Company, 1928.

McElroy, Robert. *Jefferson Davis: The Unreal and the Real*. 2 vols. New York: Harper & Brothers, 1937.

Martin, Bessie. *Desertion of Alabama Troops from the Confederate Army: A Study in Sectionalism*. New York: Columbia University Press, 1932.

Massey, Mary Elizabeth. *Ersatz in the Confederacy*. Columbia, S.C.: University of South Carolina Press, 1952.

Meade, Robert Douthat. *Judah P. Benjamin: Confederate Statesman*. New York: Oxford University Press, 1943.

Merk, Frederick. *Manifest Destiny and Mission in American History: A Reinterpretation*. Vintage Books edition. New York: Knopf and Random House, 1963.

Montgomery, Horace. *Cracker Parties*. Baton Rouge: Louisiana State University Press, 1950.

———. *Howell Cobb's Confederate Career*. Tuscaloosa, Ala.: Confederate Publishing Company, Inc., 1959.

Moore, Albert Burton. *Conscription and Conflict in the Confederacy*. New York: Macmillan Company, 1924.

Nagle, Paul C. *One Nation Indivisible: The Union in American Thought, 1776–1861*. New York: Oxford University Press, 1964.

———. *This Sacred Trust: American Nationality, 1798–1898*. New York: Oxford University Press, 1971.

Nichols, Roy F. *The Disruption of American Democracy*. New York: Macmillan Company, 1948.

———. *Franklin Pierce: Young Hickory of the Granite Hills*. Philadelphia: University of Pennsylvania Press, 1931.

———. *A Historian's Progress*. New York: Alfred A. Knopf, 1968.

Osterweis, Rollin. *Judah P. Benjamin: Statesman of the Lost Cause*. New York: G. P. Putman's Sons, 1933.

Owsley, Frank L. *Plain Folk of the Old South*. Baton Rouge: Louisiana State University Press, 1949.

———. *State Rights in the Confederacy*. Chicago: University of Chicago Press, 1925.

Patrick, Rembert W. *Jefferson Davis and His Cabinet*. Baton Rouge: Louisiana State University Press, 1944.

Phillips, U. B. *Georgia and State Rights*. Washington: Government Printing Office, 1902.

Potter, David M. *Lincoln and His Party in the Secession Crisis*. New Haven: Yale University Press, 1942.

———. *The South and the Sectional Crisis*. Baton Rouge: Louisiana State University Press, 1968.

Rainwater, Percy Lee. *Mississippi, Storm Center of Secession, 1856–1861*. Baton Rouge: Otto Claitor, 1938.

Ramsdell, Charles W. *Behind the Lines in the Southern Confederacy*. Edited by Wendell H. Stephenson. Baton Rouge: Louisiana State University Press, 1944.

Randall, James G. *Lincoln the President*. 4 vols. New York: Dodd, Mead & Company, 1945–1955.

Randall, James G., and David Donald. *The Civil War and Reconstruction*. 2nd ed. Boston: Heath, 1961.

Rauch, Basil. *American Interest in Cuba, 1848–1855*. New York: Columbia

University Press, 1948.

Reynolds, Donald E. *Editors Make War: Southern Newspapers in the Secession Crisis*. Nashville: Vanderbilt University Press, 1970.

Ringold, May Spencer. *The Role of the State Legislatures in the Confederacy*. Athens: University of Georgia Press, 1966.

Roland, Charles. *The Confederacy*. Chicago: University of Chicago Press, 1960.

Russel, Robert R. *Improvement of Communication with the Pacific Coast as an Issue in American Politics, 1783–1864*. Cedar Rapids, Iowa: Torch Press, 1948.

Sears, Louis Martin. *John Slidell*. Durham: Duke University Press, 1925.

Schwab, John C. *The Confederate States of America, 1861–1865*. New York: Charles Scribner's Sons, 1901.

Scroggs, William O. *Filibusters and Financiers: The Story of William Walker and His Associates*. New York: Macmillan Company, 1916.

Shanks, Henry T. *The Secession Movement in Virginia, 1847–1861*. Richmond: Garrett and Massie, 1934.

Silver, James W. *Confederate Morale and Church Propaganda*. Tuscaloosa, Ala.: Confederate Publishing Company, Inc., 1957.

Simms, Henry H. *A Decade of Sectional Controversy, 1851–1861*. Chapel Hill: University of North Carolina Press, 1942.

Sitterson, Joseph Carlyle. *The Secession Movement in North Carolina*. Chapel Hill: University of North Carolina Press, 1939.

Spencer, Ivor D. *The Victor and the Spoils: A Life of William L. Marcy*. Providence: Brown University Press, 1959.

Stanton, William. *The Leopard's Spots: Scientific Attitudes Toward Race in America, 1915–1859*. Chicago: University of Chicago Press, 1960.

Starobin, Robert S. *Industrial Slavery in the Old South*. New York: Oxford University Press, 1970.

Strode, Hudson. *Jefferson Davis*. 3 vols. New York: Harcourt, Brace, and Company, 1955–1964.

Takaki, Ronald T. *A Pro-Slavery Crusade: The Agitation to Reopen the African Slave Trade*. New York: Free Press, 1971.

Tatum, Georgia Lee. *Disloyalty in the Confederacy*. Chapel Hill: University of North Carolina Press, 1934.

Thomas, Emory M. *The Confederacy as a Revolutionary Experience*. Englewood Cliffs, N.J.: Prentice-Hall, Inc., 1971.

———. *The Confederate State of Richmond*. Austin: University of Texas Press, 1971.

Todd, Robert Cecil. *Confederate Finance*. Athens: University of Georgia Press, 1954.

Van den Berghe, Pierre L. *Race and Racism, A Comparative Perspective*. New York: Wiley, 1967.

Vandiver, Frank E. *Basic History of the Confederacy*. Princeton: D. Van Nostrand Company, 1962.

———. *Rebel Brass: The Confederate Command System*. Baton Rouge: Louisiana State University Press, 1956.

———. *Their Tattered Flags*. New York: Harper's Magazine Press and Harper & Row, 1970.

Warren, Robert Penn. *The Legacy of the Civil War*. New York: Random House, 1961.

Wells, Damon. *Stephen Douglas: The Last Years, 1857–1861*. Austin: University of Texas Press, 1971.

Wender, Herbert. *Southern Commercial Conventions, 1837–1859*. Johns Hopkins University Studies in Historical and Political Science, Series XLVIII, Number 4. Baltimore: Johns Hopkins University Press, 1930.

Wesley, Charles H. *The Collapse of the Confederacy*. Washington: Associated Publishers, Inc., 1937.

Wiley, Bell Irvin. *The Life of Johnny Reb: The Common Soldier of the Confederacy*. New York: Bobbs-Merrill Company, 1943.

———. *The Plain People of the Confederacy*. Baton Rouge: Louisiana State University Press, 1943.

———. *The Road to Appomattox*. Memphis: Memphis State College Press, 1956.

———. *Southern Negroes, 1861–1865*. New Haven: Yale University Press, 1938.

Winters, John D. *The Civil War in Louisiana*. Baton Rouge: Louisiana State University Press, 1963.

Wooster, Ralph A. *The People in Power: Courthouse and Statehouse in the Lower South, 1850–1860*. Knoxville: University of Tennessee Press, 1969.

———. *The Secession Conventions of the South*. Princeton: Princeton University Press, 1962.

Yates, Richard E. *The Confederacy and Zeb Vance*. Tuscaloosa, Ala.: Confederate Publishing Company, Inc., 1958.

ARTICLES

Alexander, Thomas B. "Persistent Whiggery in Alabama and the Lower South, 1860–1867." *Alabama Review*, XII (1959), 35–52.

———. "Persistent Whiggery in the Confederate South, 1860–1877." *Journal of Southern History*, XXVII (1961), 305–329.

Ambrose, Stephen E. "Yeoman Discontent in the Confederacy." *Civil War*

History, VII (1962), 259–68.

Andrews, J. Culter. "The Confederate Press and Public Morale." *Journal of Southern History*, XXXII (1966), 445–65.

Bailey, Hugh C. "Disaffection in the Alabama Hill Country, 1861." *Civil War History*, IV (1958), 183–93.

———. "Disloyalty in Early Confederate Alabama." *Journal of Southern History*, XXIII (1957), 522–28.

Boucher, Chauncey S. "*In Re* that Aggressive Slavocracy." *Mississippi Valley Historical Review*, VIII (1921), 13–79.

Brumgardt, John R. "Alexander H. Stephens and the State Convention Movement in Georgia: A Reappraisal." *Georgia Historical Quarterly*, LIX (1975), 38–49.

Carnathan, W. J. "The Proposal to Reopen the African Slave Trade in the South, 1854–1860." *South Atlantic Quarterly*, XXV (October, 1926), 410–29.

Coddington, Edwin B. "Soldiers' Relief in the Seaboard States of the Southern Confederacy." *Mississippi Valley Historical Review*, XXXVII (1950), 17–38.

Current, Richard N. "The Confederates and the First Shot." *Civil War History*, VII (December, 1961), 357–69.

Curti, Merle. "Young America." *American Historical Review*, XXXII (1926), 34–55.

Donald, David. "The Proslavery Argument Reconsidered." *Journal of Southern History*, XXXVIII (1971), 3–18.

Ezell, John. "Jefferson Davis Seeks Political Vindication, 1851–1857." *Journal of Mississippi History*, XXVI (1964), 307–321.

Fahrner, Alvin A. "William 'Extra Billy' Smith, Governor of Virginia, 1864–1865: A Pillar of the Confederacy." *Virginia Magazine of History and Biography*, LXXIV (1966), 68–87.

Fitts, Albert N. "The Confederate Convention: The Provisional Constitution." *Alabama Review*, II (1949), 83–99.

Fladeland, Betty L. "Compensated Emancipation: A Rejected Alternative." *Journal of Southern History*, XLII (1976), 169–86.

Fleming, Walter L. "The Early Life of Jefferson Davis." *Mississippi Valley Historical Association Proceedings*, IX (1917), 151–76.

———. "Jefferson Davis, the Negroes, and the Negro Problem." *Sewanee Review*, XVI (1908), 407–427.

———. "The Peace Movement in Alabama During the Civil War." *South Atlantic Quarterly*, II (1903), 114–24 and 246–60.

Freehling, William W. "Paranoia and American History." *New York Review of Books*, XVII (September, 1971), 36–39.

Greenberg, Kenneth S. "Revolutionary Ideology and the Proslavery Argument: The Abolition of Slavery in Antebellum South Carolina." *Journal of Southern History*, XLII (1976), 365–84.

Hamilton, J. G. de Roulhac. "The State Courts and the Confederate Constitution." *Journal of Southern History*, IV (1938), 425–48.

Hill, Louise B. "State Socialism in the Confederate States of America." in J. D. Eggleston (ed.), *Southern Sketches*, Number 9, First Series (Charlottesville: Historical Publishing Company, Inc., 1936).

Johnson, Ludwell H. "Fort Sumter and Confederate Diplomacy." *Journal of Southern History*, XXVI (1960), 441–77.

————. "Lincoln's Solution to the Problem of Peace Terms, 1864–1865." *Journal of Southern History*, XXXIV (1968), 576–86.

Johnson, Michael P. "A New Look at the Popular Vote for Delegates to the Georgia Secession Convention." *Georgia Historical Quarterly*, LVI (1972), 259–75.

Kerby, Robert L. "Why the Confederacy Lost." *Review of Politics*, XXXV (1973), 326–45.

Kimball, William J. "The Bread Riot in Richmond, 1863." *Civil War History*, VII (1961), 149–54.

Lathrop, Barnes F. "Disaffection in Confederate Louisiana: The Case of William Hyman." *Journal of Southern History*, XXIV (1958), 308–318.

Long, Durward. "Unanimity and Disloyalty in Secessionist Alabama." *Civil War History*, XI (1965), 257–73.

Lowe, Richard and Randolph Campbell. "Slave Property and the Distribution of Wealth in Texas, 1860." *Journal of American History*, LXIII (1976), 316–26.

McCash, William B. "Thomas R. R. Cobb and the 'Better Terms' Argument." *Georgia Historical Quarterly*, LX (1976), 49–53.

McDonald, Forrest, and Grady McWhiney. "The Antebellum Southern Herdsman: A Reinterpretation." *Journal of Southern History*, XLI (1975), 147–66.

McKitrick, Eric L. "Party Politics and the Union and Confederate War Efforts." *The American Party Systems*. Edited by William Nisbet Chambers and Walter Dean Burnham. New York: Oxford University Press, 1967.

McMurry, Richard M. "The Atlanta Campaign of 1864: A New Look." *Civil War History*, XXII (1976), 5–15.

McWhiney, Grady. "The Confederacy's First Shot." *Civil War History*, XIV (March, 1968), 5–14.

————. "Jefferson Davis and the Art of War." *Civil War History*, XXI (1975), 101–112.

Morrow, Ralph E. "The Proslavery Argument Revisited." *Mississippi Valley Historical Review*, XLVIII (1961), 79–94.

Nichols, James L. "The Tax-in-Kind in the Department of the Trans-Mississippi." *Civil War History*, V (1959), 382–89.

Owsley, Frank L. "Defeatism in the Confederacy." *North Carolina Historical Review*, III (1926), 446–56.

———. "Local Defense and the Overthrow of the Confederacy." *Mississippi Valley Historical Review*, XI (1925), 490–525.

Parks, Joseph H. "State Rights in a Crisis: Governor Joseph E. Brown versus President Jefferson Davis." *Journal of Southern History*, XXXII (1966), 3–24.

Rabun, James Z. "Alexander H. Stephens and Jefferson Davis." *American Historical Review*, LVIII (1953), 290–321.

Ramsdell, Charles W. "The Control of Manufacturing by the Confederate Government." *Mississippi Valley Historical Review*, VIII (1921), 231–49.

———. "The Confederate Government and the Railroads." *American Historical Review*, XXII (1917), 794–810.

Richardson, Ralph. "The Choice of Jefferson Davis as Confederate President." *Journal of Mississippi History*, XVII (July, 1955), 161–76.

Robbins, John B. "The Confederacy and the Writ of *Habeas Corpus*." *Georgia Historical Quarterly*, LV (1971), 83–101.

Rogers, William Warren. "The Way They Were: Thomas Countians in 1860." *Georgia Historical Quarterly*, LX (1976), 131–44.

Russel, Robert R. "What Was the Compromise of 1850?" *Journal of Southern History*, XXII (1956), 295–308.

Scheiber, Harry N. "The Pay of Confederate Troops and Problems of Demoralization: A Case of Administrative Failure." *Civil War History*, XV (1969), 226–36.

Scroggs, Jack B. "Arkansas in the Secession Crisis." *Arkansas in the Civil War*. Edited by John L. Ferguson. Little Rock, Ark.: Arkansas History Commission, n.d.

Sears, Louis Martin. "Slidell and Buchanan." *American Historical Review*, XXVII (1922), 709–730.

Sellers, Charles G., Jr. "The Travail of Slavery." *The Southerner as American*. Edited by Charles G. Sellers, Jr. Chapel Hill: University of North Carolina Press, 1960.

Shofner, Jerrel H., and William Warren Rogers. "Montgomery to Richmond: The Confederacy Selects a Capital." *Civil War History*, X (1964), 155–66.

Silver, James W. "Propaganda in the Confederacy." *Journal of Southern History*, XI (1945), 487–503.

Stephenson, Nathaniel W. "A Theory of Jefferson Davis." *American Historical Review*, XXI (1915), 73–90.

Tingley, Donald F. "The Jefferson Davis–William H. Bissell Duel." *Mid-America*, XXXVIII (1956), 146–55.

Trexler, Harrison A. "The Davis Administration and the Richmond Press, 1861–1865." *Journal of Southern History*, XVI (1950), 177–95.

———. "Jefferson Davis and the Confederate Patronage." *South Atlantic Quarterly*, XXVIII (1929), 45–58.

———. "The Opposition of Planters to the Employment of Slaves as Laborers by the Confederacy." *Mississippi Valley Historical Review*, XXVII (1940), 211–24.

Vandiver, Frank E. "The Civil War as an Institutionalizing Force." *Essays on the American Civil War*. Edited by William F. Holmes and Harold M. Hollingsworth. Austin: University of Texas Press, 1968.

———. "Jefferson Davis and Confederate Strategy." *The American Tragedy: The Civil War in Retrospect*. Hampden-Sydney, Va.: n.p., 1959.

———. *Jefferson Davis and the Confederate State*. Oxford, England: Clarendon Press, 1964.

———. *The Making of a President: Jefferson Davis, 1961*. N.p.: Virginia Civil War Commission, n.d.

Van Riper, Paul P., and Harry N. Scheiber. "The Confederate Civil Service." *Journal of Southern History*, XXV (1959), 448–70.

Wiley, Bell Irvin. "Southern Reaction to Federal Invasion." *Journal of Southern History*, XVI (1950), 491–510.

Wish, Harvey. "Revival of the African Slave Trade in the United States, 1856–1860." *Mississippi Valley Historical Review*, XXVII (1941), 569–88.

Wooster, Ralph A. "An Analysis of the Membership of Secession Conventions in the Lower South." *Journal of Southern History*, XXIV (1958), 360–68.

Worley, Ted R. "The Arkansas Peace Society of 1861: A Study in Mountain Unionism." *Journal of Southern History*, XXIV (1958), 445–56.

DISSERTATIONS

Bowen, Nancy Head. "A Political Labyrinth: Texas in the Civil War— Questions in Continuity." Ph.D. dissertation, Rice University, 1974.

Entrekin, William Frank, Jr. "Poor Relief in North Carolina in the Confederacy." M.A. thesis, Duke University, 1947.

Folk, Edgar Ester. "W. W. Holden, Political Journalist, Editor of *North Carolina Standard*, 1843–1865." Ph.D. dissertation, George Peabody College for Teachers, 1934.

Muldowny, John. "The Administration of Jefferson Davis as Secretary of War." Ph.D. dissertation, Yale University, 1959.

Nelson, Larry Earl. "The Confederacy and the United States Presidential Election of 1864." Ph.D. dissertation, Duke University, 1975.

Robbins, John Brawner. "Confederate Nationalism: Politics and Government in the Confederate South, 1861–1865." Ph.D. dissertation, Rice University, 1964.

Robinson, Armstead L. "Day of Jubilo: Civil War and the Demise of Slavery in the Mississippi Valley, 1861–1865." Ph.D. dissertation, University of Rochester, 1976.

Index

Abolitionists, 12, 29. *See also* Antislavery
Agriculture, 64–65
Alabama: secession of, 26–27, 30–31; union-ism in, 39; disaffection in, 97, 98, 115, 129–30, 185, 194, 205, 207; elections of 1863 in, 155; mentioned, 157, 158
Allen, Henry, 158
Allen, Thompson, 152–54
Anderson (S.C.) *Intelligencer*, 232
Andrews, Eliza F., 237
Antislavery: and Kansas issue, 6; Davis' views on, 6, 12–13
Arkansas: election of 1860 in, 22–23; seces-sion of, 44; disaffection in, 98, 133; men-tioned, 57, 147, 157
Atlanta *Daily Intelligencer*, 108, 124, 139, 210
Augusta *Constitutionalist*, 121

Ballinger, W. P., 133
Beauregard, P. G. T., 52, 57, 74, 169, 268
Bell, John, 16
Benjamin, Judah P.: and Confederate di-plomacy, 174; on emancipation, 245–46; mentioned, 63, 79, 95, 199, 250
Blair, Francis Preston, 221
Bocock, Thomas, 220–21
Bonham, M. L., 109, 211
Boyce, William, 74, 220
Bragg, Braxton: defended by Davis, 268; mentioned, 62, 71, 89, 175, 261, 264
Breckinridge, John, 16, 22–23
Brooks, William, 115, 172
Brown, Albert Gallatin, 10–11
Brown, John, 13, 236
Brown, Joseph E.: criticizes Confederate

policies, 79–85, 155–56; inconsistency of, 81, 89; efforts to aid poor of, 159–65; character of, 159; appeals to yeomen of, 160; appeals to planters of, 165; urges negotiations, 203–205; mentioned, 110, 131, 134, 136, 147, 179, 210, 218, 265, 266, 270
Bull Run, 52
Bureau of Conscription, 64, 71, 90, 126
Butler, Benjamin, 183

Calhoun, John C., 2–4, 21, 84, 101, 168, 229
Campbell, John A.: reaction to secession of, 91; on desertion, 126; on disaffection, 133; and Hampton Roads conference, 223–24; mentioned, 143
Charleston *Mercury*: sees despotism in North, 48; antidemocratic views of, 33*n*; criticizes Davis, 77–79, 257–58, 259; opposes eman-cipation, 248; mentioned, 102, 121, 123, 178, 184, 192, 208, 217, 218, 226–27, 237
Chesnut, James, Jr.: notes class resent-ment, 94; on arming slaves, 241, 251
Chesnut, Mary Boykin: on North, 49; on slavery, 233, 236–38; on arming slaves, 241, 244–45; on emancipation, 244–45; mentioned, 61, 77, 91, 94, 101, 114, 118, 125, 207, 217, 218, 220, 256, 258, 260, 268, 270, 271
Churches, 184–85
Clark, Charles, 192, 214
Clark, H. T., 264
Clay, Clement C.: on sentiment in Ala-bama, 130, 185; on emancipation, 253; on northern peace forces, 198, 199

291